Government and Po

Concepts and Comparisons

Ian Selby

Nelson

Thomas Nelson and Sons Ltd
Nelson House Mayfield Road
Walton-on-Thames Surrey
KT12 5PL   UK

Nelson Blackie
Wester Cleddens Road
Bishopbriggs
Glasgow
G64 2NZ   UK

Thomas Nelson Australia
102 Dodds Street
South Melbourne
Victoria 3205 Australia

Nelson Canada
1120 Birchmount Road
Scarborough Ontario
MIK 5G4 Canada

© Ian Selby 1995

First published by Thomas Nelson and Sons Ltd 1995

I(T)P   Thomas Nelson is an International Thomson Publishing Company

I(T)P   is used under licence

ISBN 0–17– 448232–9
NPN 9 8 7 6 5 4 3 2 1

Printed in Spain by Gráficas Estella

Acknowledgements
The author and publishers are grateful to the following for permission to use copyright material
in this book:

The Guardian for the graphs 'Income' and 'Spending' from the issue of 2 May 1994, the graphic
'Europe of the Regions' (7 March 1994) the graphic 'The expanding Union' (11 June 1994) and a
table from *The Guardian Political Almanack*, 1993/4;
Les Gibbard for the cartoon 'He who fights and runs away';
The Independent for the extract from an article by Peter Hennessy from the issue of 21 January
1991;

Chambers Harrap Publishers Ltd for three figures from *The Business of Government*, by J.D.
Derbyshire;

Photographs: House of Commons Library p. 47; Hulton Deutsch Collection Ltd pp. 5, 22, 28, 37;
Mirror Syndication International pp. 94, 149, 164, 189, 207, 273.

Dedication

For Mark

Contents

Preface

Politics has become an increasingly popular subject in recent years. The aim of this book is to provide a core text which supplies students with a contemporary knowledge and understanding of basic political ideas, concepts, structures and processes.

This text combines a comparative explanation of political concepts with the main topics of British politics, including the Prime Minister, the Cabinet, pressure groups, political parties. It draws simple comparisons with parallel institutions in other Western democracies.

Throughout the text are 'Key concepts' and 'Key terms' provided to give the student a better understanding of some of the more complex political ideas. Chapter 1 is designed to equip students with a clear understanding of some of the most complex of these, allowing them to identify the relationship between ideas and the reality of politics at the different levels of government and in different political systems. Some chapters are larger than they appear in more traditional politics textbooks, the main example being 'Britain and the European Union' (Chapter 9). This is a topic of growing importance which I believe deserves far greater attention than it has received in the past. This chapter deals with the development of the European Union from its beginnings through to the ratification of the Maastricht Treaty.

The text is designed to be student friendly. Each chapter contains self-test questions and essay topics. Chapter 14 gives general guidance on examination technique and in particular advice on answering data/stimulus response questions, including a number of data/stimulus response self-tests.

It is my hope that this book will provide a contemporary explanation of politics, and a foundation upon which further and more complex political study can be based.

CHAPTER 1

Political concepts

The term, 'Politics' is used to describe the process through which individual and collective decisions are made. It is the activity in which goals are agreed and pursued through policies designed to achieve these goals. It is a characteristic of most social systems; family, community, region, state and international community. When human beings form a group this leads to a discussion in order to decide what their community will seek to achieve. The discussion of different goals and priorities often leads to a conflict between competing interests. Politics is the process which resolves these conflicts. In this respect it is a constructive and practical subject examining the nature of the decision-making process. All politics involves ideas, power, authority, responsibility, representation, rights and welfare. Once aware of the basic concepts of politics, a person may understand the structure and relationships of a political system and the nature and reasoning of the decisions taken.

Example:

When a family goes shopping someone usually prepares a shopping list. Other members of the family may be allowed to add to the list, but the extent of these additions relies on a number of factors. First, economic: how much money is the decision-maker prepared to spend and to what extent is he or she prepared to overspend? Second, the nature of the additional expenditure: is it worthwhile or frivolous? Third, social relations affect any such decisions: will family welfare be increased by possession of a pet or computer game? These are all political decisions that will affect the outcome of the shopping trip, causing both beneficial and detrimental short- or long-term consequences for the family.

In state politics similar decisions face those in power and the concepts in this chapter act as points of reference, enabling students to comprehend the relationships between state institutions and the State and the citizen, and to judge the operation and effectiveness of many of these concepts in relation to the British political system:

- What is the role of British government?
- How effective is our system in ensuring representative and responsible government?

- Is our parliamentary democracy effective at holding the executive to account?
- How do the three arms of government – the legislature, the executive and the judiciary – co-exist in Britain?

Similarly, concepts are used to compare and contrast the differing political systems that exist in the world today. For example, 'civil liberties' has a similar meaning in the USA and the UK but a different meaning in China. Once you understand what a civil liberty is, you can assess whether the political systems of China or the United States encourage or discriminate against the concept, and whether the people of either country enjoy greater or lesser freedoms.

This chapter explains some of the most important concepts as follows:

1.1 **Theoretical concepts**: Ideology, democracy, liberal democracy, the majoritarian model, constitutional democracy, pluralism, corporatism, power, authority, legitimacy, sovereignty, nation-state, nation and state.

1.2 **Concepts of the State**: the separation of powers, the government, the executive, balance of power, checks and balances, representative and responsible government, parliamentary and presidential government, unitary and federal government.

1.3 **Concepts of the individual**: citizenship, civil rights, natural rights, welfare and the welfare state.

1.1 | Theoretical concepts

In Britain we live in a **democracy**. This term describes a system of government in which supreme authority rests with the people and government is conducted only by and with their consent. As United States President, Abraham Lincoln said: 'government of the people, by the people, for the people'.

A democracy may be either **direct** or **indirect**.

Direct democracy

A direct (or pure) democracy exists where the will of the people is translated into public policy (law) directly by the people themselves at mass meetings. This system operates only in very small communities where it is possible for citizens to meet in a given place and where problems of government are few and simple. Direct democracy does not exist at a national level anywhere in the world today.

Indirect democracy

Indirect democracy is the most common form that exists today in the Western world. In Britain, France, Germany and the United States there is a system called **representative democracy**. This means that the people of these countries are able to choose regularly, in free and open elections, public office-holders to act on their behalf and implement a package of policies to improve the lifestyle and security of the nation. These officials represent the interests and wishes of the people, having been elected to office by them. This is indirect democracy.

Most Western democracies are called **liberal democratic**. This term means that these democracies place a strong emphasis upon individual rights and liberties, free elections and representative government. Liberal democracies have governments that are representative and accountable to the people, but the power of these governments is limited, designed to create a balance between the rights of the minority and those of the individual against the interests and rights of the majority. This acknowledges that, in most representative democracies, elections produce majority and minority political groupings and policies are decided by a majority of representatives voting for them. This is called a **majoritarian model**.

Liberal democracies are founded upon the traditions of **liberalism**, which is a tradition of political thought centred on the value of individual liberty. Individuals are said to hold rights which exist independently of the state and form the basis for constitutional limits upon the power of government. The task of government is to respect and protect these rights, allowing individuals to pursue their own chosen goals with due regard for the rights of others. Liberalism is a broad idea which originated in the late seventeenth century through the writings of the Englishman, John Locke. Its core meaning has remained the same although liberalism in practice has changed over the past two centuries. Liberal democracies today emphasise the need for government to enable democratic participation and extend health, welfare and educational rights to encourage the development of the individual.[1]

In addition, most democracies may be described as **constitutional democracies**, meaning that their democratic principles are enshrined in a constitution that constructs an institutional, operational and legal framework, which regulates the relationships between the branches of government and between these institutions and the citizen. Democracies seek to balance competing interests and give people the power and ability to make a range of different choices, some of which are of major importance.

Example:
The United States and the United Kingdom are democracies with different systems of government. The USA is a federal republic. The form of government is based on a written constitution. Britain is a constitutional monarchy, governed by Ministers in the name of the Queen.

In making many of these major decisions, people are influenced by the different ideas put forward by those standing for public office. Candidates who stand in elections usually belong to political parties, which act as a label for people to clearly see what each candidate believes in and stands for. This creates a system of **party government** (*see Chapter 3*) and central to a party system of government is ideology.

Ideology in our context means the basic values and ideas which people hold about the nature of society and the role of politics and government within it. In political terms an ideology provides a way of analysing existing society and gives society ideals to work towards. Ideologies are associated with either political thinkers, like Karl Marx, or with political parties. Each political party possesses an ideology; a set of ideas that are commonly held and which form the foundation of each party's policies. Socialism is a central ideology of the Labour Party, and during the 1980s, 'Thatcherism' was the central ideology of the Conservative Party.

Within Western societies there are a range of competing ideologies that find expression in the political arena. This allows a political theorist to say that Britain, France and the United States are pluralist democracies. **Pluralism** seeks to encourage diversity within a political system. It accepts that society is composed of many different people and groups who may each possess both different and similar ideas. Pluralism advocates that these groups are involved in the decision-making process, with different people and interests influencing different areas of public policy. If one accepts that we live in a society where people possess a wide set of beliefs and ideas, then it is inevitable that those ideas and beliefs should influence the way in which public policy is made and implemented. In a pluralist democracy the widest possible influence on the decision-making process is open to the large variety of different groups and interests that exist. In pluralist societies, democracy is linked to competition between groups and the right to vote. Government is carried out for the benefit of the majority by representatives chosen by the people. In practice, this can mean that the powers of government lie in the hands of a single group.

Example: *The Conservatives in the UK or the Republicans in the USA.*

However, no group can rely upon the support of the electorate and compete with other groups for electoral support. In pluralist systems competition and co-operation is encouraged between groups. Pluralism encourages the establishment of **pressure groups** and their incorporation into the policy-making process, because they have a positive effect upon democracy and serve to provide the individual with alternative means of representation (*see Chapter 6*).

Similar to pluralism is the theoretical concept of **corporatism**. There are several interpretations of this term; historically, it referred to a form of social organisation that represented groups of workers and employers to the institutions of the State and had great authority over the lives of its members. The modern meaning of the term is the tendency for the State to work closely with relevant officially recognised groups in the making of public policy. In Britain in the 1960s and 1970s ideas of corporatism surrounded the making of economic policy. Both trade unions and business groups were encouraged to work with the governments then in power, to construct a policy acceptable to all three. These groups were encouraged to share responsibility with the Government in implementing the policy.

Example:
In the 1970s the Trades Union Congress (TUC) helped the Labour Government, for a time, to implement its incomes policies.

The essential difference between pluralism and corporatism is that corporatism establishes institutional incorporation into the policy-making and policy-implementing process of organised, officially recognised and relevant interest groups by those in power. Pluralism simply acknowledges the competition between different interests in society for power, and the desire to allow those interests to influence to varying degrees the policy-making process.

Figure 1 Len Murray and Vic Feather at the TUC conference 1973.

Democracy has a variety of inter-linked concepts but none are as important as the terms 'power' and 'authority', which are central to an understanding of political activity and the operation of political systems.

Power means the ability to get someone to do something which they may not wish to do. Political analysis focuses upon the ability of individuals or groups to act or to achieve goals through the compliance of others. The concept of 'power' concerns the distribution of power in a political system and identifies the nature and limits of power available to groups or institutional post-holders. Power may be exercised via authority, influence, manipulation, coercion or force.

Power is a goal which different groups in society seek to achieve. In democracies, different groups and individuals seek political office and use constitutional power contained within the offices of government to implement their ideas and achieve policy goals.

Example:
Bill Clinton, President of the USA, has sought to use the power of that office to introduce legislation to change the American health care system.

Authority is the right to rule, and is usually based upon law, convention, social status, or hereditary principles. The main basis of authority is the ability to secure assent or compliance on the grounds of legitimacy.

Example:
Teachers have the authority over their students to get them to read or work.

Forms of authority

1. Traditional. This rests upon long-standing customs and habits of a society.

    Example: The Queen has traditional authority.

2. Rational-legal authority based upon laws, conventions and rules that rest within an office of state.

    Example: The Prime Minister.

3. Charismatic authority based upon the personal qualities of the individual.

    Example:
    Many revolutionary leaders possess charismatic authority which creates an intense commitment from the population to the leader and their message. This was the case with the Chinese Communist leader Mao Zedong.

It is possible to have power without authority. Linked to both concepts is **legitimacy**. This is the idea that power is gained and authority exercised according to certain principles, or laws, or practices, or a combination of all three. Political authority exists when people believe that it is right, that is, legitimate. Legitimacy is usually conferred in Western liberal democracies through open and free elections, but it may also stem from tradition, religion, economic, and military success.

Thus legitimate government possesses authority in the eyes of the people it rules. Legitimate power has to be seen as right and good in the eyes of the people over which it is exercised.

Power, authority and legitimacy are three concepts that closely orbit each other. They are all crucial to the operation of government and a political system.

A concept founded upon power and authority is **sovereignty**. This has a dual meaning. First, it means the condition of political and legal autonomy (self-government) that a state enjoys when it is recognised by other states as being able to exercise ultimate power and authority over its own territory. This means that states are able to exist independently of each other and respect such independence. When armed forces from one state invade another, the sovereignty of the victim state is said to have been violated. This often leads to wars.

Example:
In 1982 when Argentine armed forces invaded the Falkland Islands, British sovereignty was infringed.

Secondly, this doctrine is used to denote the ultimate power of a person, group or institution within a political community to make, interpret and enforce laws binding upon all other members of that community. In Britain this means 'the Queen in Parliament' which in practice means that Parliament has supreme legislative authority and its laws cannot be challenged by any other body, including a court. It is described as sovereign. Parliament has the authority to rule Britain and make laws. In other countries it is harder to establish which institution has sovereignty. In states like Germany and the USA, a federal constitution divides and limits the powers of state institutions, and government is described as **limited**. No single institution, the Federal Government, the Federal Legislature, the State Governments or the Supreme Court, is as sovereign as the British Parliament.

Finally, the concept of sovereignty came into existence at the same time as the international political system, as we know it today, began to evolve – creating an interactive system of nation-states. A **nation-state** is a legal and territorial expression involving a population organised under one government with sovereignty over its territory and citizens. Usually such an entity comprises of a nation or perhaps a group of nations. Nation-states are legally recognised entities that have international rights and representative authority in the international system that exists throughout the world.

Example:
The United Kingdom of Great Britain and Northern Ireland is a nation-state, composed of four nations. As such, it is entitled to join international organisations such as the United Nations.

A **nation** is the name given to a group of people who come from a geographically defined region and share an ethnic identity, language, culture and common heritage. A nation has no status or existence within international law, only states are legally recognised.

Example:
Wales and Scotland are nations but they are not nation-states. They are components of the UK, which is the legally recognised nation-state.

Central to this concept is the word **state**. The term 'state' has two meanings. First, it refers to a legally recognised international actor in the international system. A state is an organisation that reserves for itself the sole legitimate right to use force within its territory and is recognised by other states as independent, e.g. Australia, Germany and Brazil. Secondly, this concept refers to a set of institutions through which public policy and laws are decided and executed. A state exercises power over its territory and peoples.

Key term: The Government.

This term has two meanings. First, it refers to the institutions of the State that have the power to exercise authority over the people, implement policies and administer laws.

Second, this term is used to describe the politically appointed section of the executive branch of government. Normally in Britain the leader of the political party with the largest number of seats in the House of Commons, which usually has an absolute majority of over 326 seats, becomes the Prime Minister, and he or she is responsible for appointing a large number of the political posts that form 'the Government'. This includes Secretaries of State, junior Ministers and their aides. This group of politicians, which total around 100, act collectively and implement the policy decided at Cabinet level. Members of the Government are

Questions

1. Distinguish between power and authority.
2. What is a liberal democracy?
3. Define (a) pluralism and (b) corporatism.
4. Define the term 'sovereignty'.
5. What is a state and what is nation?

1.2 | Concepts of the State

Underlying international political systems is the idea of the sovereign State. States operate according to a variety of different concepts. These may be based on liberal traditions or other ideological traditions such as Communism. Western democracies follow a set of liberal concepts that describe the nature of the State and its interaction and relationship with its citizens.

Perhaps the most important concept in understanding the operation of the State is that of the **separation of powers**. The French philosopher Montesquieu (1689–1755) believed that a political tyranny could be prevented if the three arms of **government** were separated. The three arms of government are:

1. **The legislature**, which creates law (in Britain this is done by Parliament).
2. **The executive**, which puts laws into effect (in Britain this is the task of the Government).
3. **The judiciary**, which judge cases of dispute between the other two arms or between one of them and the citizen, or whether a law has been broken (in Britain the role of the courts system). The powers of the judiciary vary between countries. Britain does not have a Supreme Court similar to that of the United States.

Montesquieu believed that a tyranny exists when these three arms, or functions, of government are embodied in one political office enabling the holder of that office to pass oppressive laws, rule according to them and judge people breaking them. Montesquieu believed that moderate government relied on no one person or group being able to control all three arms. He argued that each arm should be separate from the other and empowered to exert control over each branch thus creating a **balance of power** within the political system and a series of **checks and balances** (*see Figure 2*).

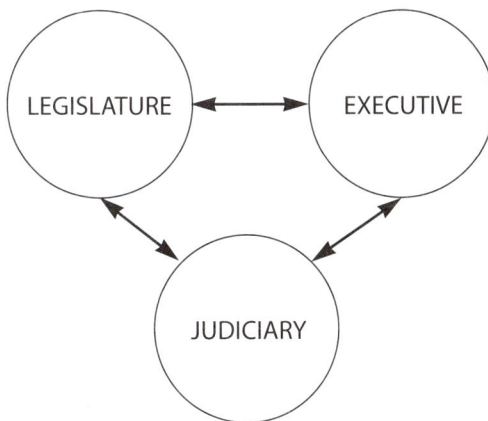

Figure 2 The three branches of government. Each branch has powers to check and balance the others.

The ideas of Montesquieu had considerable influence upon the founding fathers of the United States Constitution, who purposely instituted checks and balances throughout the United States political system. The United States Constitution provides for the three powers to be expressly exercised: by the Congress who make the laws, by the President who rules according to those laws, and by a Supreme Court which judges whether those laws have been violated or not. With some amendments this constitution has remained a successful working document to this day. The United States has a strict separation of powers.

In Britain, by contrast, there is a considerable overlap between the legislature, the executive and the judiciary. There are instances where one person or group exercise two or even all three of these powers.

bound by the conventions of collective and individual ministerial responsibility. Members of the House of Lords and the House of Commons are appointed to the Government, and every department has at least one peer attached to it so that he or she can act as spokesperson for the Government in the House of Lords. This large grouping of politicians is described as 'the Government'.

Key term: The executive

This is the institution which is responsible for the administration of government, having the power and authority to implement parliamentary laws and policies and manage the State. In some instances the executive may make laws through the tool of delegated legislation (*see Chapter 3*). In Britain, the executive comprises the Prime Minister and all other Ministers and the civil service. The Prime Minister is the head of the executive.

Key term: The balance of power

This is the idea that power within a political system should be shared equally among the three functions of government ensuring that power is not concentrated a single office, i.e. the executive.

Key term: checks and balances

Within the three branches of government, a system of overlapping powers is created to permit each branch to check, i.e. restrain or balance, the actions of the others.

Example:
The House of Lords operates legislative power and exercises judicial power because it is the highest court in the land. The Lord Chancellor is a member of the House of Lords, a judge and a member of the Cabinet (executive power) and so exercises all three powers.

That the separation of powers does not apply rigidly in the UK has not resulted in a tyranny, but many argue that the effectiveness of Parliament and the power of the judiciary are weakened and civil liberties endangered because the British executive holds such a concentration of power. Executive control over Parliament through its parliamentary majority allows it to enact any law it wants and to limit the extent of its accountability. Britain does not have a strict separation of powers.

The doctrine of the separation of powers enables us to understand the operation of government within different states but most states have a second tier of regional, local or state government. The concepts of unitary and federal states enable us to understand the relationship between these different levels of government and further categorise states.

The term **unitary state** describes a state in which all power and authority resides in one single body. In the UK this body is Parliament. Parliament makes all the laws and governs the country from a centralised bureaucracy. The British constitution invests all power in Parliament which is described as 'sovereign'. Parliament can give power to other institutions, e.g. local authorities, but these may be withdrawn at any time. Usually unitary states are highly centralised and all authority is concentrated in the institutions of central government.

Example:
Britain, France and Sweden are highly centralised unitary states.

The opposite of a unitary system exists where authority is equitably shared between the central government and the lower levels of government. This system is known as **federalism**. In a federal state the powers of the federal or national government, and the regional government are quite separate, and neither can take away the powers of the other. It should be noted that four of the largest states in the world have a federal system of government, Australia, Brazil, Canada and the United States. The federal system is normally constructed through a written constitution which outlines the parameters of the different levels of government and their interrelationships. Usually there is a sharing of power between the levels of government. Central government is responsible for external relations: defence, foreign affairs, and economic policy. The provincial and/or regional government is primarily responsible for domestic policy: education and welfare. Some functions are shared, such as trade policy, and both tiers have a law-making function with some laws made at a national level and others made at a local level to suit local needs.

In the federal system disputes often arise between the different levels of government which require arbitration, and it is the role of a Supreme Court to adjudicate and interpret these disputes in relation to the constitution (*see Chapter* 2) which usually outlines the nature of the relationship. This is the case in the United States.

Finally, the concepts of responsible and representative government help our understanding of the relationship between the citizen and the government in a democratic state. The theory of **responsible government** suggests that governments should be responsible to the electorate that elected them. Moreover, governments should be responsible to the legislature and judiciary for their actions and policies. Responsibility means having to explain, defend and answer for the policies made and decisions taken. Equally, this theory suggests that governments should act responsibly within the limits of the law, acknowledging the rule of law, and governing in accordance within its own judgement. Acting responsibly, in the interests of the nation and community is as important as acknowledging that it can be held responsible through elections for its behaviour and policies, and its successes and failures.

The British and French Governments are held responsible to the people through elections and through the national legislatures which are empowered to hold the members of the Government responsible. From this concept has arisen two interrelated concepts: individual ministerial responsibility and Cabinet collective responsibility (*see Chapter* 8).

By viewing responsible government from the standpoint of the relationship between the executive (law executing) and legislative (law making) agencies, two basic forms of responsible government can be identified: parliamentary and, in comparison, presidential.

In Britain, responsible government operates through a **parliamentary system of government**, meaning that the legislative assembly, Parliament, is not elected or appointed separately from the executive. The executive is subordinate and responsible to Parliament for its actions and policies. The leader of the majority party in the House of Commons forms a government and members of the Government are both individually and collectively responsible to Parliament. In the parliamentary form the executive composes a Prime Minister or Premier (chief executive) and that official's Cabinet. The Government remains in office only while it commands the confidence and support of the majority in Parliament.

Presidential government features a form of separation of power between the executive and the legislative branches. The two branches are independent and equal. The chief executive (President) is chosen independently of the legislature, holds office for a fixed term, and has broad powers not subject to the direct control of the legislature. In the United States a written constitution provides for a separation of powers between the branches of government.

Representative government is a system of government in which public policies are made by politicians who are selected by the electorate and held to account in periodic elections. It means government should represent the interests of those who voted them into office, acting on and reflecting the wishes of the people. Government is, however, granted a degree of discretion in taking decisions on behalf of those they represent.

British governments are representative because MPs are elected to the House of Commons. The largest party in the Commons forms the Government, ensuring a direct link between the Government and the wishes of the people through the MPs and the party.

Example:
In 1992, having won a general election with a majority of seats in the House of Commons, the leader of the Conservative Party, John Major, formed a government claiming to represent the interests of the electorate.

However, since 1945 no British government can have said to have had the support of the majority of the electorate and therefore truly to have represented their interests, because no government has been elected with over 50% of the popular vote. British governments since 1945 have taken office through a simple majority of seats in the Commons, although there have been cases where governments have taken office with not even a simple majority of all the votes cast in the general election.

This concept also means that governments and national assemblies should reflect the socio-economic composition of the electorate. Thus Parliament should contain white, black, Asian, male, female, etc., members. However, both the British Parliament and Government may be criticised for not representing accurately the true socio-economic background of the people.

Example:
In Parliament there are few black or Asian MPs and within the present Government there are very few women.

Questions

1. What is the 'separation of powers'?
2. Distinguish between unitary states and federal states.
3. Distinguish between responsible and representative government, and parliamentary and presidential government.
4. What is 'parliamentary government'?

1.3 | **Concepts of the individual**

Concepts of the citizen revolve around the meaning of citizenship and the nature of the citizen's personal relationship with the State and its agencies. The concept of **citizenship** means that a member of a state is both entitled to such civil and political rights that exist in that state and owes an obligation to respect those rights. The most obvious identification of citizenship is a passport that identifies a person as an individual from a particular state. The extent to which citizenship is conferred depends upon the political rule in any particular state. In some states in the past only those who were really wealthy or of high birth enjoyed citizenship.

Example: Before the American Civil War, slaves were not citizens.

Citizenship is granted by birth, depending either on where one was born or to whom one was born. It is also granted by naturalisation, which is a legal process by which a person becomes a citizen of another country. Some people who live in states are not citizens. These include people classified as 'residents' who have been granted permission to live in a state but are not entitled to enjoy the full rights of citizenship.

Example:
Many Turkish people living in Germany are residents, but not full citizens.

A citizen normally enjoys a number of rights.

Examples:
The right to vote, the right to have a passport to enable one to leave and return to one's state, and expectation of state protection.

Citizens are subject to the laws of the State and under certain circumstances owe an obligation to the State. For example, at times of war citizens may be called upon to join the armed forces of a country and protect their state from military attack.

The rights which citizens may enjoy are collectively known as **civil rights**. This term describes those freedoms and privileges within a society that belong to a citizen. The denial of these rights, whether on the grounds of race, religion, class, gender, or other social characteristics, is regarded as a denial of citizenship.

Civil rights vary from country to country and over time, and are sometimes known as civil liberties. They govern a citizen's relationship with the authorities of the state and relations with other citizens. They may include the right to vote, the right to freedom of speech, the right to freedom of association, the right to demonstrate, freedom of movement and freedom to join a trade union. In Europe, most states have signed the European

Convention on Human Rights which identifies many civil rights which those signatories have agreed to guarantee within their state (*see Chapter 11*).

Sometimes civil rights are guaranteed by a legally binding document, known as a Bill of Rights. The most famous Bill of Rights is contained within the United States Constitution. The first ten constitutional amendments contained a series of civil rights including freedom of expression and belief, and fair and equal treatment before the law. Britain does not have a Bill of Rights. Civil rights in the British Constitution are guaranteed in different ways (*see Chapter 2*).

Civil rights should be distinguished from so-called **natural rights**. These are rights we are supposedly born with and include the right to life, dignity, freedom and movement. Natural rights exist independently of any man-made rules and regulations; they are rights which belong to people irrespective of state definitions. However, states do have the power to deny these rights. In Britain the theory that people had rights independent of the state, in whatever form it took, developed slowly over many centuries. The first written expression of the 'rights of the person' is found in the Magna Carta of 1215. This document established the very first civil right, the right to a prompt trial.

Civil and natural rights are linked to the concepts of freedom and welfare. **Freedom** means that a person is free to do anything provided their action does not infringe the freedoms of others. John Stuart Mill defined freedom as follows: 'the individual is not accountable to society for his actions, in so far as these concern the interests of no one but himself'.

In the modern world, individuals are bound by a great variety of different laws that govern their behaviour in society.

Example:
In Britain, to drive a car a person must be seventeen years old or over and must pass a state-organised driving test to prove that they have been properly trained to operate a car on their own.

Freedom may be a negative concept, guaranteeing rights over laws that seek to limit citizens' rights. In modern societies freedom is used to guarantee the existence of certain rights, to guarantee an individuals' welfare and to guarantee against laws that restrict freedom of action.

Example:
Laws which guarantee individuals' freedoms within the criminal and civil legal machine.

In this context the term 'welfare' means the observance and existence of conditions that ensure the well-being of an individual, their prosperity, good fortune and health. This is linked to ideas of equality, justice and rights. Accordingly, laws should not encroach upon the individual's welfare or limit their ability to improve their own welfare. Moreover, according to some definitions, the State is expected to pursue social and economic policies that encourage and develop the welfare of its citizens. Originally this meant that the State would play a limited role in social and economic affairs allowing the provision of private welfare to exist. In the late twentieth century this gave rise to the idea of a **welfare state**.

A welfare state exists where a government assumes responsibility for ensuring the provision of basic economic and social necessities to its citizens through the direct provision of certain goods and services. These services are designed to ensure the well-being of its citizens. The nature and scope of the welfare state vary between countries.

This may include a combination of services, including the provision of cash payments to those who are unemployed or sick, a free and comprehensive health care service, and the supply of education, public housing and personal social services.

Today the definition includes the need for government to pursue economic policies that will cover the costs of its welfare provision and avoid problems such as poverty and unemployment. In Britain the major provisions of the welfare state include: social services, housing provisions, the National Health Service, education, social security.

Questions

1. What are civil rights?
2. Distinguish between freedom and welfare.
3. What is meant by the term 'welfare state'?

Notes and references

1.   See Eccleshall, R. et al. *Political Ideologies* (London, 1986), ch. 2.

Further reading

Eccleshall, R. et al. *Political Ideologies* (London, 1986).

Renwick, A. and Swinburn, I. *Basic Political Concepts* (London, 1987).

CHAPTER 2

The constitution

Most nation-states in the world have some form of constitution. A constitution is a system of laws, customs and conventions which regulate the relations between the organs of the state and the citizen. It often refers to a document or documents which embody the most important laws establishing the structure and principles of government.

Constitutions give structure and organisation to the processes of an institution, for example a state, a government, a party, a trade union, or even a club or society. In this chapter we will discuss state constitutions.

Most constitutions are designed to establish the framework of a state and the structures and powers, procedures and processes of the institutions of government.

Example:
The Constitution of the United States of America regulates how the President is chosen and how laws are passed. Similarly, the Constitution of the Russian Federation outlines how the offices of state are to be filled and what the powers of the President and Parliament are. These are examples of written constitutions.

There are a variety of political issues which revolve around this topic including a Bill of Rights, electoral reform,[1] devolution,[2] and the role of the monarchy. This chapter will examine the following :

2.1 Written and unwritten constitutions.

2.2 The written constitution debate.

2.3 A Bill of Rights?

2.4 The monarchy: role and reform.

2.5 Conclusions.

2.1 | Written and unwritten constitutions

So far we have talked of constitutions without classification. There are two different types of constitution.

Written constitution

A written constitution is a constitution that embodies all the rules, powers, and functions of the various organs of the state and their relationship to each other in a written form. These constitutions are described as rigid because they are difficult to change. Amending one is difficult, often involving complicated procedures.

Example:
The United States has a written constitution that has only been amended twenty-six times. To amend the United States Constitution requires a two-thirds majority in both Houses of Congress and all State legislators. However the US Constitution's flexibility is increased by the existence of a Supreme Court which has the power to interpret and re-interpret the Constitution to allow it to move with the times.

An unwritten constitution

An unwritten constitution refers to one which is not embodied in one single document and is composed of a variety of different documents.

This form of constitution is **flexible** because it can be changed through simple procedures. The British Constitution can be described as unwritten and flexible. It is drawn from five principle sources:

1. **Statute laws:** These are laws made by Parliament, i.e. Acts of Parliament and other forms of legislation made under the provisions of the original Act, e.g. delegated legislation.
2. **Common law:** Comprising customs, decisions made by the courts, and the prerogative powers. Common law has been important in establishing many individual rights and liberties.
3. **Conventions:** These are unwritten rules of constitutional behaviour. No constitution, written or unwritten, can work entirely by clearly defined rules. In every constitutional framework there are unwritten rules which are considered binding upon all those who are responsible for making the constitution work. Conventions are generally agreed practices which relate to the workings of the political system.

The characteristics of the British Constitution are:

1. There is no written constitution. It is derived from a number of different documents.
2. There is a great debate about what the British Constitution is and this is subject to many interpretations.
3. Much of the British Constitution is composed of an 'uncodified set of political practices' which govern how the country is run.
4. It is evolutionary; it has evolved over centuries and has changed as the country has altered.
5. Unlike the United States where there is a strict separation of powers, the British Constitution allows for a concentration of power at its core, i.e. the Government (executive) over both Parliament and Whitehall.

Example:
It is a convention that when a government loses a 'vote of confidence' in the House of Commons the Prime Minister and his or her government should either resign or ask the Queen to dissolve Parliament and authorise a general election.

4. **European Union law:** After joining what is now known as the European Union (EU) in 1973, Britain has been bound by the laws made by the EU Commission. These laws are another source of the British Constitution, which in the past twenty years has had a dramatic effect on the composition of the British state.
5. **Works of authority:** A variety of written works which are venerated because they give guidance and interpretation on uncertain aspects of the constitution.

Example:
The Parliamentary rule book by Erskine May (Treatise on the Law, Privileges, Proceedings and Usage of Parliament) *which outlines parliamentary practice and procedure.*

The principles of Britain's Constitution

1. It is adaptable and responsive to change. Every new Act of Parliament changes our Constitution, allowing the Constitution to evolve naturally and simply.

Example:
The Criminal Justice and Public Order Act 1994 changed the age of consent for homosexuality.[3] This was a simple process which required a majority of MPs in the House of Commons to vote in favour of the change in the law. This vote altered the Constitution without a great deal of drama and complication, illustrating that the Constitution is flexible.

2. It reflects the unitary nature of the State.
3. It invests all power in Parliament which is described as 'sovereign'. The Westminster Parliament can give powers and responsibilities to other institutions, e.g. local authorities, but these can be removed at any time by Parliament (*see Chapter 11*). However, in Britain in practice there is **parliamentary government** meaning that the executive is a component of the legislature and sovereign power is exercised by the Government through its parliamentary majority.
4. It embodies the principle of the rule of law (*see Chapter 10*).

Questions

1. Outline the possible advantages and disadvantages of (a) a written and (b) an unwritten constitution.
2. What are the main characteristics of the British Constitution?
3. Define 'sovereignty'?
4. What are the main sources of the British Constitution?

2.2 | **The written constitution debate**

The merits and demerits of the British Constitution have been debated for thirty years. The debate has arisen as the power of government has increased at the expense of parliamentary power. Critics claim that many Acts of Parliament have bolstered the powers of the executive and combined with an increase in the use of delegated legislation and Orders in Council, parliamentary power has been diminished. Since the 1960s the British Constitution has been criticised on the following grounds:

1. It is an ineffective guardian of the rights of the individual.

    Example:
    Terrorist trials where miscarriages of justice have taken place include the Birmingham Six and the Guildford Four cases. Here the wrong people were convicted of a number of IRA bombings in the early 1970s and served almost two decades in prison until their release by the Court of Appeal, which ruled that their convictions were 'unsafe'[4].

2. It is unable to provide effective controls over an all-powerful executive. This is exemplified by Lord Hailsham's reference, in 1976, to the over-mighty powers of the Government and Prime Minister. This reflected a feeling that the executive was too powerful and that Parliament was unable to exert effective control over it. These feelings have been amplified by the massive increase in the influence that government now has over the daily lives of people in Britain.

3. It possesses an inefficient and ineffective Parliament, unable to properly scrutinise government activity. The 1994 Pergau Dam and Matrix Churchill affairs reopened the debate over the weakness of Parliament. In both cases Parliament was misinformed about the Government's policy – on the export of arms to Iraq in the case of Matrix Churchill, and over the linking of aid policies to Malaysia with arms contracts for British firms in the Pergau example. In both cases, what Parliament had been told later transpired to be incorrect and showed the inability of Parliament to scrutinise the executive effectively (*see Chapter 3*).

4. Judges are too weak to be 'guardians of the law' because they do not have the power to fulfil this role.

Arguments for a written constitution

1. Critics argue that there has been a steady increase in the powers of, and exercise of power by, the executive. The use of the majority principle and strict party discipline in the House of Commons has meant that parliamentary controls over the executive have dwindled in the past thirty years. In Britain, the executive branch controls the legislature through the operation of party government (*see Chapter 3*). Supporters of a written constitution argue that if we introduced such a constitution it would give us an opportunity to separate the executive from the legislature, as is the case in the United States, and increase Parliament's powers.

2. It is alleged that the size of government and its role and influence has increased dramatically in the past fifty years. This has resulted in a vast array of frequently changing laws, that have limited the freedoms of the individual and business. Most people are unaware of how these changes affect them and the majority of citizens are ignorant of their civil rights.

    Example:
    The five Criminal Justice Acts passed in Britain since 1979 have radically altered the criminal justice system. The 1994 Criminal Justice Act contains clauses which changed the civil rights of the individual, including the removal of the right of silence of an accused person without the inference of guilt.

    In the face of such changes critics of the present arrangements suggest that we need a 'Bill of Rights' incorporated into a written constitution which would :

    - set out clearly the rights of the citizens and the rights of the state
    - provide a better guarantee for individual rights and freedoms
    - limit the powers of the State
    - help educate British citizens about their civil rights.

3. It is alleged that the judiciary is too weak to protect the citizens from abuses of power by the executive.

    The 1993 Matrix Churchill case showed how important the judiciary can be in preventing government abuses of power. The judge in this case insisted that it was wrong that certain documents had been classified as secret and withheld under **public immunity certificates** from the defence team of the accused directors of the Matrix Churchill company. As a result the public immunity certificate order was lifted and subsequently the case against the directors was dropped. The judge in this case played a pivotal role in ensuring that justice was seen to be done and in protecting the accused. Leading lawyers believe this case and others like it show that judges in Britain should have a much wider role allowing them to act as an effective check upon the organs of the State. If a written constitution were introduced, senior judges could be given the power of judicial review of legislation, rather like the Supreme Court in the United States, allowing them to strike down or set aside Acts that were deemed contrary to the constitution, and thereby protecting the rights and liberties of citizens.

4. Critics such as the civil liberties pressure group Liberty argue that during the 1980s and 1990s there has been a massive increase in the powers of government and suggest this has occurred without effective scrutiny or control by Parliament. This has led to an infringement of civil rights and choice via the use of statutory instruments and delegated legislation.

Example:
The Dangerous Dogs Act 1991 allows the Home Secretary to add to the list of dogs, which under the provisions of the Act are either banned or controlled, other breeds of dogs if he or she feels it appropriate, without having to seek parliamentary approval.

Proponents argue that the introduction of a written constitution would ensure that people know their rights and increase public confidence in the nation's constitutional arrangements.

5. The decline of Parliament as an effective check on government is a further argument for a written constitution. This is best shown by the admission of William Waldegrave, the Minister for 'open government', in March 1994 before the Treasury and Civil Service Select Committee that Ministers do not have to tell the whole truth to Parliament. Such statements encourage critics of Parliament to argue for wholesale reform because this reflects its weaknesses as the principle scrutiniser and controller of the executive.[5]

Arguments against a written constitution

1. It is argued that Britain's present constitution has adapted in the face of problems and will continue to do so. This adaptation explains its durability.
2. Proponents of the present system argue that it would be extremely time-consuming and expensive to draft a written constitution.
3. There are many problems regarding the implementation of a written constitution. Those against any reform question how a new constitution would be formulated. It is most likely that a

Key term: Public immunity certificates

These are orders signed by Ministers which are used in legal cases to prevent secret government documents from being released ahead of time. Normally most government documents are held for thirty years before they are released for public viewing. In the Matrix Churchill case the documents showed that the Government was aware that the company was selling arms to Iraq. This, once it became public, was one of the factors which led to the case being dismissed.

Royal Commission would have to be created with the purpose of defining the principles, but who would decide its membership and terms of reference? This and many other problems would have to be addressed before a written constitution could be introduced.

4. If a written constitution were introduced the whole nature of British society would have to be adapted resulting in the abolition of many traditions and conventions.

5. A written constitution would be likely to change the role of the judiciary and politicise it. Judges would have much more power to interfere in the political process.

6. The introduction of a written constitution would cause the **doctrine of entrenchment** to be scrapped.

7. It is undesirable and unnecessary. A written constitution would place tremendous power in the hands of an unelected, unrepresentative judiciary. Furthermore, constraints exist which limit the powers of the State, e.g. the doctrine of *ultra vires* (*see Chapter 10*).

8. Constitutional flexibility would be lost and it is not clear how our constitution would adapt in the face of changes in society, e.g. how would a rigid constitutional framework deal with moral and ethical issues such as embryonic research and implantations?

9. Written constitutions are held to be guarantors of individual rights and freedoms and therefore, proponents argue, the introduction of a written constitution in Britain would be a constructive development safeguarding civil rights. However, against this view, opponents of change argue that a written constitution would not safeguard civil rights or democratic government. They use two examples to illustrate this point. First, the USSR had a written constitution which in theory provided for the guarantee of civil rights but in practice did not. Secondly, the USA, despite having one of the most venerated written constitutions, has seen democratic government abused by powerful executives.

Key concept: the doctrine of entrenchment

This means that no Parliament in Britain can bind the actions of its successors. When an Act is passed it can later be repealed if Parliament desires to change it. It means that laws can be easily changed over time to meet the changing needs of society.

Example:

In 1972, during the Presidential Election Campaign, supporters of President Nixon, who was seeking re-election, were involved in a 'dirty tricks' campaign directed towards the Democratic opponent. This was known as the Watergate Affair. When the story broke, the President denied any knowledge of the affair. Later however, in his second term in office, having won the presidential election it became clear that he had known about the campaign, and Nixon was forced to resign in disgrace. This affair revealed to the American people how government power could be abused, and it forced the United States Congress to reform itself to become a more powerful and wary scrutiniser of the Federal Government.

Figure 3 President Nixon at the time of his resignation over the Watergate Affair.

Conclusions

1. It would be difficult to introduce a written constitution into Britain because there are so many problems associated with the drafting, implementation and operation of such a document.
2. It would provide improvements, removing inconsistencies and unclear conventions.
3. If Britain had a written constitution it would have to create an all-embracing agreement, acceptable to all the political parties. This would be difficult to achieve given the range of opinions and ideologies that separate many Members of Parliament.
4. Now that the post-war consensus has collapsed and a new form of consensus between the major political parties has yet to be formed, it will be much more difficult to reach agreement on a written constitution.
5. It is possible that a written constitution would mean that many centuries of development and historical constitutional material would have to be swept away.

The activities of pressure groups, such as Charter 88 for constitutional reform, have put reform onto the political agenda but none of the major parties have proposed the introduction of a written constitution, although the Labour Party and the Liberal Democrats have proposed, to varying degrees, policies which would entail limited constitutional reform. A wholesale re-write of the British Constitution does not seem to be a viable option at the present time and therefore attention has shifted to more limited goals of achieving the introduction of a Bill of Rights.

Questions

1. What are the arguments against Britain adopting some type of written constitution?
2. 'Parliament cannot bind the hands of its successors.' How does the doctrine of entrenchment affect arguments for the implementation of a written constitution?

2.3 | **A Bill of Rights?**

Out of the debate over the nature of the British Constitution and the realisation that radical and complete constitutional reform is unlikely, campaigners for constitutional reform have turned their activities to campaigning for a more limited goal of a 'Bill of Rights'.

This has been a continuing debate since the 1970s when a number of eminent authorities, including Lord Hailsham, Sir Leon Brittan,

Tony Benn and Michael Zander, began to advocate the introduction of a single all-embracing document that incorporated the liberties and rights of citizens and aimed to protect the citizens against abuses of power by an all-powerful executive. A range of pressure groups developed over the issue including the National Council for Civil Liberties and Charter 88. Leading members of the judiciary have, for some time, expressed their support for a Bill of Rights.[6]

Arguments in favour of a Bill of Rights

1. Supporters of a Bill of Rights argue that the scale and scope of Government activity has increased massively in the past fifty years. As a result the principle of parliamentary sovereignty has been used by governments from all sides of the political spectrum to legitimise and bolster their actions. With the use of the whips and strict party discipline governments have ensured that their policies have been introduced despite widespread public opposition.

    Example:
    The Community Charge (Poll Tax) and British Rail privatisation are examples of policies which have been introduced by using the parliamentary majority despite serious reservations being expressed by many leading industrialists and other organisations.

2. Attached to this criticism is the apparent weakness of the Opposition to counter government policies and the reluctance of back-benchers to act in the interests of the constituents rather than their party.

3. Similarly, proponents argue that Parliament is unable to act as the guardian of individual rights and freedoms because of the domination of party politics which gives the Government control of parliamentary sovereignty.

4. Supporters of the idea, including Michael Zander, argue that there has been a massive increase in the detail and volume of government legislation impinging upon almost every aspect of people's daily lives. Furthermore, with the scale and complexity of the annual Budget, MPs and Lords are unable to exercise effective control and scrutiny over executive financial actions and policies, enabling them to protect citizens against abuses of power.[7]

5. Supporters of a Bill of Rights argue that the rise in the presidential premier has further eroded the power of Parliament to control the executive. The Matrix Churchill case and the Pergau Dam affair illustrate this (*see Chapters 3, 6, and 7*).

6. Proponents of a Bill of Rights suggest that there are defects in the electoral system, and that, since 1945, these have resulted in governments taking office that do not possess over fifty per cent of the votes cast in a general election. Therefore, a Bill of

Rights would ensure that the interests of the majority are protected against governments which did not command majority support. Critics argue that these governments do not have the moral authority to govern and are vulnerable to resistance from sections of the electorate against their policies.

7. Critics argue that, as signatories of the European Convention on Human Rights, Britain could easily incorporate the Convention into domestic law, enabling its judiciary to deal with abuses of human rights internally, thereby avoiding the international embarrassment of having one of the worst records of all the signatories to the convention. Only Italy has a worse record than the UK. Through incorporation, moreover, British judges could interpret cases to suit domestic conditions and the European Court at Strasbourg would remain the final arbiter.

8. Supporters of this idea argue that if a Bill of Rights were introduced into the British Constitution it would raise consciousness about human rights throughout Britain.

9. Most importantly, proponents of a Bill of Rights argue that there has been a catalogue of legislation in the past twenty years that has limited the rights and freedoms of the individual which, if a Bill of Rights had existed, would have been deemed unlawful by the courts.

Example:
The introduction of Diplock Courts and the suspensions of jury trials in Northern Ireland.

Arguments against a Bill of Rights

1. Those who oppose the introduction of a Bill of Rights argue that constitutional flexibility would be lost and that the doctrine of entrenchment would be removed. The United States Constitution is often used as an example of the inflexibilities and problems that can result from a written constitutional framework.

Example:
The inability of various Presidents to alter the gun laws of the United States which are enshrined in the US Constitution.

2. Critics argue that a Bill of Rights is no guarantee of liberties. In the USSR citizens were supposedly guaranteed freedom of speech in their Constitution but they were unable to enjoy this freedom in practice.

3. Supporters of the status quo argue that a Bill of Rights would transfer responsibility for the protection of the individual from an elected Parliament to a fragile piece of paper. Opponents argue that the present system based on Parliament is quite adequate in preserving the rights of the individual. If there are

criticisms of Parliament's powers over the executive it would be more beneficial to reform Parliament rather than start down the road of widespread constitutional reform.

4. Furthermore, a Bill of Rights would increase the role and power of judges. They would move from being judicial interpreters of Acts of Parliament and case law to being arbiters of the principles of the Constitution. Many who oppose a Bill of Rights argue that judges are unfit for such a role, and criticise the judiciary for being elitist and biased in favour of the 'establishment' (*see Chapter 10*). One famous case is often cited as an example of the political bias of the British judiciary – the Ponting case.

5. Further arguments against the introduction of a Bill of Rights have been levied by a number of leading academics. Philip Norton suggests that a Bill of Rights is undesirable because it would embody the values of a particular time.[8] What is right for today's society may be wrong for a society in the future as the Bill would be an entrenched document. The resulting inflexibility could produce difficulties for future societies. Furthermore, he suggests that a Bill of Rights would politicise the law, making it the unaccountable arbiter of political matters, such as capital punishment or the homosexual age of consent, and not Parliament. Norton suggests that it is unachievable because there is no method under which an entrenched Bill of Rights could be introduced and that there is no consensus on the rights to be included. Professor Norton concludes that a Bill of Rights is held up as 'offering protection for those oppressed by public authorities. It is offered as a saviour that Parliament cannot be'. He argues that a Bill of Rights would not revolutionise the protection of civil liberties in Britain.[9]

6. Opponents argue that many of the rights which would be included in a Bill of Rights already exist, and are to be found in a variety of sources within the unwritten Constitution.

Conclusions

The practical difficulties that surround the introduction of a Bill of Rights are similar to those concerning the introduction of a written constitution in Britain. There have been a number of attempts to introduce a Bill of Rights through Private Members' Bills. None of these attempts have been successful, and only when the issue enters the mainstream popular political agenda will a Bill of Rights have any chance of being passed into law. This is beginning to happen. In the spring of 1994 Sir Patrick Mayhew, the Northern Ireland Secretary, while announcing moves to get the Ulster peace process moving again raised the possibility that a Bill of Rights could be enacted for Northern Ireland.[10] No firm proposals have yet been published but if Northern Ireland were given a Bill of Rights it would be hard for the Government to resist moves to introduce a similar Act on the mainland. In mainland Britain the issue still fails to ignite mass support.

Questions

1. What is a 'Bill of Rights'?
2. Outline (a) a case for and (b) a case against the introduction of a Bill of Rights into Britain.

2.4 | The monarchy: role and reform

The role of the monarch has changed substantially over the centuries. The institution of the monarch has evolved from being one of an absolute ruler to that of a ceremonial head of state. In the 1990s Britain has a **constitutional monarchy.**

During the 1970s and 1980s the institution, in the form of the present Queen, received a great deal of popular support throughout the UK. In the past few years this has begun to fall as the House of Windsor has become engulfed in family break-ups and controversy. These events have reopened the debate over the role and need for a monarchy, which has been ongoing since 1945. Anti-monarchists, or republicans, believe that the institution should be replaced with an elected office such as a president with strictly defined powers and responsibilities removing the present, imprecise, convention-based system.

The case for the monarchy

1. It works. Monarchists argue that the present institution works both as an effective head of state and a constitutional safeguard. When called upon, the Queen has ensured the smooth and effective operation of government in the UK. The monarchy provides an essential constitutional mechanism in the formation and dissolution of governments, especially where the result of a general election is inconclusive or leadership is in doubt.

    Example:
    When Prime Minister Harold Macmillan fell ill in 1963 the Queen visited him in hospital to seek his advice on a successor, and proceeded to call on Sir Alex Douglas Home to form the next government.

2. The monarchy provides a unifying influence above party politics. Supporters argue that the monarch is an impartial and a non-partisan symbol of national unity, whereas in other

Key concept: the constitutional monarchy

This means that in the present day the monarchy has a limited role within the constitutional framework of the UK. Its powers have mostly passed to the institutions of the Prime Minister and Cabinet. The monarch is seen as impartial and above politics, and is said to act 'on the advice' of her Ministers and thus is sheltered from political controversy. The monarchy operates a few royal prerogatives which allow for the smooth operation of the Constitution. These include the appointment of the Prime Minister, the leader of the largest party in the House of Commons, and the power to dissolve Parliament on the advice of the Prime Minister. This is perhaps its most important role, providing for the smooth process of the formation and dissolution of government in the UK.

Key concept: prerogative power

These are the powers which in legal terms are still those of the monarch in that they do not stem from Parliament. They are powers which were originally accepted by the law courts as rightfully belonging to the King (or Queen) in his (or her) capacity as ruler. Over time, most of these powers have been transferred, by convention, to Ministers, particularly the Prime Minister. The prerogative powers include the appointment of Ministers, the creation of peers, the dissolution of Parliament and acting as the source of the honours system.

Figure 4 The Queen and Prince Philip attending the State Opening of Parliament.

countries heads of state usually have a party colour and are members of politicised institutions.

Example:
In France the President is an elected person who has a political label. President Mitterrand was a socialist. In the United States President Clinton is a member of the Democrats.

The monarch presents a style, experience and professionalism which is not matched by any other head of state. It provides a symbol for the nation and the 'ceremony of monarchy' legitimises government. Some argue that the solemnity and symbolism of ceremony are essential ingredients in public life because they strengthen awareness of national identity and respect for the authority of government.

3. The Queen tenders non-partisan advice to the Prime Minister. The Sovereign has the right 'to be consulted, the right to encourage and the right to warn'. The Prime Minister meets with the Queen once a week usually on a Tuesday to discuss matters of state. The Queen has maintained a scrupulously neutral position in party political terms but she did voice her concerns in public speeches over devolution in the 1970s and social divisions in the late 1980s.

4. Monarchists argue that the Queen has a potentially valuable role to play in foreign affairs. A state visit by the Queen is often seen as an opportunity to improve diplomatic, social and economic relations with a country. When the Queen makes trips abroad a vast entourage of people travel with her including businessmen and Department of Trade officials. Royal visits can greatly improve relations and are often used to add legitimacy and prestige to foreign leaders or new regimes. Moreover, business deals often follow royal visits.

5. The monarch provides a touchstone of family behaviour. The royal family was once held to be an example to the nation of a stable, loving nuclear family. With the break-up of several marriages, this is no longer the case.

6. The royal family are involved in good works. The royals devote a substantial part of their time to good works; visiting the sick, opening hospitals, lending their weight to countless charities and good causes.

7. The Queen heads the Commonwealth. As the ceremonial head of the Commonwealth, the Queen acts as a focus and a binding influence for this loose association of states.

8. The monarchy earns money for the nation. Thousands of tourists are attracted to Britain by the monarchy, earning valuable foreign currency for the UK. The economic benefits that this brings is held by some to be their most substantial contribution to the welfare and happiness of the British people.

The case against the monarchy

1. Heads of state should be elected. It is argued that an inherited title cannot be justified as a good qualification for a head of state, and in a modern democracy the head of state should be elected.

2. The monarchy reinforces the British class system and conservative values. Supporters of change argue that the monarchy cannot be described as a non-political office because it reinforces conservative values such as wealth and inherited privilege, and support for the status quo. Furthermore, critics argue the monarchy sits at the apex of the class-based system propagating elitist values and preventing, by its continued existence, any move towards a classless society because of the privilege and position it symbolises.

3. The monarchy is expensive. The monarchy costs approximately £40 million per annum. This figure is composed of an annual grant from Parliament – the **Civil List** – to enable the Queen to meet the expenses of her royal household and other members of the royal family, the income from the Duchy of Lancaster, the income from the Duchy of Cornwall (which goes to Prince Charles for official and private purposes), Grants in Aid from government departments for the maintenance of palaces, aircraft, a yacht and a train, and the Queen's private income. Critics argue that the services the Queen and the other royals provide is not worth this level of government expenditure. The fact that until recently the Queen did not pay any tax on a personal income which made her one of the richest women in the world allowed critics to argue that the institution was too expensive and a more efficient and cheaper option would be a presidency.

4. The honours system is an absurdity. The Queen is the foundation stone of the honours system which is seen as socially divisive and absurd. The Queen dispenses these honours on the advice of the Prime Minister. However, the elevation of some men and women above their fellows for good works, position in the civil service or service to the political institutions of the country has been criticised as unfair, unrepresentative and open to abuse by political parties.

   Example:
   On leaving Prime Ministerial office Harold Wilson gave his secretary a life peerage. Some considered this an abuse.

5. The functions of the monarchy are meaningless. The royal prerogatives have all been usurped by the executive in virtually every respect. In theory the Queen can do a variety of things without Parliament's consent, e.g. declare war, but under our present constitutional arrangements she does not, in reality, have this power.

Key term: the Civil List

This is the amount of money which Parliament votes to give the Queen and her immediate family to cover their duty expenses. The present Civil List was reorganised in 1991 and presently amounts to a payment of £7.9 million a year for the next ten years.

6.   The monarchy is an anachronism. If we wish to see a classless society within a modern and efficient democracy then the monarchy is an institution which holds back progress and democratic development because it is founded on historical traditions, nostalgia and archaisms. The monarchy is seen as a barrier to the development of constitutional reform.

7.   The contribution of the monarchy to diplomacy and foreign relations is insubstantial. A royal visit to another state does not result in the overnight resolution of the problems between that state and the UK nor does it substantially benefit trade relations with that country.

8.   The royals' contributions to 'good works' and the tourist industry has to be acknowledged but it is an elaborate and expensive system.

9.   The royal family was once held to be the model family. Now it is seen as an example of much that is wrong with the contemporary family.

Conclusions

To date, pressure for a radical reform of the institution of the British head of state has never developed. In the early 1990s an orchestrated press campaign over the level of the Queen's personal wealth led to her volunteering to pay tax on her income. The Prime Minister, John Major, announced this decision, claiming that the Queen was bowing to public opinion. Moreover, the repairs to Windsor Castle following the fire that damaged it have brought about a new chapter of partnership between the Government and the monarch, with the Queen opening Buckingham Palace in order to contribute to the costs of the repairs of £60 million. These events demonstrated how the popularity of the institution has declined in recent years as the 'perfect family image' has collapsed.

The debate over the reform or abolition of the monarchy has tended to centre on the costs of the institution. The reform of the Civil List has gone some way to appeasing critics. The financial arguments must be weighed against the possible costs of a president. This institution would entail the same level of demand for services; transport and travel, personal staff, housing, and would require a salary to be paid. The method of choosing a president would incur additional cost as would the institutional transition from a constitutional monarchy to a presidency. It is likely that a presidency would cost probably slightly less than the present system, but the overall savings would be minimal and the process would involve a great upheaval.

The monarchy has now entered a serious stage in its development towards the twenty-first century, and its survival is dependent on the interpretation of its role by Elizabeth II's successor. John Major has successfully instituted a number of reforms which have given both the nation and the monarchy time to reflect, e.g. taxation and reforms of the Civil List. There is now an opportunity to create a new style of monarchy, perhaps similar to that of the Netherlands; 'a Bicycle monarchy', less pompous and elitist, closer to the ordinary citizen, with an accompanying remodelled social role breaking down class rigidities and snobberies. It seems likely that the monarchy will remain, if in a different form, so long as the British people believe it to be a worthwhile institution. The words of Lord Atlee, referring to the House of Lords, may perhaps be applied to the monarchy: 'Leave it alone, it works'.

Questions

1. What is meant by the term 'constitutional monarchy'?
2. Define the term 'prerogative powers'.
3. Outline (a) a case for and (b) a case against retaining the monarchy.

2.5 | Conclusions

1. Constitutional reform has been placed on the political agenda but it remains at the periphery.
2. Both the Conservative and Labour Parties have acknowledged the need for some form of constitutional renewal, but the Tories have taken a much more conservative attitude to reform than have Labour.
3. It is debatable whether constitutional issues will ever be great vote winners. In the 1992 General Election a debate over the introduction of proportional representation between the Labour Party and the Liberal Democrats in the event of a hung Parliament occupied a proportion of the final week of campaigning and detracted from the main issues of the election. This damaged the Labour Party's campaign and helped contribute to its failure in 1992 (*see Chapter 12, section 7*).
4. Charter 88 and other pressure groups have helped to place aspects of our constitution under public scrutiny but it remains to be seen whether after the next general election the British Constitution will undergo a complete overhaul.

Essay topics

1. 'A wholesale and complete reform of the British Constitution is necessary'. Discuss.
2. Discuss the view that a Bill of Rights is neither necessary nor desirable.

3.   Outline the arguments for and against reform of the monarchy?

4.   Discuss the problems involved in drawing up a written constitution for Britain.

5.   'The British Constitution is what happens.' Discuss.

Essay planning

5.   'The British Constitution is what happens.' Discuss.

This essay topic is asking you to explain the nature and characteristics of the British Constitution, with particular reference to the way our constitution changes.

(a) Explain the nature and characteristics of the British Constitution.

(b) Explain the mechanisms for changing the constitution, i.e. Acts of Parliament.

(c) You should argue throughout the essay that it is flexible – unwritten characteristics allow the Constitution to change daily: every time a Bill is passed the Constitution changes, every time a judgement is made the Constitution changes, every time a convention is broken the Constitution changes.

(d) Thus, you conclude that in the British system what happens in the branches of government affects the contents of the Constitution.

Notes and references

1.   See Chapters 11 and 12.

2.   See Chapters 11 and 12.

3.   *The Guardian*, 22.02.94.

4.   McKie, D. *The Election: A Voters' Guide'* (London, 1992), p. 162.

5.   *The Times*, 09.03.94.

6.   Norton, P. 'A Bill of Rights: The Case Against', *Talking Politics*, Vol. 5., No. 3., 1993, p. 149.

7.   See Zander, M. 'A Bill of Rights: The Debate Continues', in *'Social Studies Review,'* Vol. 1., No. 3., 1986, pp. 32–6.

8.   Norton, P. 'Should Britain have a Bill of Rights?', *Talking Politics*, Vol. 1, No.1, 1988, pp. 149–52.

9.   See ibid., pp. 149–52.

10. *The Times*, 24.02.94.

Further reading

Holme, R. and Elliot, M. (eds) *1688-1988: Time for a New Constitution* (London, 1988).

Madgwick, P. and Woodhouse, D. 'The British Constitution', *Talking Politics*, Vol. 6, No. 1, 1993.

Madgwick, P. 'The Monarchy in Contemporary Britain', *Talking Politics*, Vol. 6, No. 2, 1993.

Morton, A. *Theirs is the Kingdom: The Wealth of the Windsors* (London, 1990).

Nairn, T. 'Should Britain abolish its Monarchy', *Social Studies Review*, January 1989.

Norton, P. *The British Polity* (London, 1991).

CHAPTER 3

Parliament

Key term: bicameral

This term describes legislatures that have two chambers. The first chamber is normally chosen by direct election and the second chamber by some form of indirect election, nomination or hereditary principle. The second chamber has a different constituency representing different interests. Bicameralism ensures that there are checks and balances within legislatures and that minority interests are represented. Some bicameral chambers are weaker than others. The British House of Lords is subordinate to the House of Commons. In other political systems the two chambers are co-equal, e.g. the Senate and the House of Representatives in the United States Congress.

The term unicameral describes a legislature that has one chamber. Unicameral legislatures exist in many liberal democracies, including New Zealand and the Nordic countries.

The British Parliament is the legislative branch of our political system. Parliament consists of the House of Commons, the elected chamber, and an unelected second chamber, the House of Lords. This is a bicameral legislature. The British political system is described as a parliamentary democracy, because the people elect Members of Parliament (MPs) in free and open elections to represent them in the House of Commons.

Parliament is a legal body having the legal and legitimate authority to pass laws and make rules for Britain. It can change any aspect of the British Constitution and is the seat of power in the British system of government because it possesses sovereignty. This means that Parliament has absolute power to govern the country and make any law for the UK. Theoretically, Parliament makes the laws, which do not need to be approved by another institution. Parliament, therefore, is said to be supreme. However, this is not entirely correct because since joining the European Union (EU) in 1973 the institutions of the EU have been able to make laws for Britain without reference to Britain's Parliament. This has been seen as a weakening of parliamentary sovereignty and the issue of Parliament's absolute power is at the heart of the debate about the future development of the EU. Nevertheless, Parliament is the major institution of British democracy and this chapter will examine the following :

3.1   The role of the House of Commons.

3.2   The role of the opposition.

3.3   Question Time.

3.4   The role of an MP – delegate or agent?

3.5   Select Committees.

3.6   How Bills are passed.

3.7   The role of the House of Lords.

3.8   Reform of the House of Lords.

3.9   Parties in Parliament.

3.1 | **The role of the House of Commons**

The British Parliament consists of two chambers, the House of Lords and the House of Commons, and the Crown (the Queen) in Parliament. Although the Lords is described as the Upper House, it is the Commons that holds the most power because it is the elected chamber. This has been the case since the turn of this century when the Commons became the dominant partner after the 1832 Reform Act and became much more so following the Parliament Act of 1911. The 1911 Act radically changed the nature of the British Constitution, making the elected Commons supreme and reducing the powers of the Lords.

The House of Commons consists of 651 elected MPs who each represent a constituency. All MPs now belong to a political party and, following a general election, the leader of the political party with the most seats in the House of Commons is asked by the Queen to form a government. Customarily, after a general election one party wins a majority of seats in the Commons, i.e. over 326. This is known as an overall majority. However, sometimes no party achieves an overall majority. The existence of a party system in both the Commons and Lords affects their operation and this is discussed later.

The Commons performs the following functions:

1. Representation

The Commons is elected by the people of Britain in general elections to represent their interests. Britain is thus a representative democracy. MPs are elected to represent the interests of their constituencies, their party and, sometimes, with other MPs from their area of the country, regional interests. The Commons should theoretically represent and reflect the social and ethnic composition of Britain but it does not achieve this, and is criticised because it is predominantly composed of white, middle-class, middle-aged males.

Key term: legal and legitimate authority

This means that an assembly is granted the legal authority to pass laws and govern the country. In Britain there are a vast number of legal documents that give Parliament the legal right to make laws and govern. These include the Bill of Rights, 1689, the Acts of Settlement 1701, the Reform Act 1832, and the Parliament Acts of 1911 and 1949. These give legal authority to the actions of Parliament but legitimate authority originates from the popular elections that allow the citizens of Britain to elect its representatives to the Parliament at regular intervals. Legitimacy to govern is derived from the consent of the people.

Key term: the Speaker

This is an MP, chosen by the Commons to become the Chairperson of the Commons. The Speaker is responsible for the smooth running of the Commons and for maintaining order in the Chamber.

2. Legislation and legitimisation

The prime role of the Commons is to represent the interests of the people, but its secondary role is to pass laws. Representation and legislation are perhaps the most universal functions of all assemblies across the world. The United States Congress, the French National Assembly and the German Bundestag possess elected memberships that represent a range of different constituencies and political parties and which pass laws. In Britain the Commons does not initiate legislation, except in the form of Private Members' Bills. The executive produces legislation which is presented to Parliament for approval in the form of a Bill. The Commons may scrutinise and amend legislation before approving it (a majority vote in favour), but it does not write Bills.

Therefore, one may claim that the Commons merely legitimises the legislation of the executive. The strict party system in the British Parliament means that the Commons normally gives its consent to government legislation because the party in office is supported by the majority of MPs in the Commons. It is in their own interests to support their government in office and so its actions, policies and legislation are approved (legitimised) by the majority of MPs on the grounds of party dictate and loyalty rather than necessarily on merit. This is known as **party government** and has led many to criticise our parliamentary system because it means that the legislature is controlled by the executive through the operation of the party system. The Commons is organised along party political lines and if one party has an absolute majority of MPs it can count on their constant support to ensure that its legislation is passed, that it receives parliamentary approval for its actions, and that it retains office until the next general election. The domination of the party system upon the activities of the Commons, and to a lesser extent the Lords, cannot be stressed enough.

Sometimes, however, governments take office with a small majority or two parties are forced to accommodate each other, forming a coalition government. This can mean that supporters in the Commons can desert the Government, in which case it may lose power. Coalition government is more common on the Continent, e.g. in Germany.

Example:
Since 1979 the Conservative Governments have lost only a handful of very minor votes in the House of Commons, although the fear of losing vital votes during the closing stages of the European Communities Amendment (Maastricht) Act in 1993 forced John Major to employ extreme tactics to ensure 100% support from his Conservative MPs.

3. Critique and scrutiny

The Commons has a responsibility to be critical of the Government and to scrutinise its actions, and those of other public bodies, on behalf of the electorate. This means that the Commons can explore and examine government policies, questioning Ministers and holding the Government accountable. The Commons is equipped to perform these functions through Departmental Select Committees, Ministerial and Prime Minister's Question Times, and so on. The Official Opposition plays an important role in relation to this function of the Commons (*see section 3.2*).

MPs from all sides of the Commons can scrutinise and criticise the executive. Conservative MPs have divided loyalties, between on the one hand being supportive of their Government and on the other expressing criticism when necessary. Sometimes it is better to advocate constituency interests, to ensure their place in the Commons, than to support a policy that could damage their chances of remaining in the Commons at the next general election.

Example:
A number of Conservative MPs have been highly critical of John Major's Government on such issues as economic policy and the Coal Mine Closure Plan of 1992.

Figure 5 The main debating chamber of the House of Commons.

4. Debate

The Commons is a debating chamber where issues, policies and legislation are discussed. Normally such discussions operate within the framework of an argument written in the form of a motion. Motions endorse or condemn the Government's policy or they initiate discussion on a matter where the Government does not have a view. MPs or peers from all sides have the opportunity to speak in the debate, at the end of which they vote in favour of the motion or against it.

5.   Financial responsibility

The House of Commons assumes primary responsibility for the financial affairs of the country. It has the power to 'grant supply' and raise taxes, i.e. to permit the Government to spend and raise public money through taxes. The Annual Budget is introduced to the Commons in November each year and it is debated and scrutinised over a number of months before it is approved and sent to the Lords. The Commons has the power to approve the estimates, i.e. the amount of money to be spent by each department. Furthermore, the Commons is responsible for scrutinising the spending of taxes through the system of Select Committees, in particular the Public Accounts Committee.

However, the complex nature of government finances means that most members of the Commons are poorly equipped to deal with such matters and the Commons is not an effective scrutiniser of financial affairs.

6.   Redress of grievances

A traditional role of the Commons is to actively remedy the complaints of the people against public institutions. It is a primary role of MPs to deal with the problems of their constituents and as members of the Commons they have a range of powers that can be employed to seek redress.

Example:
In a problem over social security payments an MP may write a number of letters on behalf of the constituent to the Department of Social Security, or take the matter up personally by meeting with the Minister responsible. Alternatively the MP may refer the matter to the Ombudsman (see section 3.10).

7.   Recruitment of Ministers

The Government contains around 100 posts. The mass of these are filled by MPs chosen by the Prime Minister from the majority party. The Commons is a training ground for potential members of the executive and most MPs hope to prove themselves worthy of promotion into the Government.

The functions listed above are the roles of the House of Commons, some of which are performed individually by MPs (*see section 3.4*). It cannot be over-stressed that the operation and success of these roles are tempered by the existence of the strict party system. This is one of the problems with the Commons that is perhaps not always the case in other legislatures. By comparison in the United States the Congress operates a party system but it is not as strict as in Britain. Democrat and Republican members of Congress often vote together on issues and legislation against a Democratic or Republican President (the executive), even though in theory Congressional members should support their partisan President.

Example:
Such a cross-party alliance defeated the initial draft of President Clinton's Crime Bill in August 1994.[1]

Questions

1. List and explain two functions of the House of Commons.
2. What is meant by the term 'party government'?
3. (a) What is meant by the term 'legal and legitimate authority'?
   (b) How is this applicable to Parliament?
4. Distinguish between unicameral and bicameral legislatures.

3.2 | The role of the opposition

The British democracy has a unique feature, an officially recognised opposition to the Government. The second largest party in the House of Commons is accorded a special place as 'Her Majesty's Official Opposition' and the leader of the Opposition is paid a salary under the Minister of the Crown Acts. This group of MPs sit opposite the Government.

The Official Opposition has a number of roles:

1. It acts as an alternative government, selecting a leader and shadow Cabinet who in theory, can form a government immediately if the opportunity arises.

   Sometimes, though unusually, it can force a general election upon a Prime Minister and the governing party through a vote of 'no confidence' in the Commons. If successfully carried, a general election has to take place to allow the people to choose a new government if they wish.

   Example:
   The Labour Government in 1979 lost a 'vote of no confidence' in the Prime Minister, James Callaghan, forcing a general election. The Conservatives won and formed a new government.

2. The Opposition seeks to oppose and criticise the Government. The Opposition has a duty to oppose the Government and present legitimate criticism of the Government's policy. The Opposition has a number of days allocated to it on which it may chose the topic for debate. These are known as **Opposition Days**.

Key term: Opposition Days

These are days in the Parliamentary timetable set aside for the Opposition to choose the subject and nature of the debate. There are twenty Opposition Days; seventeen are allocated to the Official Opposition, and the remaining three are given to the second largest Opposition Party.

3.   The Opposition attempts to modify government policy through winning arguments in debates or in Standing Committees. However this is very hard to achieve when the Government has a majority – especially a large majority in the Commons – although in the Lords the Opposition has in recent years been far more successful in modifying policy.
4.   Constructive role. The Opposition does work with the Government in two ways:
(a) Ensuring that parliamentary practices and procedures work.

Example:
The Chief Whips of both parties, and the leader and shadow leader of the House work together to help arrange the parliamentary timetable. However, from December 1993 to the summer of 1994 this co-operation was suspended over Government use of 'the Guillotine'. Informal relations between the party's business managers was curtailed and Labour insisted on full votes on even the most uncontentious of items on the daily agenda and the pairing system was suspended.[2] Co-operation was renewed in the summer of 1994.

(b) On some policies – generally foreign and security policy – the Government and the Opposition tend to have similar views, although co-operation sometimes occurs on domestic policies, e.g. Northern Ireland.

However, this bipartisan aspect of Government–Opposition relationship broke down when the post-war consensus collapsed after 1979. By 1994 there were clear signs that a consensus between the two parties was re-emerging on domestic policy.

Example:
Both major parties in 1994 talked of a commitment to policies designed to create full employment in the UK.[3]

The effectiveness of this role is tempered by the following factors:

1.   The limited resources, research provisions and support services that help the Opposition perform its role.
2.   The Government is in control of the civil service and access to considerable research and back-up services are denied to the Opposition. Furthermore, the Government has the advantage of initiating policy and timing its presentation to Parliament.
3.   The Government has the power to shape events whereas the Opposition can only respond and possesses only limited possibilities to initiate.

Key concepts: bipartisan

This term refers to the phenomena of political parties working together and supporting each other on certain policies. Often parties are divided on many issues, but in some they adopt similar approaches and co-operate with each other, usually defence and foreign policy. In Western democracies it is a common phenomenon to find close comparisons between different political parties on these two areas. Parties more usually differ over the means of achieving a common policy goal rather than over the aim. In Britain there has been a fairly bipartisan approach to the Northern Ireland problem.

Questions

1.   What is the Opposition in British politics?
2.   Give a brief account of the role of the Opposition.

3.3 | **Question Time**

All Ministers are responsible to Parliament for the work of their departments. They are drawn from both Houses of Parliament allowing members of each House to question them about the activities of their department. Question Time is a procedure in the parliamentary timetable that allows both peers and MPs to question Ministers, in an oral and written form.

It takes place on four days of the week, from Monday to Thursday, beginning in the Commons shortly after prayers and finishing at 3.30pm. Ministers answer questions on a rota basis, e.g.:

MONDAY	TUESDAY	WEDNESDAY	THURSDAY
Welsh questions	Education	Scotland	Foreign Affairs
	3.15pm – Prime Minister		3.15pm – Prime Minister

This means that every few weeks MPs have the opportunity to question each ministerial team. Every Tuesday and Thursday, as indicated above, there are questions to the Prime Minister. MPs may table either written or oral questions; MPs may only table eight questions for oral answer in every ten sitting days whereas there is no limit to the number of questions that they may table for written answers.

Written questions can result in MPs being provided with longer answers containing detailed information: 241 written questions are tabled every day by MPs and cost £97 each to answer.[4]

Oral questions have to be precise, and are phrased as a question and addressed to the responsible Minister. There is a list of topics on which questions cannot be asked including purchasing contracts and arms sales. Questions are printed in the daily 'Order Paper', but now only the first thirty questions are printed. Usually between twenty and twenty-five questions are answered and each MP has the opportunity to ask a supplementary question even in reply to the Minister's answer. Another MP may be allowed by the Speaker to ask a supplementary question even though their name is not on the Order Paper, if they catch the Speaker's eye. During Ministerial Question Time, the Opposition shadow spokespersons are allowed to ask a question.

At Prime Minister's Question Time, MPs table an 'open question'. A list of MPs wishing to ask the Prime Minister a question is printed and usually only the top ten MPs on the list have the opportunity to ask the Prime Minister a question. The open question means that the Prime Minister is asked to list his or her engagements for the day and having done so the MP asks a supplementary question on any area of government activity. This means that the Prime Minister may be asked a question across a broad range of topics. The Leader of the Opposition has the right to ask the Prime Minister a question and reply to the answer.

Question Time is an important opportunity for back-benchers to question Ministers about policies and raise constituency issues. It is one of the few occasions when the executive has to face MPs in a direct confrontation and answer for its actions. Recently, the value of this procedure has been queried because of the increasingly adversarial nature of British politics. Critics argue that it has become an opportunity for scoring political points off opponents. Moreover, Ministers come to the House well briefed and prepared by civil servants and Prime Ministers have been known to spend considerable time preparing for their duel in the House twice a week.

Critics argue that the original purpose of question time has been subverted by practices like planted questions, lengthy replies and downright evasion of answers. Time is so short that information given out is very scanty.

In June 1994, John Major, raised the possibility of reforming Question Time to allow MPs to submit a specific, topical or substantive question the night before Prime Minister's Question Time, allowing more information and accurate answers to be delivered.

Question

What is Question Time? Is it an effective institution?

3.4 | The role of an MP – delegate or agent?

The role of an MP is closely linked to the role of the House of Commons and therefore some of the points are similar to those in section 3.2, although they are expressed in individual terms and not collectively.

1. Representative

(a) *Constituency.* MPs are elected to represent the people and interests of their constituency. An MP represents everyone in the constituency regardless of whether they voted for him/her or not.

(b) *Party.* All MPs belong to a political party. In Britain most candidates in an election belong to some form of political party and the successful candidates in general elections normally belong to one of the major parties. Therefore MPs represent the views and ideas of their party, and in Parliament an MP will support his or her party. This means that MPs sit with other members of the party on one side of the Commons and take the party whip, voting with their party in the lobbies of the House of Commons. This is very important if the party has a majority in the Commons and is the Government. MPs may face a dilemma by representing both the party and the constituency because sometimes their interests clash. In these cases an MP will usually support his or her party.

Example:
In 1992 the Conservative Government proposed the closure of 31 coal mines. Although there was a backlash against this policy it was approved by a majority of MPs after a short delay. Many Conservative MPs voted with their Government, although this policy may have had a detrimental effect on their constituents. They voted for the interests of their party and not necessarily for those of their constituents.

(c) *His/her own views.*

2. Legislator

An MP is a key player in the legislative process in Britain. He (or she) can vote in favour of or against Bills, sitting on standing committees which consider them. MPs may amend a Bill by tabling amendments in the various stages through which a Bill goes, and persuading their fellow MPs to support them.

Example:
During the passage of the Criminal Justice Act 1994, Edwina Currie MP tabled an amendment to reduce the homosexual age of consent to 16. Although a majority of MPs supported an alternative amendment to reduce the homosexual age of consent to 18, the Currie amendment opened a debate on homosexual rights that led to a change in the law. This is an example of the power that an ordinary MP can exert on the legislative process.

An MP may also use a device known as the Private Members Bill to attempt to introduce his or her own legislation, or the procedure known as the **Ten-Minute Rule Bill**.

Key term: the Ten-Minute Rule Bill

On a Tuesday or Wednesday afternoon after Question Time, an MP can make a short speech (ten minutes) in favour of a Bill he or she wishes to present. If any MP wishes to oppose the Bill he or she may make a short speech against it. If a vote in favour of the Bill is carried, it is deemed to have received its first reading. Then it is scheduled for a second reading. However, these Bills normally fall at a later stage and reach the statute book. It is not a particularly practical legislative procedure but allows MPs the opportunity to highlight an issue and test opinion on controversial matters.

3.   Redresser of grievances

MPs hold regular 'surgeries' in their constituency, which are opportunities for people to meet with the MP and ask him or her to deal with a particular personal problem. MPs are expected to use their position or 'offices' to help. The average MP's workload involves a high proportion of constituents problems with local government, the Department of Social Security and the Department of Health.

4.   Criticiser and scrutiniser

An MP can criticise a Department of State or other institution, having the means to scrutinise the activity of both governmental and non-governmental organisations. MPs from all sides of the House may carry out this role effectively, although those who belong to the governing party do not pursue this role as actively as members of the Opposition parties. An MP may use questions, both oral and written, to criticise and scrutinise the activities of the Government, and through membership of Select Committees may question and scrutinise the actions and decisions of members of the Government.

These parliamentary tools allow MPs to produce critical reports and comments on the activities of the Government. They can scrutinise the actions of the Government to ensure that it is acting legally. Furthermore, it allows MPs to act as the guardians of the public interest, ensuring that the Government does not become too powerful or dictatorial and that it listens to public opinion and valid criticisms.

5.   Careerist

Most MPs are ambitious and on entering Parliament they attempt to act in the interests of furthering their own careers.

6.   Legitimiser

MPs support the government in office voting in favour of its policies and legislation and therefore legitimising its functions. Although the majority of MPs who support the Government normally belong to the governing party, Opposition MPs often support the Government in office at times of national adversity, i.e. during wars. Generally, in Britain, on matters of defence and foreign policy there has been a degree of bipartisanship between the different political parties.

In Britain, an MP performs these roles both as a representative of the people and of the party. However there is debate in the British system on whether an MP is a **delegate** or an **agent**.

With reference to these definitions, it can be seen that an MP does not easily fit into either categorisation. In the British system it would be correct to say that an MP is more an agent than a delegate.

Once elected an MP is responsible for his or her actions. MPs can be held responsible by their constituency party, the national party and their wider constituents. These controls still allow a high degree of freedom of action and interpretation on the majority of issues. Primarily an MP follows the directions of the party whip in the Commons voting according to their instructions. Failure to follow the directions of the whip can mean disciplinary action will be taken against the offending MP. In this respect an MP could be said to be a delegate of his or her Party.

The party is the strongest influence upon an MP but in many other respects MPs are free agents. In many cases, they are able to choose how they will vote, in free votes, and what they should say in the chamber. They are free to ask whatever questions they wish of the Government and table any amendments to Bills that they wish. They may decide to support the ideas and interests of a particular pressure group or may choose to become consultants for a particular industry or business. Furthermore, they may choose to speak in an adjournment debate, introduce any Ten Minute Rule Bill or Private Members Bill they wish, all without recourse to their constituents. They are able to make up their own minds on a whole range of issues and ideas, such as the issue of capital punishment.

MPs are not obliged to refer everything back to the constituency for ratification before they act or comment. In leadership campaigns MPs can freely decide which candidate they will support. Sometimes they do refer back to the constituency party for advice, although this is not often the case.

In practice, most MPs spend weekends in their constituencies where they do discuss matters and problems, but this does not equate their position with a delegate. They are not delegates except in the loosest sense in reference to the party. They are free agents sent to Parliament to represent constituencies, though this freedom is restricted by the membership of a political party.

Questions

1. What is an adjournment debate?
2. Explain two roles of an MP.
3. What do you understand by the terms 'agent' and 'delegate'?

Similarly an *agent* is a representative but by comparison, receives only the briefest of instruction, consisting usually of a general outline of what he or she should aim to achieve. Agents have almost complete freedom of action on how to represent the interests of their constituents but they must remember that they can be held accountable for their actions when they return to their constituency. Agents have a great deal of freedom of action.

Key term: adjournment debates

This is a procedure in the Commons that allows an MP or group of MPs to raise a particular issue at the end of the parliamentary day. Before the House adjourns, MPs may raise an 'important matter that should have urgent consideration'. Usually in these half hour debates other members may make a contribution and as a rule a government Minister will respond.

3.5 | **Select Committees**

During the 1960s and 1970s criticisms were levied that MPs were unable to perform effective scrutiny of the executive. Question Time and debates were regarded as ineffective tools with which to scrutinise the actions and policies of the Government. During this period a number of possible improvements were discussed by MPs and in 1979 the House of Commons approved the creation of a system of permanent fixed-jurisdiction scrutiny committees, called Departmentally Related Select Committees.

These committees are similar to the system of committees which exists in the United States Congress. In Congress there is a system of specialised committees with fixed jurisdictions over particular policy areas, such as foreign affairs, defence, etc. The new House of Commons' committee system was modelled on the congressional system.

Select Committees have existed in the Commons for many years, the oldest being the **Public Accounts Committee** which dates back to the nineteenth century. This Committee oversees government expenditure, ensuring that taxpayers' money is spent as Parliament intended. This Committee contains MPs from all sides of the House who attempted to work together in a bipartisan manner.

The powers of the Select Committees
1. The right to send for persons, papers and records and examine them.
2. The right to make reports.
3. The right to appoint persons with technical knowledge either to supply information or explain complex matters.

These Committees, however, do not have any legal right to demand that Ministers and civil servants attend and answer questions. Civil servants cannot divulge information on advice offered to Ministers or express opinions on policy. However, the Conservative Government refused to grant the committees such power and only gave an undertaking that 'maximum co-operation would be forthcoming'. Although the committees do not have the power to compel ministers to attend, ministers in practice have usually felt it politically wise to accept an invitation to appear before a committee. There have been a number of examples, however, where Ministers have either refused to attend or been prevented from doing so by the Prime Minister.

Example:
In the 1980s Margaret Thatcher prevented William (now Lord) Whitelaw from attending a committee hearing into prison break-outs while he was Home Secretary.

These committees usually consist of eleven members each and the chairpersonships of the committees are shared between the parties: Conservative ten and Labour six. Members of these committees seek to work together across the political divide and unlike standing committees which work on an adversarial format these committees sit around a horse-shoe shaped table emphasising the element of co-operation (*see Figure 6*).

Figure 6 House of Commons Committee Room 15.

MPs now aspire to become members of Select Committees because of the increased public profile that it affords; chairing a commitee can afford an even greater public profile and power. Independently-minded chairpersons, including the Conservative MPs Nicholas Winterton, Chair of the Health Select Committee 1983–92 and Robert Adley, Chair of the Transport Select Committee from 1992 until his death in 1993 have proved to be a thorn in the side for the Government, and were critical of government policy in the areas covered by their committees.[5]

Some committees hold long-term inquiries while others adopt short-term inquiries. Generally there is a mixture of the two. Often Ministers are summoned to make reports on general or more specific matters.

When the Committee has finished its inquiry into a particular issue it produces a report which usually receives quite high levels of

Key term: the Public Accounts Committee

This is the oldest Select Committee and consists of fifteen members and is usually chaired by an Opposition MP with financial experience. This committee's work is retrospective, as it scrutinises past government expenditure to ensure its legality, but it also checks for efficiency and 'value for money'. The Committee works closely with the National Audit Office. It has discovered some notable examples of wasteful expenditure. In February 1994 the Committee completed an investigation which revealed £200 million pounds had been lost due to waste and incompetence by central government.[7]

Example:
The Public Accounts Committee have succeeded in persuading Whitehall to alter the way in which taxpayers' money is spent and accounted for. As a result of the Pergau Dam affair (see page 50), from July 1994 onwards the Government agreed to implement a recommendation of the Public Accounts Committee, that when a dispute occurs between a Cabinet Minister and a top civil servant in which the Cabinet Minister overrules a top civil servant forcing them to spend public money, the dispute has to be reported to National Audit Office, Parliament's financial watchdog, without delay. This means that any repetition of the Pergau Dam affair will be reported to Parliament straightaway.[8]

publicity. Most of these reports call on the Government to adopt a new policy or approach to a problem. Many contain numerous recommendations and are highly authoritative. Between 1979 and 1992 they issued over 900 substantive reports.[6] Many of these have contained thousands of recommendations, some of which are adopted by the Government.

Assessment

By 1992 there were sixteen Departmental Select Committees established but this figure has increased with the creation of a Select Committee on Northern Ireland. After the 1992 General Election, the Energy Committee was abolished and a National Heritage Committee and a Science and Technology Committee were established.

The new system has provided MPs with an alternative career structure and an opportunity to build up specialist knowledge. The committees have become an alternative authoritative source of information for MPs, the Government, pressure groups, the media and the public. The new committees have increased the scrutiny power of Parliament and have become a major feature of the post-1970s House of Commons, holding Ministers and civil servants accountable for their actions and policies.

During the 1980s there were some notable successes, including the case of the Defence Select Committee which was extremely critical of the Fortress Falklands policy of the Thatcher Government and the method of defence procurement employed by the Ministry of Defence in the early 1980s. This led to the creation of a specialised team within the Ministry of Defence, with technical and scientific knowledge specifically responsible for defence procurement, now known as the Defence Procurement Agency.

The success of the new committees depended on a number of factors:

1. The chairmanship was central to the direction and level of activity that each committee took. The attitude and ambitions of the chairman could give a committee either a high or low profile. Michael Mates (Conservative), the former Chairman of the Defence Select Committee adopted a high profile whereas David Marshall (Labour), Chairman of the Transport Select Committee in the Parliament of 1987–92, adopted a low profile.
2. Party affiliation can obviously influence the actions of the Chairman and the membership of the committees. There has been substantial bipartisanship on these committees; however, this has not been without incident.

Example:
The leaking of the Health Select Committee Report that called for the slowing down of National Health Service reforms in 1991 to the Department of Health by an MP's researcher, is a clear indication of where ultimate loyalty lies.

3. The success of these committees may be judged in terms of the number of recommendations adopted by the Government. This has been hard to assess, as it depends upon the issue, its public and political importance and the debate surrounding it. In 1986, in a parliamentary written question, the Prime Minister, Margaret Thatcher, listed 150 recommendations made by Select Committees in the period March 1985 to March 1986 that the Government had accepted. The following example is new evidence.

    Example:
    Between 1989 and 1993 the Trade and Industry Select Committee produced fourteen reports containing 210 recommendations. The Government has accepted 154 recommendations in whole or in part, or has noted where no further action was sought.[9]

4. The attention that the media has given to Committee reports and recommendations, although hard to measure, can account for their success in highlighting issues and increasing public awareness and debate. This may be a rather intangible factor, but greater public discussion has resulted from their investigations and reports on issues such as homelessness and animal welfare.

5. Civil servants have been forced to publish more information about government activities and to explain to MPs how they made their recommendations and advised Ministers. However, the 1980s were not a catalogue of success for Select Committees. The lack of a statutory right to demand the presence of Ministers or force them to answer questions is a critical weakness. In the Westland inquiry, the former Defence Secretary, Michael Heseltine, refused to answer eight questions. Equally there have been problems concerning the taking of information and evidence from officials, especially in relation to the Westland incident.[10]

In 1990, a House of Commons Procedure Committee reviewed the ten-year operation of the Select Committee system. The Committee found that, 'the system as a whole has proved itself a valuable and cost effective addition to the House's ability to perform its proper function of holding Ministers to account'.[11] But this report did have its critics and was described as 'complacent' by Lord St John of Fawsley.[12]

The report was not able to comment on the Maxwell case, which revealed in 1991 the limits of Select Committee power to elicit responses from private individuals.[13]

Between 1990 and 1995 the system of Departmental Select Committees played a positive role, allowing MPs to scrutinise the activities of the executive and hold its members accountable. The level of media attention paid to these committees has increased since 1992 because they have played a crucial role in analysing some of the policy failures of the Conservative Government.

Example:
The October 1992 the Coal Mine Closure Plan provoked widespread outrage. The proposed closure of thirty-one pits making 30,000 miners unemployed caused a political storm in Westminster. A swell of public support for the miners' case saw widespread demonstrations throughout the country. Many of those on these marches were not typical public demonstrators; 'The donkey jackets of the 1984/5 strike were replaced by Barbours, marching with miners to show their distaste at Government proposals.'[14] Consequently, the Government agreed to launch a wholesale review of Britain's energy policy and simultaneously it asked the Trade and Industry Select Committee to launch a similar review. The Committee took evidence from all sides and consulted a range of experts. Its report made a series of recommendations of which the Government's own review was forced to take account.[15]

Michael Heseltine, when he published the White Paper in March 1993, maintained that this document matched most of the recommendations made by the Trade and Industry Committee,[16] although this was disputed by its Chairman, Dick Caborn.[17]

Other notable issues that have been the subject of highly publicised Committee inquiries in recent years have included: the Arms to Iraq Affair, leading to the establishment of the Scott inquiry; an investigation into CD prices; the Pergau Dam affair, which broke new ground when members of the Foreign Affairs Select Committee were taken to see confidential papers in the Foreign Office in 1994.

Example:
In July 1994 the all-party Foreign Affairs Select Committee produced a report highly critical of the Government's policy in 1988 linking British overseas aid for a Malaysian dam to a £1 billion arms deal between Britain and Malaysia. The Committee found that Ministers failed to keep Parliament properly informed about the deal in 1988 and that answers to MPs questions were 'less informative than the House has a right to expect'.[18]

Clearly the most important development since the 1992 General Election for Select Committees was the Government's decision to ask the Trade and Industry Committee to examine the options for the coal industry in 1992. Whatever one's views of the outcome of the review and subsequent events, on which opinion is divided, the fact that a Departmental Select Committee was perceived to have the status to be given the task is recognition of the way in which the Committee system has proved its worth in the last fifteen years. Furthermore, with a smaller majority in the Commons all opposition to the Government has a greater chance of success and subsequently it is possibly now the case that the Government does have to be more sensitive towards committees. *The Guardian* newspaper commented in July 1992, that MPs' power to hold the Government to account had drained away during the Thatcher years, 'but here is an opportunity to take it back. MPs should seize it with both hands.'[19]

Select Committees are now seen as powerful tools for ordinary MPs to use, especially in the conditions of small majority government. In January 1993 the *Financial Times* said 'Some Parliamentary Select Committees are beginning to exercise a degree of influence over the administration that they had previously only dreamed of.'[20] It seems that the opinions of both Select Committees and back-benchers are now being solicited and listened to by Ministers. This has not happened since the 1970s. Since April 1992 there has been an increase in the power, influence and prestige of the Parliamentary Select Committee.[21]

Questions

1. What are Select Committees?
2. What was the aim behind the creation of Select Committees and has this been achieved?

3.6 | How Bills are passed

The legislative process in Britain is quite simple although it seems complex because of the many stages through which a Bill passes before it becomes an Act (*see Figure 7*). This is a popular question and students should use the breakdown below as a revision device.

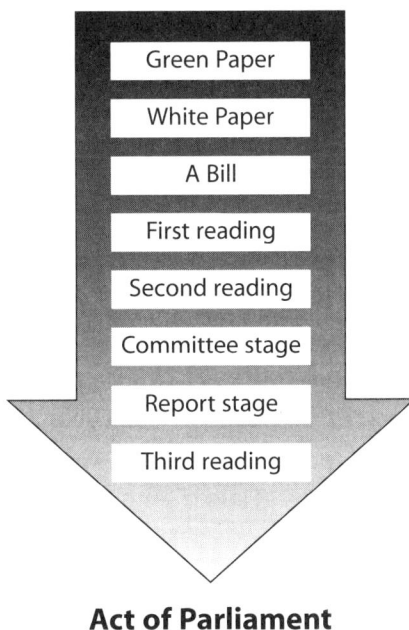

Green Paper

White Paper

A Bill

First reading

Second reading

Committee stage

Report stage

Third reading

Act of Parliament

Figure 7 The stages of a bill.

Green Paper

This is a consultation paper published by the Government which outlines its thinking on a particular issue. It usually outlines a number of options and legislative ideas, ideas which the Government would like to see incorporated into law, or present laws adapted to suit the needs of today's society. The Green Paper invites comments from the public and interested parties like pressure groups.

White Paper

The White Paper is published a few months after a Green Paper and contains 'firmed up' proposals for legislation or policy commitment. A White Paper is an expression of the Government's intentions. Normally there is a consultation period for comment but there are not usually massive differences between the contents of a White Paper and a Bill.

Example:
The White Paper on Open Government, Cm 2290 July 1993, outlined the Government's policy to increase the openness of Whitehall's processes to public scrutiny: 'The White Paper builds on the Government's commitment to make government in the UK more open and accountable.'[22]

A Bill

This is published a few months after a White Paper and is a legally drafted document that contains a variety of clauses and provisions, relating to its subject area. However, not all Bills are preceded by a Green or White Paper. A Bill normally deals with one area of activity and seeks to change the law or invent new laws. Most Bills are Public Bills that concern the whole community.

Example:
The 1994 Coal Industry Bill abolished British Coal and established a coal authority to license private mine operators.

The clauses of the Bill change various aspects of law, or lay down a framework of operation for a new body to work through. A Bill is normally published after its first reading.

First reading

This marks the formal introduction of a Bill to Parliament. The title of the Bill is read out and it is accepted by the House. Bills can be introduced into either the Lords or the Commons. No debate occurs because the first reading is a formality after which a date is set for the second reading.

Second reading

During this stage the Bill is debated in principle, i.e. its main aims and measures are debated. Most Bills are given a half or full day's debate. These debates are opened by the Minister responsible for the measure, and he or she is responsible for ensuring the smooth passage of the Bill through its legislative stages in the House, be it the Commons or the Lords.

Example:
David Mellor MP was responsible for ensuring that the 1988 Children Act reached the statute book in the form which the Government desired.

After the Government Minister has introduced the debate in second reading, the Opposition spokesperson replies and a debate on the principles of the Bill ensues in which any MP may express their opinions. After the debate is wound up the House divides for a vote if the Bill is contested. Once approved, it is sent for detailed scrutiny in the Committee stage.

Committee stage

The majority of Bills are sent to a **Standing Committee.** The purpose of this Committee is to examine each clause of the Bill, scrutinise its wording and possible interpretation, and amend the Bill where necessary. The Committee decides any amendments to a clause before approving or rejecting the particular clause of the Bill. It cannot reject or make amendments that run counter to the principal of the Bill that was approved by the House in the second reading.

Discussion in the Committee will often follow the adversarial lines of debates that are followed in the House of Commons. Generally, much time is taken up with the controversial clauses of the Bill and each Committee resembles both in composition and structure the House of Commons. Each Committee consists of between eighteen and twenty-two MPs, and the Government always has a majority, reflecting its majority in the House of Commons. These Committees are temporary and only exist for this stage of the Bill. They are known by a letter rather than by the title of the Bill, and are called Standing Committee A, Standing Committee B, etc. Sometimes a Committee stage is held on the floor of the House of Commons like the Committee stage in the Lords. This means that every MP can have a say in the detailed scrutiny of the Bill.

Example:
The European Communities (Amendment) Bill (The Maastricht Bill) 1993 went through a Committee of the whole House.

Once the Bill has gone through this stage it passes to the report stage, and a new Standing Committee is appointed to consider the next piece of legislation.

Report stage

In the report stage the changes made to the Bill are brought to the attention of the House and MPs may again make amendments. Often the Government uses this stage to introduce further amendments to the Bill. If a Bill has been heard by a Committee of the whole House it does not have a report stage.

Third reading

In this final stage, known as the third reading, the Bill as amended is debated and the House gives its final approval. Debates are usually short but if the Bill is not contentious no debate takes place. After it has been approved the Bill goes to the 'other place', i.e. the House of Lords. In the Lords the Bill will go through a series of similar stages with some subtle variations. If the Lords make any amendments to the Bill it returns to the Commons for MPs to consider the Lord's amendments. These amendments are either accepted or reversed and the Bill is then reconsidered by the Lords. Normally Peers accept the Bill in the form that the Commons desires and do not press their amendments.

Example:
In November 1993, The Lords re-amended the Rail Privatisation Bill against the wishes of the Government at the close of its legislative stages. The Bill was rushed back to the Commons to have the Lords' amendments removed and then the following day the Bill was accepted by peers. This was because Ministers threatened to invoke the provisions of the 1911 and 1949 Parliament Acts, allowing the elected chamber to overrule the Lords on a money bill that was also a manifesto issue, if Peers did not pass the Bill.[23]

Key concept: the Statute Book

When a Bill becomes an Act it can be called a statute and it is described as having been placed in the Statute Book. It is then published with all the other Acts passed in a parliamentary session in a series of bound volumes of legislation called the Statute Books.

Once passed by both Houses of Parliament the Bill goes to the Queen for royal assent whereupon it becomes an Act of Parliament.

Students should note that all Bills, with the exception of Private Members' Bills and Private Bills, go through this procedure. Bills are primary legislation.

Delegated legislation

When an Act of Parliament is passed it does not necessarily include all the rules and regulations required to put it into effect. Instead the new Act commonly confers powers on Ministers or their departments to work out necessary details. These powers are commonly known as 'delegated legislation' and the term 'statutory instrument' is used to describe the documents that grant delegated powers.

Parliament has sought to scrutinise the growth in the size and use of delegated legislation in the post-war period by establishing a

Select Committee on Statutory Instruments. This Committee has the power to draw Parliament's attention to any instrument that appears to make unusual use of the power conferred by the original Act.

There are two other forms of Bills of which students should be aware. These are known as Private Members' Bills and Private Bills.

Private Members' Bills

Private Members' Bills are introduced and sponsored by ordinary MPs who are responsible for ensuring the passage of the Bill through its legislative stages in the Commons. When the Bill goes to the Lords the MP will form an alliance with a Lord who is responsible for ensuring its passage through the 'other place'.

Space in the parliamentary timetable is very limited, so only a small amount is set aside for Private Members' Bills, – or PMBs – which are normally considered by the House of Commons on a Friday. Subsequently, at the beginning of each parliamentary session in November, a ballot is held of all the MPs and those whose names are drawn at the top of the ballot stand the best chance of introducing a Bill and seeing it reach the Statute Book.

Often the most non-controversial ideas stand the best chance of succeeding as PMBs. Sometimes, however, Bills are introduced which are controversial and radical, but are not opposed by the Government: rather they receive quiet support. These relate to issues which political parties cannot address in manifestos because they would be politically divisive and damaging, such as abortion. Thus in 1967 abortions were legalised via the PMB procedure resulting in the Abortion Act 1967. This procedure allows the Government to test the opinion of the House or ensure a reform of the law without being held responsible for the reform which could be politically damaging.

Usually only around ten to twenty PMBs reach the Statute Book every year. Sometimes PMBs fail because they do not complete their stages through lack of parliamentary time. In other cases delaying tactics are employed by MPs opposed to the Bill to kill it.

Example:
The 1994 Private Members' Bill entitled the Disabled Persons Rights Bill was killed off by the Government and led to a controversy over the role of a member of the ministerial team at the Department of Social Security, Nicholas Scott. The Government claimed that the Bill would cost billions of pounds to implement.[24]

Private Members' Bills allow:

1.   MPs to act as legislators in their own right;
2.   issues to be addressed which political parties cannot sponsor;

3.   a close link between MPs and some pressure groups who provide the ideas for some Private Members Bills.

Private Bills

These are Bills that are sponsored through Parliament by private organisations, who require parliamentary approval to take a certain action. They normally affect only a section of the community, be it a local authority, a business or an individual.

Example:
Hypothetically, an oil company may ask Parliament to grant it special powers to lay a pipeline across Wales, causing disruption to a large number of people.

Most Private Bills are sponsored by local authorities or large businesses. These Bills are introduced into either House and are sometimes supported by an MP or Lord with an interest. Sometimes the organisation responsible for the Bill conducts a large-scale lobbying exercise to persuade peers and MPs to support the Bill. The Bill follows the normal legislative stages but in the Committee stage, a Committee of four to five members acts as a jury, taking evidence from both supporters and opponents of the Bill. Barristers are often used to present arguments for or against the Bill to MPs or peers. The Committee recommends whether the Bill should be approved or disapproved by the House.

Key term: a hybrid Bill

Hybrid Bills are Public Bills which are classified by the Speaker as having a particular effect on one section of the community. They follow the same procedure as Public Bills except that after the second reading the Bill goes to a small select committee where a procedure similar to a Private Bill Committee is followed. The Bill then proceeds along the normal Public Bill procedure.

The most controversial Private Bill of recent times was the Bill sponsored by the Cardiff Bay Development Corporation to seek permission to build a large permanent barrage across Cardiff Bay, creating an artificial lake. This Bill raised many environmental concerns and was first introduced in 1987, although it did not succeed in gaining royal assent until November 1993. The Bill was introduced four times, and was only successful when the Government re-introduced it in April 1991 as a hybrid Bill and sponsored it through its legislative process.[25]

In the case of most Private Bills there is little party politics and MPs are able to act with complete legislative freedom.

Questions

1. Distinguish between an Act and a Bill.
2. What is role of a Standing Committee?
3. Explain the legislative process.
4. What are Private Bills and Private Members' Bills?

3.7 | The role of the House of Lords

Composition

The House of Lords consists of hereditary peers and life peers, bishops and law lords. None of its members are elected and so critics argue that it is an anachronism in a modern liberal democracy. The continued existence of the Lords is the subject of a debate about parliamentary reform.

There are about 1,200 peers eligible to sit in the Lords. Of these 800 are hereditary peers, about 350 are life peers, 19 are Law Lords and 26 are Archbishops and Bishops. At the start of each parliamentary session all peers are asked if they intend to be an active participant in the forthcoming year and normally between 400–800 peers respond affirmatively, although the majority of this number only attend once.[26] Since the 1970s the attendance number of active peers has risen. In the 1970s an average of only 250 peers attended daily; by comparison, today the average daily attendance is over 300 peers. Under the terms of the Life Peerages Act 1958, attending peers are paid an 'attendance allowance', now worth over £100 a day. The Lords has a Conservative majority, meaning Conservative peers outnumber Labour peers four to one, although this does not mean that the Conservatives have a constant majority in the House.

Example: Political affiliation of peers in 1993

Party	No. of peers declaring affiliation
Conservative	476
Labour	115
Liberal Democrat	58
Cross-benches	279

Functions

It is important for students to note the differences between the powers of the Lords and the powers of the Commons.

1. The Lords does not have a role as a redresser of grievances.
2. It does not to have a representative role similar to the Commons because it is not elected. It may be argued that through the creation of life peers it reflects, better than it once did, the social and ethnic make-up of Britain, but this is still limited. It is representative in the following respects:
(a) Many peers represent their own differing interests and actively support the interests of various pressure groups. Many peers work with a range of different pressure groups speaking on their behalf in debates and tabling amendments drawn up by these pressure groups to government legislation.

Key term: hereditary peers

These are people entitled to sit in the House of Lords because they inherited their title which passes from one generation to the next. The range of this type of peer includes Dukes, Barons and Earls, e.g. The Duke of Norfolk, Lord Bath.

Key term: life peers

These are people who are created Lords for only their lifetime and when they die their title and right to sit in the Lords dies with them. It is not passed on to their descendants. This form of peer was introduced through the Life Peerages Act 1958 which allowed the Crown to appoint life peers. The Act was an attempt to democratise the Lords by altering its composition to create a better political balance. A large number of former Labour MPs and eminent supporters have been created life peers, e.g. Lord Callaghan and Lord Healey. In addition, a large number of eminent people from all sectors of the community have been made life peers: actors, lawyers, retired civil servants, bankers, business executives, writers, journalists, trade unionists, etc. This has allowed these individuals to bring their expertise and influence into the legislative process.

Key term: cross-benchers

These are Lords who do not declare a political affiliation and sit on the middle benches in the chamber. Normally those who have never expressed a political preference in their previous employment sit on these benches and this means that they can swing the balance in important debates because a government majority may not necessarily be guaranteed. For example, former civil servants sit on these benches.

Example:
Lord Ashley works in the Lords for a number of charities for the deaf and hard of hearing.

(b) They represent the interests of the British elite and, to a much lesser extent, working-class interests via the numbers of trade unionists and former Labour MPs who are life peers.

3. It does have a legislative and legitimisation function. The Lords passes Bills in the same way as the Commons. Most Lords' amendments are drafting amendments, correcting the language used, and are accepted by the Commons. All Bills go through a similar procedure although there are some subtle differences:

(a) Sometimes the Bill can be moved from second reading to third reading without a Committee stage. This is used for bills where there is no desire to present amendments.

(b) The Committee stage is normally taken on the floor of the House, and all amendments tabled are debated. The emphasis in this stage is to ensure that the Bill is well drafted and coherent. Sometimes a Bill may be referred to the equivalent of a House of Commons standing committee for consideration. These are known as **Public Bill Committees** and they have only been used twice – most recently in 1992.

(c) Most Lords amendments are drafting amendments, correcting the language used, and are accepted by the Commons.

In its capacity as a legislator the Lords is effective and efficient. Many non-contentious government Bills are introduced into the Lords first, and having completed their stages, they can be dealt with by the Commons quite quickly because all the hard work of ensuring that the clauses of the Bill are correctly drafted and effective has been completed beforehand. The existence of the second chamber saves the Commons a huge amount of time.

Through this legislative function, the Lords legitimises the functions of government by approving new laws and endorsing policy. However, the legislative powers of the Lords are limited as compared with the Commons. They may:

(d) *Amend and scrutinise legislation.* Since 1979 the Lords have been keen amenders of government legislation. They have inflicted a number of defeats upon the Government over a vast range of areas.

Example:
During 1993–4 the Government suffered regular defeats in the Lords during the passage of the Criminal Justice and Public Order Act 1994. Furthermore, between 1979 and 1991 the Lords inflicted 173 defeats upon the Conservative Government. Many of these were successful because of the numbers of cross-benchers voting against the Government.

(e) *Debate legislation and approve legislation.*

(f) *Delay legislation for up to one year.* The Lords are only empowered to delay legislation for one year according to the Parliament Act of 1949. This is perhaps the most controversial aspect of its functions and powers.

The Lords once enjoyed full legislative power enabling them to vote against a Bill and defeat it. However this power has been reduced since 1911 when the first Parliament Act was pushed through by the Liberal Government after a bitter and drawn-out fight with the Lords over the Budget of 1910. Under the terms of this Act the Lords were only empowered to delay legislation for two years. Furthermore, the Act reduced the powers of the Lords over **'money' Bills.** Any 'money' Bill would become law one month after leaving the Commons whether it was approved by the House of Lords or not.

The provisions of this delaying power were further reduced by the 1949 Parliament Act to one year: it is a very rare occasion when the Lords exercises its delaying power. Although they may be keen amenders of government legislation they are not keen delayers of legislation for which an elected government can claim to have a mandate. However, the Lords have seen fit to overturn Bills that are not backed by the popular mandate, and passed by the Commons on a free vote.

Example:
In 1990 the Lords rejected the War Crimes Bill, which allowed the prosecution of alleged Nazi war criminals living in the UK. The Bill, which was eventually passed, was delayed by the Lords for one year.

(g) Exercise an absolute veto on any Bill to prolong the life of Parliament beyond five years.

4. The Lords has a critique and scrutiny function. It is an effective scrutiniser of government action and legislation, complementing the work of the Commons acting as an effective reviser of legislation and scrutinising the work of the Government, in debates, Question Times, etc. In Question Time, government Ministers seated in the Lords answer both written and oral questions. Equally, the Lords can express criticisms in debates and question times.

Debates in the Lords discuss motions which may take three forms:

(a) *Motions which express a particular viewpoint.*

(b) *'Take note motions'*: allowing discussion of matters on which the government wishes to hear the views of peers.

(c) *Call for papers motions*: this a convention through which backbenchers can place a particular issue on the agenda for a day ensuring a debate in the House. At the end of the debate it is customary for the motion to be withdrawn.

Key term: a veto

This term describes the power to reject or forbid a proposed measure. Many legislatures across the globe are able to veto and/or reject a proposal including the United States Senate which may veto the appointment of a member of the Supreme Court or the European Parliament, which may veto the EU Budget (*see* Chapter 9).

Debates in the Lords:

(a) can be highly informed, less politically charged than is the case in the Commons and critical of government policies;

(b) can give government Ministers opportunities to explain and justify policies and reveal ideas under consideration in their department;

(c) can fulfil an expressive function, allowing issues to be raised which are not often raised in the Commons.

> **Example:** *A debate in 1993–4 session on UFOs.*

5. It has a judicial function. The House of Lords is the highest court of appeal in the UK. In practice this is not performed by the whole house, rather it is carried out by a judicial committee comprised mainly of the Law Lords but includes the Lord Chancellor, ex-Lord Chancellors and peers who have held judicial office. Cases are heard in a committee room by five to ten Lords, and their decisions are delivered in the Chamber.

6. Members of the Lords become members of the Government representing departments to their Lordships and occupying, in some cases, Cabinet office. Normally two members of the Cabinet come from the Lords, the Lord Chancellor and the Leader of the House of Lords. The Lords can supply fresh blood to the Government: in 1992 Lord Goschen became a government whip in the Lords at the age of 27.

7. The Lords may pass Private Members' Bills. Private Members' Bills from the Commons have to be passed by the Lords and require a peer to sponsor the Bill through the legislative process. Peers may introduce Private Members' Bills but only a small number are successful.

In 1990–91 only one peer's Private Members' Bill successfully reached the Statute Book.

The Lords committees

In addition to legislative committees the Lords may create a number of other committees.

Ad Hoc Select Committees
These consider certain legislative proposals and issues of public policy. They are temporary and examine a range of policies and issues, including murder and life imprisonment.

Sessional Select Committees
These are appointed each session. Two that are re-appointed each session are the European Union Committee and the Select Committee on Science and Technology.

The European Union Committee
This was created in 1974 and its role is to scrutinise draft EU

legislation, identifying those proposals which raise important questions of principle or policy. The EU Committee has a system of sub-committees which are staffed by over sixty peers. It scrutinises the draft proposals and recommends which should be debated by the whole House. It is highly regarded and many of its reports have been highly influential both on MPs and across Whitehall.

Questions

1. Compare three functions of the Lords with their equivalents in the Commons.
2. What is the role of the Lords in the legislative process?
3. Describe the system of committees which exist in the Lords.

3.8 | Reform of the House of Lords

Reform of the House of Lords is a debate which has raged for most of the century. In the post-war period it has oscillated between those who want either further reform or outright abolition. The essence of the argument against the Lords is the critique that in a modern liberal democracy it is an anachronism to have a second legislative chamber whose composition is, in the majority, hereditary peers who inherit their position through birth. It is unrepresentative and has no electoral mandate. The two major parties stand at opposite poles on the future of the Lords.

1. The Conservatives are content with the status quo so long as the Lords does not inflict too many defeats, or too big a defeat, on a Conservative Government.
2. By comparison, the Labour Party has been committed to reform of the Lords for some time. In 1969 the Labour Government introduced a Bill that sought to phase out the hereditary element. It failed to reach the Statute Books.
3. The Liberal Democrats propose creating a new second chamber; a Senate primarily elected by the nation's citizens, with the power to delay all legislation except money bills for up to two years.[27]

Arguments in favour of the present House of Lords

1. **Reforms so far instituted**
   The Life Peerages Act, 1958 and the Peerages Act 1963 reformed the Lords.[28] The creation of life peers has gone some way, supporters argue, in democratising the Lords by introducing fresh blood, new faces and new expertise. This has broadened the socio-economic background of the Lords and weakened the 'conservative' approach of the second chamber.

2. **Opposition to government**

Some argue that during the 1980s the Lords were the only effective opposition to the Conservative Government. The range and number of defeats that the Lords have inflicted on both Margaret Thatcher and now on John Major have been significant. If one of the purposes of a bicameral legislature is to ensure a balance of power between chambers, the House of Lords has successfully achieved this goal despite its weaknesses, acting as a break upon 'the elected dictatorship' that can exist in the Commons.

Example:

The Criminal Justice and Public Order Act 1994 was quite radically amended by the Lords forcing the then Home Secretary, Michael Howard to reconsider a number of issues.

This success has led Government Whips to employ '**backwoodsmen**' to ensure the Government's majority, and to anticipate movement and reach compromise over matters of dispute.

The results of increased activity:

(a) The Lords is now a greater target for lobbying by pressure groups than previously. More and more pressure groups are seeing the Lords as a place where their views may find expression and support.

(b) The Lords have been seen to be more responsive to public concerns and pressure than the Commons, especially during the 1980s.

3. **The hereditary principle**

Some supporters of the Lords argue that the hereditary principle is a virtue because it allows peers to take an independent and objective line in the conduct of the affairs of the Lords. Peers do not owe their position to anyone and do not have to become entangled in party politics. This independence is beneficial for British democracy because it acts as a counterweight to the Commons, which is controlled by a 'party' government holding a majority of seats in the Commons. Many hereditary peers have modest incomes and modest homes. Supporters argue that because the Lords now reflects a wide spectrum of British society, it can bring a variety of experiences and independent points of view into the legislative process.

Arguments against the present House of Lords

1. **The hereditary principle**

The most vociferous opponents of the Lords, mainly from the left of the Labour Party, argue that Britain is the only Western

Key term: backwoodsmen

This term refers to those peers who do not attend the Lords very often and only attend when their political party needs their support in a vote on a particular policy or Bill. The majority of this reservoir of Lords are Conservative peers and in recent times have attended to ensure that the Conservative Government pushes important Bills through the House of Lords, e.g. the Community Charge Bill 1989.

liberal democracy that has a second chamber composed of people chosen through birth rather than democratically elected. They suggest that the reforms instituted so far do not go far enough. Life peers are not elected, they are appointed by the Queen on the advice of the Prime Minister and the system is open to abuse. Critics argue that for the unelected chamber to have the power to delay the legislation of the elected chamber is a monstrous anomaly in a modern democracy.

2. **Conservative majority**

The Lords has had and still retains a Conservative majority, although this has been reduced since the 1960s. The Conservatives still possess over 450 peers, many of whom only attend when absolutely necessary, perhaps once a year – the 'backwoodsmen' mentioned above. When a Labour Government has held office this has created problems. Between 1974–79 the Conservative majority in the Lords inflicted 347 defeats upon the Labour Government and delayed a number of important pieces of legislation, including the Race Relations Act.

3. **Patronage**

The power of patronage can lead to a manipulation of the composition of the Lords. Patronage is not open to democratic influence or control but is open to abuse. Critics argue it would be fairer to have a democratically elected second chamber with clearly defined roles and powers.

Public confidence in the Lords can hardly be described as high, but it is higher than it has been for many decades. If the Labour Party had won office in 1992, its manifesto contained a variety of commitments to Constitutional Reform including a Freedom of Information Act, Reform of the Lords and a Bill of Rights. Whether, in the lifetime of one Parliament, it would have been able to complete all three aims, and whether it would have a large enough majority to carry reform of the Lords through, is very debatable.

The debate has moved from retention, and from complete abolition, to reform. Arguments concerning the abolition revolve around the need for a second chamber at all and suggest that Britain's democracy could exist perfectly well with a single chamber or unicameral legislature.

The future of the Lords

As the reform debate has rumbled on during the past few decades, the role of the Lords within the British democracy has become increasing valuable. In the 1980s it was seen to be an effective, if unelected, opposition to the high majority Conservative Governments. It effectively scrutinised and amended much government legislation and the public image of the Lords improved dramatically. Its internal composition has changed through the Life Peerage Act and in the 1980s it appeared to be more in touch with public opinion than did the Commons. In the period 1992–5 the Lords continued to act as a keen reviser of government legislation and it forced the Major Government to think again over many aspects of its legislation. In the 1992–3 parliamentary session peers defeated the Government on twenty occasions. In all but seven cases the defeat was reversed in the Commons or ignored.[29] Much of the Major Government's law and order legislation of the 1993–94 parliamentary session came under fierce attack in the Lords. This included the Police and Magistrates Court Act 1994 and the Criminal Justice Act 1994. Moreover, in November 1993 the Lords almost caused a constitutional crisis when they rebelled three times during the closing legislative stages of the Rail Privatisation Act 1993.[30]

The activities of the Lords in recent years have to some extent placated calls for reform or abolition but in the light of Tony Blair's 1994 public commitments to reform the second chamber, students should be aware of past and present proposals and the problems associated with **reform**.

Examples: Two examples of reform proposals:

1918 The Bryce Commission–246 MPs were to be elected by members of the Commons grouped into regions and using the single transferable vote. Each member would serve twelve years and eighty-one peers would be elected for a similar term by an all-party committee of both Houses.

1968 Crossman all-party talks resulted in an agreement to create a two-tier structure of 230 voting peers of whom the Government would have the largest number but not an overall majority, and peers over the age of 72 who would not be able to vote. The right of hereditary peers to sit in the Lords would be abolished although all existing peers would be able to sit as non-voting members for their lifetime, and in this way they would be phased out. The period of legislative delay would be reduced to six months.

If the Lords are to be reformed the following should be born in mind :

(a) If elected, the second chamber will have to be given a greater powers and a defined role because it will have democratic legitimacy.

(b) If elected, it could become a challenger to the primacy of the Commons and this could cause greater conflicts than we see today.

(c) The method of election and the constituency is a matter of debate.

(d) What will the new chamber be called? Is there a need to rename the Lords or not?

(e) If it is not given any new powers or roles will it attract the right calibre of politician?

Questions

1. What are 'backwoodsmen'?
2. Explain two proposals for reform of the Lords.

3.9 | Parties in Parliament

In Parliament political parties organise their activities and supporters through three institutions; the *whips, party meetings* and *party committees*.

The whips

The whips organise each party in Parliament and enforce party loyalty on the back-benches. The whips' offices consist of a Chief Whip, who is a primary adviser to the leader and a number of deputy Whips. The Chief Whip in the Conservative Party is appointed by the leader and in the Labour Party by the Parliamentary Labour Party.

1. The whip's main task is administrative producing a weekly outline of parliamentary business which indicates the degree of importance attached by the party to the various items on the parliamentary agenda, and outlines forthcoming business on parliamentary committees and party committees.

   This document is called a **documentary whip** and helps organise the party in Parliament. An MP's required attendance is indicated by the number of lines under each item. Minor items are underlined once, important items are underlined twice and very important items are underlined three times, indicating that an MP must attend. This is called a **three-line whip**. Whips therefore enforce discipline among the MPs, making sure MPs both vote and work with the party. MPs disregard the whip at their own peril, especially the three-line whip. If an MP wishes to be absent for a vote he must find a member of the opposing party who also wishes to stay away. This is known as 'pairing' and requires the consent of the Chief Whip.

2. The whips act as a line of communication between the back-benchers and the leader of the party. The whips advise the leaders on what the party will or will not stand for and offer advice on how to head off back-bench rebellions.

3.   Whips act as persuaders and attempt to persuade MPs to support their party in the lobbies. Whips may entice MPs with offers of advancement up the ministerial ladder if they support the party in the lobbies or use threats against rebel MPs. Sometimes they are unsuccessful.

Example:
During the Maastricht Treaty Debates of 1992/3 the Conservative Whips were unable to persuade a number of Conservative MPs to support the Prime Minister and the Conservative Party in the Commons.

Party meetings

All the parties organise weekly meetings of back-bench MPs to ensure communication between different members. The Parliamentary Labour Party, which includes members of the Commons and Lords, meets each week to discuss policy and to work out new tactics. The leader of the Party and his or her colleagues in the Cabinet or Shadow Cabinet attend if they wish.

The Conservative and Unionist Members Committee (often known as **the 1922 Committee** after a meeting in 1922, when the Conservatives decided to end their coalition with the Lloyd George Liberals) consist of all the Conservative back-benchers, i.e. those who do not hold posts in the Government and sit on the back-benches in the Chamber. When in power members of the Conservative Government may only attend if invited. The purpose of the 1922 Committee is to protect the interests of back-benchers. Opinions may be expressed and forthcoming business can be discussed. Both the Parliamentary Labour Party and the 1922 Committee help communication within parties. Disputes and differences can be settled at meetings.[31] In the Conservative Party, the 1922 Committee is very influential and the chairman of this committee has great influence on the Prime Minister and senior Cabinet members. In some cases, where Ministers are under pressure to resign, the formal support of the 1922 Committee can save a Minister's career.

Example:
In 1992 David Mellor resigned from the Government when the 1922 Committee refused to support his staying in office after allegations about his personal life became the focus of media attention.

Party committees

Each large party has a number of specialised committees on which their MPs sit which are a part of the parliamentary parties.

1. These committees mirror the subject area of the departments, have elected officers and meet regularly to discuss forthcoming business.
2. They allow for further scrutiny of government activity and provide MPs with additional means of influencing government.
3. There are twenty-four Conservative subject committees and fourteen Labour committees. The Conservative committees have a reputation for being influential and in recent years the chairpersonship of these committees has been a highly significant goal of the different wings of the party. Since 1992 the right wing of the party has sought to gain as many chairmanships as possible.
4. Conservative committees are open to all MPs and have no fixed membership. Only when a controversial topic is being discussed will large numbers attend.
5. The whips attend these meetings as they are a means of transmitting views back to leaders. If a committee is opposed to a Minister's policy idea, the Minister will often reconsider.

The whips, party meetings and party committees act as a channel of communication between front-bench MPs and back-bench MPs.

Questions

1. What is the 1922 Committee?
2. What are the functions of Party Committees?
3. What are (a) the whips, and (b) a three-line whip?

3.10 | The role and function of the Parliamentary Commissioner for the Administration (or Ombudsman)

During the 1960s it became clear that MPs were unable to adequately perform their role as redressers of the people's grievances given the sheer size of the Whitehall bureaucracy, the post-war expansion of the British State, and the amount of time and resources available to each MP to deal with constituency-based matters. This led to calls for Britain to adopt an Ombudsman system based on the Scandinavian model of a citizens' trouble shooter with a remit to investigate complaints against the central bureaucracy. In 1961 the Wyatt Report made this recommendation which was implemented in 1967, via the Parliamentary Commissioner for the Administration Act 1967. Since 1967 the idea has been extended to cover the health service, local government and Northern Ireland,[32] and private industries have created their own system of ombudsmen covering insurance and banking. Other countries have Ombudsmen: New Zealand has a Parliamentary Commissioner and Germany has a Parliamentary Commissioner for Military Affairs.

The Parliamentary Commissioner for the Administration investigates cases of maladministration within the Government. (The other commissioners investigate maladministration within their own fields, e.g. health.) In practice this means that if a citizen claims that he or she has been unfairly treated and suffered an injustice because of maladministration the Ombudsman can investigate the complaint. However, unlike the Scandinavian system where members of the public may approach the Ombudsman directly, in Britain cases are referred to him by MPs. When the legislation was debated MPs imposed this restricted access because they jealously guard their role as redressers of the people's grievances. This means that only if an MP is unable to solve the complaint and if he feels that the Ombudsman may help is the case referred. Only the Health Service and Northern Ireland Ombudsmen can receive direct complaints from the public. In the case of local government, complaints used to be referred via local councillors, but direct access was introduced by the Local Government Act 1988. In 1989 the PCA received only 766 complaints whereas the Commissioner for Local Administration in England currently receives around 11,000 complaints every year.[33]

The PCA has limited powers of investigation:

1.   He can interview witnesses and compel them to appear.
2.   He may examine the necessary files and question officials.

The PCA, however, is handicapped by limited resources, limited public awareness of his role, limited access to files and no formal powers of enforcement.

3.   When an investigation is completed and maladministration has been found, a report will be issued which may contain a series of recommendations. A copy is sent to the MP and the Department concerned. If maladministration is found, the relevant Minister may be pressured to implement the report's recommendations.

Perhaps the biggest problem for the PCA is what constitutes maladministration. The term is vague in order to allow flexibility. It can be defined as injustice caused by 'incompetence, delay, bias, neglect, inattention and arbitrariness'.[34] Injustices as a result of suspected maladministration are the criteria that must be present before the PCA may become involved. Generally, cases brought to the attention of the PCA involve social security payments, income tax problems, and other problems with Government departments.

Critics have argued that this institution is under-used but in 1994 the PCA reported that record numbers of people were complaining about the standards of public services since the launch of The Citizen's Charter. In 1992–3 the PCA handled 208 investigations, the highest number for twelve years. A record 986 people complained to their MP about a problem with a public service that had been passed to the Ombudsman. Top of the league for complaints was the Department of Social Security with nearly a third of all complaints.

Example:
The Social Security Department's mishandling of claims for disability living allowance resulted in 258,000 people not receiving their allowances for months.[35]

This increased success shows that the Ombudsman has created a new avenue for aggrieved citizens to use to rectify complaints against government. Indeed, some reports have brought about important legislative changes.

Example:
The right to have interest paid on delayed tax repayments followed a PCA inquiry.

Officials in local and central government are aware of the remit of the Ombudsmen and have improved accordingly their administrative practices to limit the likelihood of a complaint resulting in an Ombudsman investigation. The Ombudsman has brought benefits to the British democracy but it must be emphasised that the office has a limited role, with MPs remaining the primary avenue citizens use to redress grievances.

Question

What are the roles and powers of the Ombudsman?

3.11 | **Conclusions: A Critique**

This chapter presented the main characteristics, functions and roles of Parliament. Parliament is a multi-faceted organisation with two primary purposes: legislation and scrutiny. Given the range of its powers and responsibilities can it be said that Parliament is effective?

Parliament has two main powers: to hold the executive in Britain to account, and to be free to pass effective, workable legislation. The House of Commons is a powerful legislative chamber, but its powers are limited by the existence of party government which restricts its abilities to scrutinise, represent and criticise. Some critics of the

Commons argue that it now has little more than a ritual role regarding the formulation of government policy, the control of public expenditure, holding the executive accountable and the passing of legislation.[36] The power of Parliament is limited.

The limitations on the power of Parliament

1. **The growth and power of the Party**

    The party system permeates the whole parliamentary system. The operation of party government means that MPs act along party lines limiting their objectivity and freedom of action. Equally, the effective amendment of legislation passing through Parliament is hampered by the party system. Standing committees operate along party lines with a government majority on each ensuring opposition amendments will fail unless the Government agrees.

    Example:

    In the 1987–92 Parliament MPs passed the Bill to introduce the Community Charge even though this new tax was heavily criticised. When, by 1990, it had become clear that the new tax was unworkable the same House of Commons voted to replace the Poll Tax with the Council Tax. Both measures were implemented via the principle of the parliamentary majority and the effectiveness of the party system.

    Critics argue that the history of this legislation shows how ineffective Parliament is as an efficient legislative body. Conservative MPs were aware of the problems with the Poll Tax and yet they supported the implementation of what amounted to a bad law, until it became abundantly clear that it would not work. The whole exercise cost billions of pounds and showed that parliamentary common sense is restricted by the operation of the party system.

2. **A weak scrutiniser**

    Parliament is not an effective scrutiniser of executive action because the tools at its disposal are in themselves weak, but through the operation of party politics they are made even weaker. MPs do not have the resources in either personnel or finances to act as effective scrutinisers of government. Nor do they have the time necessary to fulfil this role.[37]

    Question Time is little more than political theatre before the television cameras. Even John Major has admitted that it is not fulfilling the task for which it was designed. Only written questions effectively supply MPs with information on executive decisions and actions, but even this is limited.

    The Select Committee system has gone some way in addressing the scrutiny deficit that exists in the Commons but it remains hampered by limited powers and recent reforms which have seen the creation of more Quangos (*see point 7 in this section, page 72*) and Next Steps Agencies (*see Chapter 8*). The lines of accountability for Next Steps Agencies are blurred and their development has created a new tier of government, separated from departments which the Select Committees now have to find time to scrutinise. This is proving difficult.

3. **Redresser of grievances**
   Parliament is more effective as a redresser of the people's grievances. MPs, because of their position, do command respect and influence. They can 'get things done' for a constituent or a group of constituents. Equally they may take up a cause, working with a pressure group, maintaining public awareness and pressing for action. Success may be slow to arrive, but is achievable.

   Example:
   The campaign to persuade the Government to pay compensation to those who contracted the HIV virus via infected blood serum ran for many years, supported by a group of cross-bench MPs. Eventually the Government agreed to compensation.

4. **Post-war centralisation**
   Since 1945, Britain has been subjected to a gradual centralisation of power in the hands of the executive, which Parliament has been unable to prevent or influence. The creation of the 'Next Steps' agencies is a good example. These new agencies have a semi-autonomous status and their relationship with the elected assembly is unclear.

5. **The size and secrecy of government**
   Since 1945 the size of government activity has grown enormously and much of what takes place in Whitehall is shrouded in a veil of secrecy. Critics argue that MPs are powerless to scrutinise all the activities of Whitehall effectively because of the restrictions of time, financial resources and personnel. Moreover, MPs are excluded from examining many decisions of government if they are classified as matters of national security. The most MPs may do is examine certain areas of activity or topical issues as they arise. Scrutiny of every single function and decision of government is impossible.

6. **Membership of the European Union**
   This has reduced Parliament's position as the primary legislator for Britain. Since 1973 the institutions of Brussels make laws for Britain that do not need the approval of Parliament. Equally Parliament has been forced to change English law to bring it into line with European Law (*see Chapter 9*).

Key concept: quangos

These are 'quasi-autonomous non-governmental organisations'. They constitute a form of indirect government and consist of state-related organisations which are influential in making or applying government policy. Some quangos have a regulatory function, e.g. the Commission for Racial Equality; others have an advisory function, e.g. The Parliamentary Boundary Commission. Some quangos have a legal function, e.g. the Social Security Benefits Tribunal, while still others are responsible for the provision of public services, e.g. National Health Service Trusts. These bodies are appointed by Ministers and their staff are un-elected. They are not part of a government department. They have limited public accountability and are secretive. Quangos are a political institution which lie somewhere between a Department of State and a public corporation.

7. **Quangos**

The development of the quango has further reduced Parliament's ability to scrutinise and criticise many aspects of government policy. Although the number of quangos has decreased in the last fifteen years, their powers and scope of activity has increased. Quangos now account for over one-fifth of all public spending (£47.1 billion a year) and have responsibility, for example, for university funding, hospitals (National Health Service Trusts) and the control of employment training nationwide via training and enterprise councils.

The number of public functions being administered by quangos has increased dramatically (*see Figure 8*) in recent years. Critics argue that they are a new form of indirect government over which Parliament has limited powers of accountability and scrutiny. There have been a number of cases where public money has been wasted by quangos and responsibilities have been abused, e.g. the Welsh Development Agency in 1993. However, despite worries about the size, influence and abuses of quangos, quasi-indirect government remains a useful way of making decisions and providing services.[38]

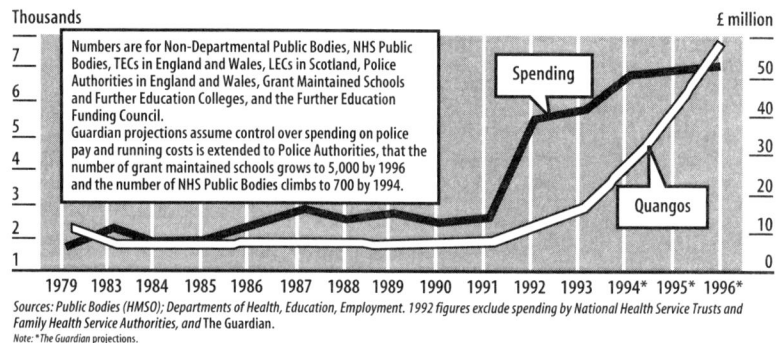

Thousands / £ million

Numbers are for Non-Departmental Public Bodies, NHS Public Bodies, TECs in England and Wales, LECs in Scotland, Police Authorities in England and Wales, Grant Maintained Schools and Further Education Colleges, and the Further Education Funding Council.
Guardian projections assume control over spending on police pay and running costs is extended to Police Authorities, that the number of grant maintained schools grows to 5,000 by 1996 and the number of NHS Public Bodies climbs to 700 by 1994.

Spending / Quangos

1979 1983 1984 1985 1986 1987 1988 1989 1990 1991 1992 1993 1994* 1995* 1996*

Sources: Public Bodies (HMSO); Departments of Health, Education, Employment. 1992 figures exclude spending by National Health Service Trusts and Family Health Service Authorities, and The Guardian.
Note: *The Guardian projections.

Figure 8 The growth of quangos.[39]

8. **The growth in the power of the executive**

Through the operation of party government the Prime Minister and Cabinet are able to control the work of the Commons. This is done through:

(a) the Leader of the House who is a Cabinet rank Minister responsible for organising many of the activities of the House;

(b) the whips;

(c) the power of patronage. All MPs aim to climb onto the ministerial ladder, but in order to do so they must not upset the Prime Minister who appoints the 100 or so government positions from within his or her own party. The majority of MPs will not act independently of their party, unless allowed to in free votes, for fear of risking their career prospects. Their aims can limit their objectivity.

9. **Financial control now rests with the executive**

   The executive constructs the annual Budget in secrecy, presenting MPs with a finalised version, and many of its provisions come into effect as they are announced. Critics argue that MPs have only limited powers to scrutinise and amend one of the most important annual Bills, the Finance Bill.

10. **Parliament is handicapped by its own rules and practices**

    Many of these are simply outdated and do not enhance Parliament's credibility and efficiency. In 1993 the Hansard Society's Commission on the legislative process recommended a series of changes to the legislative process. Other reformers argue that both chambers should undergo a complete organisational reform, including:

- different hours of sitting;
- better working conditions and resources for MPs;
- better resources for the Commons and its committees;
- the replacement of nineteenth-century customs and conventions with updated procedures and rules.

Reform of the Commons is now on the political agenda, although it is close to the bottom, and it remains to be seen whether any radical reform will occur in the next few years. However, until a political consensus between the two major parties develops regarding the issue, radical reform is unlikely to take place. The Liberal Democrats are enthusiastic for change and in 1992 proposed a range of reforms including boosting the powers of Select Committees and improving staff back-up for back-benchers.[40] The Conservatives have introduced some radical reforms including the Departmental Select Committee system in 1979, but presently they are only prepared to consider minor reforms, e.g. different hours of sitting. The Labour Party have in the past advocated a variety of reforms and in the next few years may publish new reform proposals. If the Lords are to be radically reformed in the next ten years this may act as a catalyst igniting public opinion in favour of reform of the Commons as well.

Essay questions

1. In what ways is Parliament still an effective institution?
2. 'Delegate or agent? The role of an MP fails to fulfil either of these roles.' Discuss.
3. 'Select Committees have strengthened the scrutiny power of the Commons.' Do you agree?
4. Should the House of Lords be reformed?
5. How is the Government accountable to Parliament?
6. What recent developments have (a) strengthened, and (b) weakened Parliament's controls over the executive?

Essay planning

Should the House of Lords be reformed?

This essay requires you to explain the arguments for and against the reform of the House of Lords.

(a) In an introduction you could explain briefly the origins of the reform debate.

(b) Use the material in section 3.8 'Reform of the House of Lords', to explain the arguments for and against reform in brief.

(c) In the conclusion you should consider including analysis of:
- where the debate stands today. Possibly explaining that it is part of a large debate about constitutional renewal;
- the positions of the major parties on reform;
- the recent record of the Lords, which has deflected some traditional criticisms, assess the impact of this on record on the debate.

How is the Government accountable to Parliament?

This essay requires the student to explain the devices which enable Parliament to hold the executive accountable for its decisions, domestic and foreign policies, legislation, and future policies. In this answer students need to suggest that Parliament fails to hold the executive accountable and analyse why this happens.

(a) This would include an explanation of how each of the following enable Parliament to hold the Government accountable:
- Question Time
- Select Committees
- Standing Committees and debates
- the role of the MP.

(b) It would also include an explanation as to how the executive may avoid accountability and that the above devices do not fully work (*see section 3.11*) because of:
- The operation of party government.
- The size of the Government compared to the size of parliamentary resources to enable better scrutiny.
- The weakness of the Opposition.
- The weakness of MPs.
- The working patterns of Parliament.

(c) In concluding this essay you would be advised to explain the nature of the debate about strengthening the power of Parliament over the executive.

Notes and references

1. *The Times*, 13.08.94.

2. *The Guardian*, 10.12.93.

3. *The Times*, 06.07.94.

4. *The Guardian*, 15.06.94, p. 24.

5. Robert Adley severely criticised the Rail Privatisation plans, calling them 'the Poll Tax on wheels'.

6. Norton, P. *Does Parliament Matter?* (London, 1993), p. 100.

7. *The Guardian*, 28.04.94.

8. *The Guardian*, 07.07.94.

9. Reply to Parliamentary Question from Author, Question No. 218, 27.05.93.

10. House of Commons Background Paper No. 298, September 1992, pp. 40–43.

11. House of Commons, 19–viii, 1989–90, para. 363.

12. BBC Radio 4, *Analysis* 21.11.91, Transcript 7.

13. *The Daily Telegraph*, 14.01.92.

14. Jex, M. *The New Statesman and Society*, 30.11.92.

15. *On The Record*, BBC Television, 28.03.93.

16. *The Guardian*, 26.03.93.

17. *On the Record*, BBC Television, 28.03.93.

18. *The Guardian*, 21.07.94.

19. *The Guardian*, 24.07.92. 'What has the Citizen's Charter done for us?' Commentary by Hugh Bailey.

20. *Financial Times*, 29.01.93. Commentary by Joe Rogaly.

21. See Gavin Drewry (ed.) *The New Select Committees: A Study of the 1979 Reforms*, 2nd edn (Oxford, 1989) also Michael Rush, 'Select Committees' in Michael Rush (ed.) *Parliament and Pressure Groups* (Oxford, 1990) and also Nevil Johnson, 'The Departmental Select Committees', in Michael Ryle and Peter Richard (eds) *The Commons under Scrutiny* (London, 1988).

22. Cm 2290, p. 1.

23. *The Guardian*, 'Lords Spark Rail Bill Chaos', 04.11.93.

24. *The Guardian*, 16.07.94.

25. Information from interview with the lawyers for the Cardiff Bay Development Corporation, 04.07.94.

26. Shell, D.R. and Beamish, D.R. (eds) *The House of Lords at Work* (Oxford, 1993), p. 10.

27. *The Liberal Democrat Manifesto 1992* (London, 1992), p. 48.

28. The 1963 Peerages Act allowed peers to renounce their title for their lifetime. It was enacted as a result of pressure by Tony Benn MP, who stood to loose his Commons seat because he had inherited his father's title.

29. *The Guardian*, 24.04.94.

30. Students should see *The Guardian*, 05.11.93.

31. See HMSO Educational Sheet, No. 4 'The House of Commons: general information'.

32. The Commissioner for Complaints Act 1969 (Northern Ireland), Parliamentary Commissioner Act 1969 (Northern Ireland), the Health Service Commissioner Act 1973, the Local Government Act 1974.

33. Thompson, K. 'Redressing Grievances: The Role of the Ombudsmen' in *Talking Politics,* Vol. 6, No. 1, 1992, p. 18.

34. As defined by Richard Crossman House of Commons Deb. Vol. 734 (18.10.66.) Col. 51.

35. See the Parliamentary Commissioner for the Administration Report for 1993.

36. Read Walkland, S.A. and Rye, M. (eds) *The Commons Today* (London 1981), pp. 279–304.

37 See P. Norton, 'The Post Thatcher House of Commons', *Talking Politics*, Vol. 6, No. 2, 1994.

38. See Robbins, L. *Politics Pal 1994* (Leicester, 1994), p. 10, *Indirect Government: Quangoland* (Leicester, 1994) and Jones, B. 'The Unknown Government: The Conservative Quangocracy', *Talking Politics*, Vol. 6, No. 2. 1994.

39. *The Guardian*, No. 2, 1994.

40. *The Liberal Democrat Manifesto 1992* (London, 1992), p. 48.

Further reading

Dorey, P. 'The Role of Party Whips', *Talking Politics*, Vol. 5, No. 1, 1992.

Drewry, G. (ed.) *The New Select Committees* (Oxford, 1989).

Griffith, J.A.G. and Ryle, M. *Parliament* (London, 1989).

Jones, B. (ed.) *Political Issues in Britain Today* (Manchester, 1994).

Jones, B. 'The Unknown Government: The Conservative Quangocracy', *Talking Politics,* Vol. 6, No. 2, 1994.

McKie, D. *'The Guardian Political Almanac, 1993/4* (London, 1993).

Norton, P. *Does Parliament Matter?* (London, 1993).

Norton, P. 'The Post-Thatcher House of Commons', *Talking Politics,* Vol. 6, No. 2, 1994.

Norton, P. 'Understanding Parliamentary Change', *Talking Politics,* Vol. 6, No. 1, 1993.

Robbins, L. *Politics Pal,* 1994 (Leicester, 1994).

Rush, M. 'Select Committees', *Talking Politics*, Vol. 3, No. 3, 1991.

Thompson, K. 'Redressing Grievances: The role of the Ombudsmen', *Talking Politics,* Vol. 6, No. 1, 1993.

CHAPTER 4

Political parties

Political parties are an important part of the political landscape of any country. In Britain the modern party has only existed since the turn of the century. In France it dates from the creation of the Fifth French Republic in 1958, and in the USA the modern party system dates from 1933. Today, parties are centralised ideological machines with mass memberships and political funds totalling millions of pounds.

In this chapter we shall examine:

4.1   What political parties are.

4.2   The role and function of political parties.

4.3   The ideologies of the two major parties.

4.4   The structure and organisation of the two major parties.

4.5   The role and structure of the smaller parties.

4.6   The issues of party funding.

4.7   The debate over the two-party system.

4.1 | What political parties are

Today, parties in Britain are professionally run marketing machines which encourage political participation. They try to persuade people to join them and ultimately stand as party candidates in elections. A simple definition of a political party is :

> A group of people who have a set of common ideas and beliefs who seek political office at a local and/or national level with the aim of implementing their ideas to the benefit of the locality or nation as a whole.

The eighteenth-century MP and conservative philosopher, Edmund Burke, defined political parties as:

> 'A body of men united for promoting by their joint endeavours the national interest upon some particular principle which they are all agreed.'

Both of these definitions are useful. The Conservative Party is a body of men and women united in their beliefs. They aim to further the national interest, as they see it, by implementing their ideas. Parties are not pressure groups. Parties seek elected office, while pressure groups seek to influence those in office.

Political parties have at their heart a set of beliefs and values to which all their members adhere. However, the turning of those beliefs into policies leads us to talk about the various 'wings' of a party. In every party there exists a diversity of views and opinions that are categorised as right wing, left wing, centre-right or centre-left.

1. **Right wing** refers to people who have some degree of belief in the free market or capitalist socio-economic theories.
2. **Left wing** refers to people who have some degree of belief in socialist, welfare-orientated socio-economic theories.

One complication is that although we can identify political parties according to the above, there are wings within all parties.

Centrists

Centrists believe in the core values of a party and can agree with either wing of the party on the method to use to pursue those values through policies that take a sensible approach.

Right wingers

The right wing of the party tend to advocate free market orientated policies adapted to suit their party's core values.

Example:
The right wing of the Labour Party advocates a balanced approach of mixing some aspects of capitalism with socialism. The former deputy leader of the Labour Party, Roy Hattersley, comes from this wing. They would favour retaining private schools whereas the left wing would not.

Left wingers

The left wing of any party believe that the State has a greater role to play in all aspects of society, from industry to health care. Left-wing Conservatives favour greater state intervention and protection of the welfare state, and greater public spending for the good of society.

Left-wing members of the Labour Party have more extreme beliefs including greater state invention, the nationalisation of industry and higher taxation for the richest members of society.

There is no relationship between the left wing of the Conservative party and the left wing of the Labour party, but left-wing Conservatives have a political outlook ideologically closer to right-wing Labour members, as shown in Figure 9:

Figure 9 The political spectrum.

Labour Left ↔ **Centre** ↔ **Labour Right** → **Conservative Left** ↔ **Centre** ↔ **Conservative Right**

Questions

1. Define the term 'political party'.
2. What is meant by the phrase, 'the wings of a party'?

4.2 | The role and function of political parties

A political party allows people to identify with and support a set of ideas or beliefs. A person who votes 'Conservative' in Britain is both acknowledging his or her belief in what the Conservative Party and its leader stand for, and expressing a desire that the Conservative Party should be in power to implement its ideas and policies.

There are two different types of party systems that exist in the world today: one-party systems and multi-party systems.

One-party system

A one-party system exists where the politics of the State is dominated by a single party. The one-party system has been a feature of politics in the Third World.

Example:
Some African states have one-party systems, including Zimbabwe. Most Communist countries are also examples of one-party systems. In the old Soviet Union the only party was the Communist Party of the Soviet Union, and in 1995 China, Vietnam and North Korea remain one-party states.

Multi-party system

Multi-party systems exist where two or more parties compete for power. Often this takes place through democratic elections. The Western European countries are all examples of this system.

Example:
France has a complex party system. In French national politics there are three ideological groupings, left, centre and right which have produced the major political parties. French politics is dominated by four major parties of the left and right wings. The right of French politics is divided between the Conservative UDF, 'Union pour la Démocratie Française´ and Gaullist RPR, 'Rassemblement pour la Republique'. The left is divided between the Socialists and Communists and the Socialist Party is the dominant partner. However, it is harder to distinguish a dominant

partner of the right. France has a multi-party system in which the main right- and left-wing parties compete in elections to the National Parliament, the Office of the President and local elections across the country.[1]

Sometimes countries move from being one-party systems to multi-party systems, e.g. the newly democratised nations of Eastern Europe.

We have a tendency to see parties as organs that are normally associated with democracies. Political parties also exist in Communist countries. Essentially, they fit Edmund Burke's definition but their method of operation is different. In the past few years there has been a massive growth in the number of political parties across the world with the democratisation of the former Soviet Union and Eastern Europe. In Poland, Hungary and Russia itself there are now many and various political parties representing a huge spectrum of political ideas and beliefs.

Across the world in liberal democracies political parties serve a number of important functions.

Functions of political parties

1. **Encourage popular interest and participation in politics through the formulation of policy**

   Parties are highly organised political machines that offer people ideas and choices. Individual parties design their policies in accordance with a core set of beliefs, e.g. socialism or free market economics, which they believe will solve national problems and improve the standard of living.

   Example:
   *That state-owned industries in Britain should be sold off into the private sector was an idea which the Conservatives placed in their 1979 manifesto. This policy was called **privatisation** and is seen by Margaret Thatcher and John Major as one of the most successful Conservative policies of the 1980s.*

The ideology and policies of the party are used:

- to encourage people to participate in politics, to join and become active members of the party. Individuals cannot influence the governing process alone, but as a group or body they have a better chance of doing so. The degree of political participation can be very low, from attending a few meetings rising to a higher level of activity in various party organisations and conferences and ultimately standing for public office. It is important to note that the two major parties in Britain have suffered declining membership over the past two decades.

Key concept: policy

A simple definition is that a policy is any course of action designed to improve, maintain or prevent some state of affairs. Policies are normally the operational plan by which an idea is implemented in a business or political arena.

- to attract media attention, exposing parties to public scrutiny encourage political debate about the choices available and issues facing the people.

2. **To seek political power in elections by encouraging members to stand as candidates for office**

   Every party, of whatever size, seeks the power of elected office, so that it can put its ideas into practice.

   Parties encourage members to stand for political office. Parties are an avenue for political recruitment and they encourage members to stand in elections for public office with the party label attached to their names. This often provides candidates with a foundation of support from which to win office, by having the 'party machine' working for them.

   This is not to suggest that people who do not belong to a party cannot win elections. In general and local government elections independent candidates can and do stand. In the 1993 Christchurch by-election there were nine independent candidates.[2] However, the time of independent MPs has passed, whereas in local government 'independent' councillors remain part of the political spectrum.

3. **To present choices to the electorate**

   In two-party and multi-party systems different parties have different ideas and policies. This presents the electorate with a choice. Parties often publish policy documents which publicise the ideas and policies of the party and during elections **manifestos** are produced, designed to attract voters to support their candidates for office. In Britain the party that gains a majority of seats in the House of Commons is said to have won the general election, becoming the governing party democratically empowered to form the Government and implement its manifesto. This is known as party government (*see Chapter 3*).

4. **To provide the functions of government**

   In Britain the governing party carries out the process of government by implementing its policies and staffing and organising the executive.

   Example:
   In Britain there are 100 or so Cabinet and non-Cabinet government positions. In the USA the President makes over 2,000 governmental appointments which are directly accountable to him.

Party government is more easily achieved if one party is controlling all the levers of power, providing for a coherent, well-managed, centralised and accountable system of government. The members of a government, coming from one party, will share the same interests and beliefs and generally they will work together as a

Key term: manifesto

This is a policy document usually published at the beginning of an election campaign. Manifestos clearly outline the ideas and policies of each party, allowing the electorate to make an informed choice. Additionally, most candidates produce a smaller manifesto which outlines their ideas and aims and incorporates the main points of the national manifesto.

team. In Britain, with its constitutional opposition, the party in opposition uses all the dynamics of the party system to provide an effective and co-ordinated official opposition to the governing party.

5. **Channels of communication**

   Parties provide a channel for the leadership and the membership to remain in touch and aware of each other's ideas and views. Equally, parties maintain a link between the wider public and the membership and leadership of the party, acting as a channel through which the ideas and views of the population can find expression. It is debatable whether modern parties perform this function particularly well. Both the Conservative and Labour Parties are now large bureaucratic organisations. This, critics claim, restricts the channels of communication among their own memberships as well as to the public.

6. **Representation**

   Parties are representative institutions. A party represents its ideology, policies and members and the interests of those who voted for it. If a party wins power it is said to have a mandate to govern and implement its policies. Its elected representatives are meant to act as representatives of both the party and their constituents. This can cause a conflict of interest and in modern politics loyalty to the party has a tendency to come before loyalty to the constituency.

Modern parties are constantly reviewing their policies in order to maintain or make their party a popular choice with the electorate. The Labour policy review of the late 1980s was designed to do this as was John Major's 'Back to Basics' campaign.

Questions

1. What in your view are the two most important roles that a political party performs? Explain your choice.
2. Define the term 'policy'.
3. What is meant by the terms 'multi-party system' and 'one-party system'? Give an illustration of each.

4.3 | **The ideologies of the two major parties**

Parties are umbrella organisations which encompass a large spectrum of views, from right to left. However, these terms can be confusing if the main ethos of a party is not first established. The Conservative Party in Britain can be described as a right-wing party. This means that people who join the Conservatives adhere to some or all of its central ideas which include a strong belief in private enterprise, stability and law and order, strong national defence and the encouragement of individuals to provide for themselves. These beliefs can be applied to other right-wing parties across Europe and in the United States.

Example:
In France the Conservative UDF and Gaullist RPR can be described as having a similar set of ideologies as the Conservative Party in Britain as can the Republican Party in the United States. However, these similarities should be qualified by the fact that ideologically similar parties in other countries have a different historical development and raison d'être. *Despite being in the same ideological family they can adopt different approaches to similar problems because of differences in their culture, language, heritage, constitutions and political history. The conservative governments in France in the 1980s did not adopt a radical non-interventionist policy towards French industry in a similar fashion to the policy pursued by Conservative government in Britain.*

The Labour Party in Britain is a left-wing party which believes in equality, the redistribution of wealth, a measure of state control and a bias towards the protection and furthering of the interests of the lower classes in Britain. Similarly, the Socialist Party of France believes in such ideas, but has adopted different techniques to gain power and turn ideology into workable government policy.

Both of Britain's major parties do from time to time generate fresh interpretations of these central ideas and the policies necessary to further their declared interests. Therefore as the needs of the country change, so parties must change their policies, and sometimes their principles, to meet the new challenges.

Conservative principles

The Conservative Party can be described as a very pragmatic party. This means that the Conservatives are more concerned with policies which are practical rather than for attempting to implement theoretical ideals. Such qualities have enabled the party to survive and succeed, being in office in one form or another for

Table 15.7 *Pressure groups and democracy: for and against*

For	Against
• **Participation and political access** PGs increase participation and access to political system, thereby enhancing the quality of democracy. They enable the *intensity* of feeling on issues to be considered, opinions to be weighed as well as counted.	• **Sectionalism and selfishness** PGs improve participation, but *unequally*, benefiting the well-organised but disadvantaging the weakly organised. They benefit 'those who shout loudest' against the rest.
• **Improvement of government** Consultation with affected groups is the rational way to make decisions in a free society: the information and advice provided by groups helps to improve the quality of government policy and legislation.	• **Anti-parliamentary democracy** Secret, behind-the-scenes consultations between government and groups enables covert 'deals' to be made thereby detracting both from open government and the legitimate influence of elected legislators in Parliament.
• **Social progress** PGs enable new concerns and issues to reach the political agenda, thereby facilitating social progress and preventing social stagnation.	• **Pluralistic stagnation** Group opposition can slow down or even block desirable changes, thereby contributing to social immobilism.
• **Pluralism** PGs are a product of freedom of association, which is a fundamental principle of liberal democracy: its obverse is autocratic or tyrannical suppression of interests. Freely operating pressure groups are essential to the effective functioning of liberal democracy: they serve as vital intermediary institutions between government and society, assist in the dispersal of political power and provide important counterweights to undue concentration of power.	• **Elitism** Group system only *apparently* functions on 'level playing field'; in practice reinforces existing class and power structure – 'in the pluralist heaven the heavenly choir sings with a strong upper class accent' (Schnattschneider, 1960, cited Grant, 1989, p. 26).
• **Social cohesion** PGs increase social cohesion and political stability by providing 'safety-valve' outlet for individual and collective grievances.	• **Social disharmony and dislocation** Inegalitarian operation of groups increases social discontent and political instability by intensifying sense of social frustration and injustice felt by disadvantaged and excluded sections of the population.
• **Opposition** PGs assist surveillance of government by exposing information it would rather keep secret, thereby reinforcing and complementing work of official opposition through political parties.	• **Failure of opposition** True in theory but only to limited extent in practice: in contemporary Britain, groups and parties combined are unable to mount effective opposition to government policies because often lack adequate information.

over two-thirds of this century. Normally, it is the party leader who is able to redefine 'Conservatism' to suit the times but there are some central ideas.

1. **Class divisions**

    The Conservatives do not place the same emphasis on class as Labour and they do not believe in social equality which they suggest reduces and restricts personal freedom and initiative.

2. **An emphasis on national unity: 'one nation Toryism'**

    The Conservatives believe that policies should be followed which benefit the whole nation and not just particular sections of the population. This has been called 'One Nation Toryism'. They believe very strongly in the union of the nations of Britain: Scotland, Northern Ireland, England and Wales. During the 1992 General Election, John Major stressed his belief in and support for, this concept of the 'union'.[3]

3. **The authority of government**

    The Conservatives are the party of the status quo. They believe in the principle that central government should be responsible for governing the whole country, pursuing tight control over areas such as the economy and local administration. The Conservative Party is opposed to economic planning and greater state intervention. This was demonstrated by Margaret Thatcher who said in 1979 that she was going to 'roll back the frontiers of the State'. Moreover, the Conservatives believe in strong defence and law and order policies.

4. **Social reform**

    The Conservatives, since the late nineteenth century, have followed policies which are intended to benefit and improve the social conditions of all the people. But they do believe in a hierarchical principle, seeing society as a pyramid with a ruling elite trained by background and education to supply the qualities of responsible leadership. The established institutions – monarchy, House of Lords, Judiciary and Anglican Church – are all regarded as part of the basis of a stable British nation which must be maintained.

5. **Freedom and liberty**

    Conservatives believe strongly in the freedom of the individual to make choices and the freedom of private enterprise, i.e. the free market. Therefore Conservative Governments pursue policies designed to increase individual choice, e.g. private education and private health care. Conservatives believe that private enterprise can be encouraged via reduced state intervention, lower taxation and deregulation. During the years of the post-war consensus, 1945–79, these ideas were diluted by an acceptance of the welfare state, greater co-operation with trade unions and degrees of state intervention in industry by state ownership and industrial subsidies.

Key term: one nation Toryism

The Conservative Prime Minister Disraeli (1874–80) believed that the Tories had to implement policies which benefited the ordinary man and maintained the unity of the nation. He is credited with founding the concept of 'one nation Toryism'.

However, under Margaret Thatcher there was a return to the purer form of Conservative ideas on freedom and liberty. Under John Major this continues.

Example:
The 'Heseltine' Deregulation Act 1994 is designed to free private enterprise from the shackles of government regulation by removing many layers of red tape (regulations) which limit business's freedom of action.

Although these are the main principles of the Conservative Party, the nature of their influence on Conservative leaders and politicians varies according to personalities and the pragmatic nature of the Party itself.

Under Margaret Thatcher's leadership the Party embraced the thinking of the **New Right**, which marked a shift to the right in the Conservative Party and a break from the post-war consensus.

Thatcherism

Margaret Thatcher was an ardent supporter of New Right ideas along with her colleague Sir Keith (now Lord) Joseph. The Thatcher Governments implemented many New Right policies including privatisation of state industries, a monetarist economic policy, the reduction of state subsidises, and policies designed to the release free market forces into the British economy, which Margaret Thatcher believed would benefit individual freedom and free enterprise. The policies which Margaret Thatcher's Conservative Governments pursued were called collectively **Thatcherism**. Thatcherism was economic liberalism given political flesh.[4] The Thatcherite policy agenda included the following :

- Privatisation of state-owned industries.

- Reduction and elimination of industrial subsidies.

- Reduction of the size of the State, reducing the numbers of civil servants and introducing market reforms into Whitehall's practices and routines.

- Reduction in the powers of sectional interests in society.

  Example: Trade union powers.

- Embracing a monetarist economic policy which suggested that by controlling the money supply (the amount of bank notes and credit available in the economy), inflation – the scourge of the British economy of 1970s – can be controlled. The ideas of Milton Friedman lay at the heart of Thatcherism. This policy incorporated a number of additional aims, including the reduction of public spending and the reduction in the power

Key concept: the new right

This term is used to describe the movement which evolved in the 1970s in Britain in reaction to the alleged stagnation of the post-war consensus. The New Right were a group of people who believed in the removal of sectional interests in society, the pursuit of policies by government which provided for greater freedom of choice, a belief in the virtues of the free market and a monetarist economic policy, and a distaste for state intervention. The New Right was not just a British phenomena. It also evolved in the United States and France. It was inspired by writings of the monetarists Milton Friedman and Frederick Hayek.

of Labour interests by legislation and the creation of a new industrial culture called **economic realism**. Employees and their unions would learn that they could not demand large wage increases if the rate of their production did not provide for such increases, workers would realise that by indulging in high wage demands they could price themselves out of the marketplace and bankrupt their company. This aspect of Thatcherite economic policy was matched by a general distaste for trade unions which provoked legislation designed to limit their power.

- Increased choice for people on how to use their money, e.g. private education, private health care and pensions.

- A belief in strong but limited government, designed to give people greater freedoms in the choices which they make for themselves and their lives. Thatcherism claimed that it would reduce the level of state bureaucracy and introduce market forces into the state sector, at both central and local government levels, to make it more competitive and responsive to the needs of the public.

- A policy to encourage the creation of an enterprise culture. Government should create conditions for enterprise and initiative to flourish by reducing red tape and bureaucracy.

- A belief that people should be encouraged to help themselves and not rely on state support. Margaret Thatcher believed that state welfare is excessive, expensive and inefficient. Her Government sought to pursue policies to create wealth and provide opportunities for everyone to build their own wealth. Thatcherism supports a change in the tax burden from direct to indirect taxation and has a distaste for policies specifically aimed at reducing economic inequalities.

These policies have been described as **popular capitalism**.

As part of this revolution Margaret Thatcher was able to gain a large proportion of the working-class vote in the three general elections which she won (*see Chapter 13*).

During her tenure at No. 10 Downing Street, Conservative policy shifted away from many of its traditional ideas; others, such as law and order and strong defence, remained constant. These were seen as central planks of 'Thatcherism' but they were traditional Tory ideas simply finding new expression.[5]

John Major has attempted to shift to the centre ground of Conservative ideology by talking of a 'classless society'.[6] He has continued to pursue many Thatcherite economic policies but he has attempted to construct his own 'Majorism' for the 1990s, through the 'classless society' policy and the Citizens' Charter

Key concept: popular capitalism

This terms refers to the policy pursued by the Thatcher Governments of the 1980s. Capitalism until the 1980s had been a term which referred to the activities of mainly the richest echelons in society and included the ownership of shares and private health care. Margaret Thatcher was an advocate of the thinking of the New Right which considered, among other things, that the role of government was to restore 'choice' to people across a range of social and economic activities. The Conservative Government believed that one of these choices was to allow people to create wealth for themselves by reducing direct taxation and increasing people's monetary choices. This included buying a house, investing in private pensions and health care and owning shares. The Thatcher Governments implemented policies designed to increase home and share ownership, e.g. the sale of council houses and the public privatisation of nationalised industries including British Telecom, British Gas, BP and the Regional Electricity Companies. These policies became known as popular capitalism and were summed up by the phrase, 'A home-owning, share-owning democracy'.

Initiative (*see Chapters 6 and 8*). This has been followed by 'Back to Basics', which was designed to be the Conservative policy agenda for the mid-1990s.[7]

In the October 1993 Conservative Party Conference, John Major said that Conservatives 'stand for self-reliance, decency and respect for others'. He promised, 'The Conservative Party will lead the country back to basics across the board – sound money, free trade, traditional teaching, respect for the family and the law. And above all, lead a new campaign to defeat the cancer that is crime.' This policy statement was followed by a Queen's Speech which outlined a range of policies which encompassed the new approach: a new tougher Criminal Justice and Public Order Bill; a crackdown on the dependency culture of the welfare state; a renewed emphasis on religious education in schools. John Major's 'Back to Basics' was in line with traditional Conservative ideology, combined with 'Thatcherism' and his own policy inventions. However, this new agenda became subsumed by arguments about personal morality and scandals involving Conservative Ministers who were forced to resign because of the incompatibility of their private lives with the perceived ethos of 'Back to Basics'. The majority of this new policy agenda was dropped in 1994.[8] Perhaps the only policy to originate from 'Back to Basics' which was implemented with a degree of success was the anti-crime policy contained in the Criminal Justice and Public Order Act 1994.

Labour's principles

Labour's principles are rooted in a set of doctrines known as **socialism**.

The Labour Party is a unique product of British experience and history. It is a radical coalition of interests, all socialist to varying degrees. The Labour Party was created by groups outside Parliament in 1900 including the Fabians, the Co-operative movement and the trade unions to secure social improvements for the working classes of Britain through parliamentary channels. This has been called democratic socialism. Labour is made up of both a right wing and a left wing and it still contains radical elements.

Examples: The Tribune Group and the Manifesto Group.

1. **Traditional values**
    *   Labour is the party which is dedicated to the overthrow of the status quo. It believes in social opportunity and individual freedom.
    *   Labour believes in social and economic equality. This policy is enshrined in the Labour Party Constitution. During 1945–51 nationalisation was a necessary and popular policy. Now it has been superceded by privatisation, and when a Labour

Key concept: socialism

This is a set of ideas which have many variations. Broadly speaking socialists are committed to the idea of equality and to policies intended to bring it about. These traditions include collective ownership of the economy, state ownership of industry or nationalisation in Labour's case, and extensive welfare measures. Socialists can be divided in two ways. First, by the method they adopt to implement their ideas – between those who generally reject revolution as a means of achieving socialism and use parliamentary methods to gain power to build the socialist state, and those who seek power via revolutionary means. Secondly, by the degree of equality which they envisage creating, e.g. Communists are more egalitarian than mainstream British socialists.

government is next elected it is unclear if any of the privatised industries will undergo re-nationalisation.

- Labour has always identified itself with the working classes whose fortunes it wished to improve by laying stress on greater improvements in education, health, social security and housing. Keir Hardie, the party's first leader said that 'socialism is much more an affair of the heart than the intellect', emphasising the tenet of Labour ideology precisely. Labour believes in constructing a welfare state which will help the worse off in society.

- A belief in the virtue and necessity of a National Health Service (NHS), free to all at the point of delivery. Labour developed the NHS in the late 1940s and believe it to be a fundamental construct of post-war Britain.

2. **Post-1983 new thinking**

   With the election of Neil Kinnock as leader in 1983 the Labour Party began to recover from the convulsions of the early 1980s which had seen it shift towards the left, and it began to move back towards the centre ground of politics. Kinnock moved the Party towards the Conservative-set agenda, with no more talk of nationalisation or unilateral nuclear disarmament. Labour would become enthusiastic Europeans and adopt a new approach through which capitalism was to be managed. This process gave rise to a division within the Party between those who believed in the Kinnock reforms and wished to see further reforms, *the modernisers,* and those who wanted only limited reform and the preservation of many traditional ideas, *the traditionalists*. The Kinnock reforms and policy review did not prove to be enough to win Labour the 1992 General Election.

In 1994, having lost four general elections (1979, 1983, 1987, 1992) the Party has moved further towards the centre ground claiming to be the party of social opportunity.

Labour is now embracing the free market economics of the Conservatives but with social good attached to the creed, which consists of:

1. The creation of an economy in which all can benefit. A more productive and competitive economy, with low unemployment and low inflation. Labour now supports self-reliance and individual opportunity. Labour still believes in state intervention but in the 1990s this means active government policies for employment, investment and industry. It believes that governments must act to stimulate employment, promoting investment, and work with industry to make more efficient use of our economic resources.

2. Labour is now enthusiastically in support of Europe. It believes in pursuing a policy of co-ordinated economic action with Europe aimed at expanding the European economy.

Key concept: democratic socialism

The Labour Party can be described as a democratic socialist party. This means that it seeks to construct a socialist-inspired state through democratic means. From its very beginnings Labour has sought power through the ballot box and has aimed to introduce its socialist policies through Parliament and not through revolution.

3. Labour now believe in Constitutional reform and increasing the rights of citizens.

4. A central policy of the Labour Party has always been the creation of better living and working conditions via better health care, social security, etc. This remains the case today. The Labour Party of the 1990s believes that the fulfilment of individual potential can only be fully realised within a strong and cohesive community. It believes in the provision of good public services, high quality health care and education and in the security of safe, crime-free streets. Furthermore, Labour is a strong proponent of Government-inspired interventionist policies to improve the environment.

5. Labour has renewed its concern for social justice, believing that each individual has a valuable part to play in British society. It suggests that conditions of poverty, unemployment and low pay prevent millions of people participating fully in society and suggests that, if in government, it would pursue policies designed to give people opportunities to improve and free themselves from these conditions, reinforcing and supporting self-reliance and overcoming human and economic waste.

This summarises present Labour ideologies and policies. Labour has certainly embraced the language of the Conservatives and added the principles of the mixed economy to its ideology. The new leader Tony Blair, a moderniser, has spoken of an **ethical socialism**, more adaptable to changing circumstance than the dominant Labour approach of most of this century. This form of socialism is based upon social justice, equality of opportunity and community combined with a strong ethical market economy.[9] His statements so far equate with the approach adopted under Smith but future policy proposals will incorporate more of Blair's thinking.

Both major parties in Britain appear to have moved into the centre ground which is occupied by the issues of crime, health, and the economy. The Labour Party has shifted towards the Conservative agenda, which remains right of centre. In the next few years the Conservatives will wish to place some clear water between themselves and Labour in the run up to the next general election.[10]

Questions

1. What do socialists mean by equality?
2. How does a Conservative view hierarchy?
3. What is 'democratic socialism'?
4. What is 'one nation Toryism'?
5. Distinguish the Conservative and socialist (Labour Party) views of social class.

4.4 | The structure and organisation of the two major parties

This area of study is popular with examiners as short answer material or compare and contrast essay questions. The Conservative and Labour parties have similar organs but their structure and the focus of power within each party is different.

The Conservative Party

The Conservative Party structure is a pyramid with all the power in the Party being centred on the Party representatives in Parliament and its leader (*see Figure 10*). The party extends itself outwards and downwards from this Parliamentary base into the country. In many ways the Conservative Party is decentralised when compared to Labour's structure.

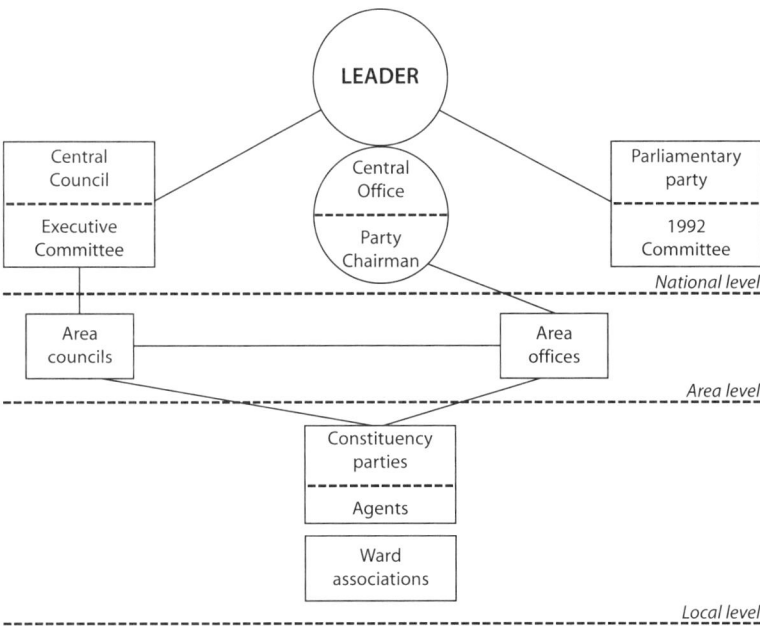

Figure 10 Conservative Party organisation.[11]

The Leader

Conservative Party leaders have potentially much greater power than any other party leader. The whole organisational structure of the Conservatives is designed to serve the leader who is responsible for the creation of Party policy and the election manifesto. However, it is not the case that with this power comes security of tenure in office. More Conservative leaders have resigned or been dismissed than in any other political party.

The leader of the Conservative Party is responsible for the strategy to be followed by the Party to win power and retain office. The leader has the right to choose the Cabinet (or the Shadow Cabinet when in Opposition). There are a number of constraints similar to those on the Prime Minister, e.g. representatives from the different wings of the Party must be included. The leader appoints the Chief Whip who is responsible for organising the party in Parliament and ensuring discipline among MPs. Through this appointment the leader is able to exert great controls over his or her MPs ensuring their support for the policies which the leader is following.

Outside the precincts of Parliament, Conservative Central Office, which is the national headquarters of the Party, and the Conservative Research Department are under the personal direction of the leader. The leader appoints the principal officers and the Party Chairman. The Chairman is responsible for organising the party nationally and managing general 'day-to-day' affairs. In the months prior to a likely general, European or local council election, the Chairman is responsible for organising and preparing the party for the election campaign. He works with the leader and a team in Central Office to decide the strategy to be followed in each election.

Through the Chief Whip and the Party Chairman the Conservative leader is able to exercise a higher degree of control and influence of his or her party than the Labour leader. The structure of the Party reflects this. It is a pyramid structure with all power concentrated at the top. Each layer beneath the leader is designed to allow the leader to have the resources and support to win a general election. The leader has tremendous influence and power over the Party. When in office these powers are amplified because the leader becomes Prime Minister.

With all this at the leader's disposal it is not surprising that the Party has a darker edge which is used unmercifully when power is not achieved or in danger of being lost. The events of 1990 serve to demonstrate that if the Party feels that a leader's time is up then it will drop that individual however many elections he or she may have won for the Party.[12]

Leadership election

The leader is chosen by all the Conservative MPs in the House of Commons. Before the introduction of a formal election procedure in the 1960s, Conservative leaders were said to 'emerge' from within the ranks of the parliamentary party.

Now, a formal election takes place in which all Conservative MPs vote to choose the leader. The procedure has been altered since 1990, when Margaret Thatcher was toppled, to make it harder for a sitting leader to be challenged.

The Constitution of the Parliamentary Party requires that an election for the leadership of the party occurs at the start of every parliamentary session in November. For a resident leader it is normally a formality. If they were unpopular, however, a challenge could still be mounted.

1. Each candidate has to have two named sponsors and the backing of another thirty-two named MPs – a total of 10% of the parliamentary party, whose names would be given to the Chairman of the back-bench 1922 Committee.
2. An election would then take place. A process of three ballots may occur. On the first ballot a candidate requires 50% of the vote of the parliamentary party plus 15% more of the votes than any other candidate. If these conditions are not met, as in 1990 when Margaret Thatcher failed to achieve the plus 15%, nominations are reopened, other candidates may enter and a second ballot takes place a week later. Again a candidate requires a 15%-plus majority, but if no-one succeeds a third ballot takes place. In this final ballot the top three candidates are entered and a form of proportional representation is used and a winner declared.[13]

The National Union
This body, created in 1867, is designed:

1. to represent the constituency associations in England and Wales (there are separate bodies for Scotland and Northern Ireland);
2. to organise the Annual Party Conference.

The central council of the National Union is composed of Conservative peers, Members of the European Parliament (MEPs), prospective MPs and representatives of regional bodies and advisory committees. It meets once a year to elect officers to a smaller executive committee. It is a weak institution which only acts as a channel of communication between supporters in the country and the leadership.

The Annual Conference
The role of the Conference is advisory. About 3,000 – 4,000 delegates attend. Each constituency association is allowed to send up to seven delegates. The Conference is little more than a rally for the faithful and a public relations exercise in which the leader receives a standing ovation and an impression of unity is portrayed for public consumption. In recent years the Conference has been used by the leadership to outline new policies and give the party a sense of direction. In 1993 John Major and his Cabinet outlined a range of new policies which became known as 'Back to Basics.'[14]

Usually the Conference is a stage-managed affair and it is unusual for Ministers to get a rough ride. Debates are strictly organised and cover each Minister's area of responsibility (e.g. defence, law and order) but dissenting speeches are kept to a minimum and votes are taken at the end of debates.

Figure 11 The Conservative Annual Party Conference, 1991.

The Conservative Party Annual Conference is not a decision-making body unlike the Labour Party Conference. It does not have any of the powers of the Labour Conference but it is often used by the leadership as a litmus test for future policies. Therefore, it is important and the leader now attends the whole of the Conference rather than, as in the 1960s, just one day to make his rallying speech to the masses.

Importance of the Annual Conference:
1. It is an opportunity for the leadership to meet with the membership.
2. It can be used as a national platform which has comprehensive media coverage to launch new ideas and policies.
3. Fringe meetings are held, which are smaller gatherings of the different groups which make up the Party outside the main conference arena, and are now used by Ministers and other MPs and members to discuss problems and future policies. They receive less media coverage and are opportunities for senior members of the party to 'think out loud' in private.
4. The conference can generate a 'mood' which indicates to the leader the popularity or unpopularity of policies, e.g. the unpopularity of the Poll Tax, the popularity of the 'Back to Basics' agenda.
5. It is important to note that legislation often follows a Conference.

Central Office

This can be described as the co-ordinating body for the national party and it provides a 'civil service' for the Party. The Chairman is responsible for Central Office, and he is aided by a vice-chairman.

Central Office is an important organisational link between the Party at large and MPs at Westminster. It controls Party offices in twelve provincial areas, and provides a range of advice and support services. Central Office is responsible for the appointment of Party agents for each constituency and draws up the list of approved candidates for electoral office.

The Research Department, which has been based in Central Office since 1965, provides secretarial support for the Shadow Cabinet when the Party is in opposition, supports policy groups, undertakes long-term research, provides research materials and briefs for the Party's elected representatives (MPs, MEPs, and local councillors), and produces a wide range of publications, e.g. the pre-election campaign guides. This department plays a very important role in policy formulation and it has been the launch-pad for a number of successful political careers, e.g. Chris Patten.

Attached to Central Office is the Conservative Political Centre which was a research group established to concentrate on long-term issues within the Party.

There are a number of external research organisations which support the Conservative Party and orbit around Central Office but are not part of it. These include the Centre for Policy Studies and the Institute for Economic Affairs.

Constituency associations

Constituency associations provide the people-power for the Party to launch and win election campaigns. These associations recruit members, organise social events and fund-raising activities, and in elections provide a range of voluntary support services including canvassing the electorate and distributing leaflets.

Local associations are responsible for the selection of candidates for office. Candidacy in local elections is often not very contentious or highly contested, but in parliamentary elections, especially in safe seats, hundreds of applicants usually apply. Sometimes the constituency associations can have candidates foisted upon them to stand in an election.

Example:
In Cheltenham in 1992 in preparation for the general election, a black candidate, John Taylor, was imposed upon the local constituency party by Central Office to contest the seat in the general election.

Groups within the Conservative Party

Both parties have a variety of different groups within them reflecting the range of opinions within the umbrella of the party. In the Conservatives there are both left-wing and right-wing groups. For example, the Bow Group, formed in 1951, accepts the principles of the welfare state and Keynesian management of the economy, and is on the left of the Party. Other groups are the Tory Reform Group, the Monday Club and the No Turning Back group.

The Labour Party

The Labour Party structure reflects a socialist ethos of democracy, egalitarianism and collective decision making. This is clearly demonstrated in the powers and roles of the leader, who at first appears to be less powerful than his Conservative counterpart.

The leader

Labour did not have a modern style leader until 1922 when Ramsay MacDonald was given the title of 'Chairman and Leader'. Until 1922 the concept of a 'leader' was an unacceptable idea to the majority in the Labour movement. This serves to illustrate the position of the Labour leader. He is not in complete control of the party machine and when in opposition he is unable to chose his own Shadow Cabinet. According to the Constitution the Labour Party Annual Conference decides policy, which the leader is supposed to implement, and the Labour head office is responsible to the National Executive committee (NEC).

If Prime Minister, the Labour leader does have wider and more discretionary powers. Upon taking office he would have to include all those elected in the last parliamentary Labour Party election to the Shadow Cabinet in his Cabinet, but thereafter he has greater freedom of choice by virtue of being Prime Minister. Theoretically, the Labour leader is supposed to abide by and implement the decisions of Conference and the NEC, but when in office Labour's leaders have often ignored the decisions made by these bodies, taking decisions and making initiatives on the basis of their powers as Prime Minister. Atlee, Wilson and Callaghan reasoned that their ultimate responsibility was to Parliament and the nation, and not to outside bodies like the NEC and Conference. This represents an awkward conflict of interest which does not arise in the Conservative Party. During the Wilson/Callaghan Governments of 1974–9 a great deal of resentment arose within the rank and file of the Party because of the way in which the leadership often ignored the wishes of Conference. This resentment laid the foundations of the internal conflict that occurred within the party in the early 1980s.

Leadership election

Until 1981 the method for electing the Labour leader was similar to that of the Conservative Party, a ballot of Labour MPs. With the 1979 General Election defeat the Labour Party entered a period of reform and recrimination.

In the search for greater democratisation the Party held a special Conference in January 1981 which led to the adoption of an electoral college for the election of the Labour leader and deputy leader, and mandatory re-selection of sitting Labour MPs within the lifetime of each Parliament. In 1990 this was altered. Re-selection can only take place if requested in a ballot of constituency party members. The central aim of these reforms was to increase the powers of the extra-parliamentary elements of the party over MPs. The electoral college was split into three parts with each having a percentage of electoral college votes as follows: trade unions 40%, MPs 30% and constituency parties 30%. In 1983 Neil Kinnock was elected leader using this method, followed by John Smith in 1992.

The 1981 rule changes also provided better security for the leader, requiring 20% of the Parliamentary Labour Party to be in favour of a leadership challenge. When in government a challenge requires a majority of 66% at the Annual Conference to be in favour.

This method of electing the leader created a number of problems for the Party. The proportion of the electoral college vote given to the trade unions left Labour vulnerable to Conservative attacks that the trade unions were still the masters of Labour by virtue of their block vote. This is a vulnerable area which was used by John Major in the 1992 election. Moreover, this reform began a process whose ultimate goal was to allow every member of the Labour party to vote in the leadership election. This became known as *one member one vote* (OMOV).[15]

Electing a new Labour leader

| Labour MPs | Trade union members | Labour Party members |

How they vote

| $\frac{1}{3}$ | $\frac{1}{3}$ | $\frac{1}{3}$ |

266 Labour MPs plus **45** MEPs

7 Million votes Trade union members plus affiliated organisations.

253,000 votes Party members vote in their areas.

Figure 12 Electing a new Labour Party leader.[16]

After the 1992 General Election defeat the Labour Party moved to address the problem of the trade union block vote which had made it so vulnerable during the election campaign. At the 1993 Annual

Conference a number of constitutional reforms were introduced which took the democratisation process further by reforming Labour's links with the unions (*see Figure 12*). Conference decided that:

1. All Labour parliamentary candidates are to be elected by Party members only. This means that the trade unions will still use their block vote at the stage of nomination of candidates, but that selection within the constituency will be made by 'one member one vote'. John Smith believed that the rule changes for selecting parliamentary candidates were absolutely central to Labour's strategy for winning power.[17]

2. Women candidates should be chosen as parliamentary candidates in half of Labour's vacant seats. The rule change, which could mean up to a quarter of the Parliamentary Labour Party being women after the next election, had been advocated by women who had already succeeded in becoming MPs and had the support of John Smith. This has meant that there will be all-women short lists of possible candidates in half of Labour's winnable vacant seats at the next general election. However, in an opinion poll conducted for *New Century* magazine in December 1993, 61% of voters opposed the scheme and only 28% endorsed it. Some Labour MPs, including the Party's former deputy leader, Roy Hattersley have openly attacked the rule change, predicting that it will prove unworkable against grassroots resistance in the regions.[18]

3. The electoral college for the selection of leader and deputy leader will remain but the proportion of the vote of each section will change from its previous arrangement of 30% for the Parliamentary Labour Party and the constituencies and 40% for the trade unions, to an equal third for each group. Supporters of this change claim that it would reduce the power of the trade unions, weaken the labour–union link, and distribute power within the Labour Party more evenly between the different sections.[19]

   This now means that Labour's electoral college gives a third of the vote to MPs and MEPs, a third to paid-up party members and a third to political levy payers in unions affiliated to the Labour Party.

However, in order to stand in the leadership election, a candidate must be nominated by a proportion of the Parliamentary Labour Party (PLP). In the case of a challenge to the leadership a candidate requires 20% of the PLP to nominate them, but in the case of a vacancy, as in 1994, a candidate must be nominated by at least 12.5% of the PLP.[20]

In 1994, with the death of John Smith, the new formula was tested successfully through the election of Tony Blair as leader and

John Prescott as deputy leader. In this election the following voted: 779,426 trade union members, 172,356 Labour Party members and 327 MPs/MEPs. Tony Blair won the leadership contest with 60.5% of the MPs/MEPs vote, 58.2% of the membership vote and 52.3% of the trade union vote.[21]

Annual Conference

This is the supreme decision-making body of the Labour Party. Its composition reflects a federal structure representing the different sections which make up the Party (*see Figure 13*).

1. Each constituency party can send one delegate for every 5,000 members or part thereof. If the women's membership of a constituency exceeds 2,500 it may send a women's delegate.
2. Each affiliated trade union may send one delegate for every 5,000 members or part thereof, provided they are paid-up members.
3. Other affiliated national organisations like the Fabian Society can send delegates.

The Conference is very important because any votes taken on the issues for debate are binding on the Party and if the votes achieve a two-thirds majority these decisions have to be placed in the next election manifesto. In the early 1980s the Conference voted by a two-thirds majority in favour of a policy of unilateral nuclear disarmament. This was included in the manifesto of 1983 and this policy commitment was partly responsible for the huge Labour defeat in that year.

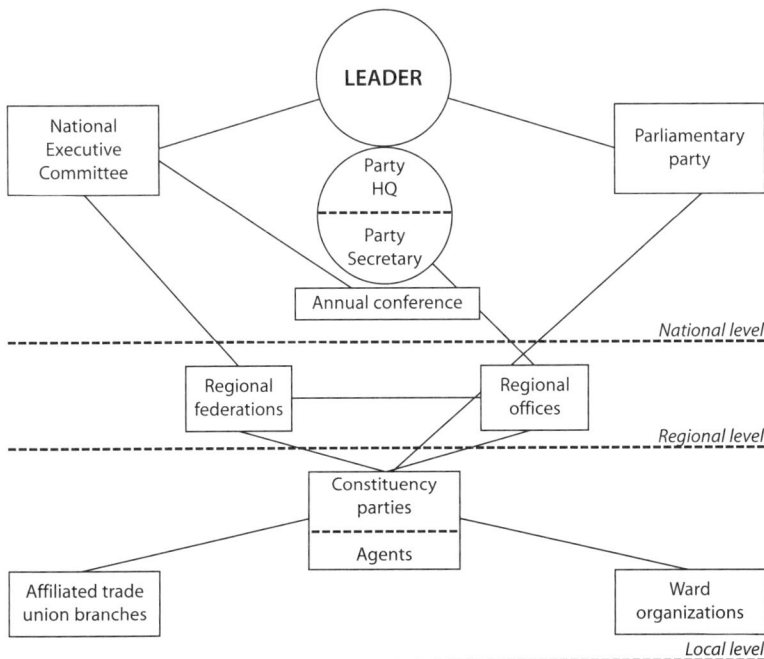

Figure 13 Labour Party organisation.[22]

The Conference does have the power and will to act independently, but it is usually willing to accept the policies of the leadership, e.g. one member one vote (OMOV) in 1993. Sometimes, however it has taken decisions which have caused problems.

It is worth noting that the power of the trade unions within the Labour Party has reduced gradually on account of internal reform and falling membership numbers.

The National Executive Committee (NEC)

This committee runs the Labour Party between each conference and seeks to uphold and implement Conference decisions.

Composition

- 29 members with the leader and deputy leader as ex-officio members. The members are elected at the Annual Conference.

- 12 are elected by and for the trade unions (many trade union members of the NEC are MPs, and the leaders of the big trade unions and members of the General Council of the TUC are not allowed to stand).

- 7 by and for the constituency parties

- 1 by and for the socialist and co-operative societies

- 5 women elected by the whole conference.

Role

1. The NEC is responsible for the day-to-day running of the Party, its administration and organisation. The NEC effectively controls the Labour Party. The leader often seeks to get a majority of his supporters onto the NEC, ensuring that the Party organisation comes under his indirect control, following his lead and implementing his ideas. During the 1980s Neil Kinnock was able to stamp his authority and policies upon the Party with the aid of an NEC which was filled with his supporters. The leader's authority and abilities can be greatly enhanced if he has an NEC which is solidly behind him.

2. The NEC oversees the work of the Labour headquarters and the work of its research and finance departments.

3. The NEC is responsible for party discipline and the work of local parties, including the endorsement of candidates. During the 1980s the NEC became more involved in work of this kind because of the action taken against the Militant Tendency.

   Example:
   In 1991 the NEC chose to expel two sitting MPs, Terry Fields and Dave Nellist, from the Party, which resulted in their immediate de-selection. Both lost their seats in the 1992 General Election.[23]

4. Closer to elections the NEC can be involved in the drafting of the manifesto. However, this role has often brought it into

conflict with the leader and the Cabinet, if Labour are in power. Both Harold Wilson and James Callaghan had problems with the NEC when it came to writing the election manifesto.

The roles that the NEC possess can give it great power over the direction and policies of the Party. This power varies according to the popularity of the leader, whether the Party is in office and on the leading personalities within the Party. When in office it has often come into conflict with Labour Cabinets. The NEC is concerned to see Conference decisions and policies followed through whereas a Labour Cabinet has to prioritise the needs of the Government and the whole country. This means that the two bodies and their members can become torn by conflict when Labour is in power. This was certainly the case in the late 1960s and 1970s when many NEC decisions were simply ignored by the Prime Minister and Cabinet.

The constituency Labour parties (CLPs)

Constituency Labour parties perform similar functions to their opposite bodies in the Conservative party; primarily responsible for the recruitment of members, organising supporters to help in election campaigns, the raising of funds and the selection of candidates for elections.

Within the Party they seemed to have a minimal role until the constitutional changes of 1981 strengthened it by the introduction of mandatory re-selection of MPs. CLPs have always had the powers to de-select sitting MPs but this power was never widely used. The re-selection procedure was reformed because the Kinnock leadership in the late 1980s became increasingly alarmed at the number of leftist candidates being selected. This was amplified by the problems which the Party faced with the **faction** known as the Militant Tendency.

The Parliamentary Labour Party (PLP)

Originally the Parliamentary Labour Party (or PLP) grouping within the Party was not accorded much prestige or importance. MPs themselves, however, have never accepted such a lowly role. Labour MPs form another component within the Party which can give a leader strong backing to pursue his policies, sometimes against the wishes of Conference and the NEC as happened under Harold Wilson. The PLP does little more than act as a supporter of the leadership and represent the MPs at various levels within the Party structure.

The parliamentary party probably best serves the role of organising the MPs as a block within the Party itself and within Parliament. Within the party in Parliament Labour MPs have formed a number of different groupings, each belonging to the different strands within the Party itself.

Key concept: faction

A faction is an organised group which has its own membership and exists within a larger body. Factions are most commonly found in political parties. The Militant Tendency was an organised extreme left-wing group within the Labour Party. In the early 1980s its membership rose to over 4,000 and its newspaper outsold the Labour Tribune. With its activities causing harm to the image that Neil Kinnock was trying to cultivate in the mid-1980s the Party began to take action against its members and it is now officially outlawed by the Party.

Groupings in the Labour Party

The Labour Party was founded by wide and very diverse range of groups coming together. Today within the Party there are a wide range of groups which have both extra-parliamentary and parliamentary origins, and range from the right to left of the Party. These include the Fabian Society, the Manifesto Group, the Tribune Group and the Campaign Group. The Fabian Society, for example, is a centrist group which founded the Labour Party. It acts as a think tank for the Party producing policy papers on a variety of subjects. Many members of the PLP are members of the Society. The Manifesto Group is a moderate 'centrist' group and was founded in 1974. It promotes moderate policies including membership of the European Union and multilateral nuclear disarmament. Its members were in favour of OMOV.

Questions

1. (a) How do the Conservative and Labour Parties replace their leaders?
   (b) Which of the two procedures is the most effective?
2. How is the leader of the Labour Party selected and to what extent is it a democratic process?
3. What is the role of groups within both major parties?
4. Distinguish between the powers and roles of the Conservative Annual Conference and the Labour Annual Conference.

4.5 | The role and structure of the smaller parties

The Liberal Democrats

The Liberal Democrats – the 'third party' – were formed in 1988 with the amalgamation of the old Liberal and Social Democratic Parties when Paddy Ashdown was elected leader.

The Liberal Democrats take the 'centre ground' in British politics believing in a combination of ideas and policies from both ends of the political spectrum. Central to their core is the belief that all government whether local, national or European should be bound by the rights of the individual and should be fully accountable. The Liberal Democrats have a foundation of strength in local government achieving greater success there than in general elections. They have a very strong belief in the 'liberal' tradition of the rights and duties of the individual citizen.

1. Economically, the Liberal Democrats believe in the free market, but suggest that the role of the government is to ensure that the market operates fairly and openly. The Liberal Democrats wish to promote free competition and choice by regulating the market. By comparison the Conservatives believe in de-regulation.

2. The Liberal Democrats believe that in some policy areas market forces should be restrained and that it is the responsibility of the government, not private enterprise to spend money and invest in a public transport system, education and health.

3. The Liberal Democrats are very strong environmentalists. They believe in implementing a strong and effective long-term environmental policy.

4. They describe themselves as an internationalist party. This means that they believe in building in the wider world an international society founded on mutual co-operation, political liberty, and shared prosperity. Within this vision they are very committed Europeans, believing that 'the UK can only be secure, successful and environmentally safe if we play our full part in building a more united and democratic Europe'.

5. They are reformists promoting constitutional reform including devolution (creating Scottish, Welsh and English Regional Parliaments), electoral reform, the introduction of a Bill of Rights and Freedom of Information Act and reform of the House of Lords.

6. Finally, Liberal Democrats state that they put people first, aiming to create

> 'a society in which all men and women can realise their full potential and shape their own success . . . We must change our political system to give the citizen more power and the government less; our economic system to confer power on consumers and to provide employees with a share in the wealth they create; our public services to guarantee choice and dignity to each of us; and our education system to equip us better for the modern world.'[24]

Structure

The Liberal Democrats have a federal structure comprising of three state parties for Scotland, Wales and England and a federal organisation at its centre with a Federal Executive Committee, Conference and Policy Committee (*see Figure 14*).

Figure 14 Liberal Democratic Party organisation.[25]

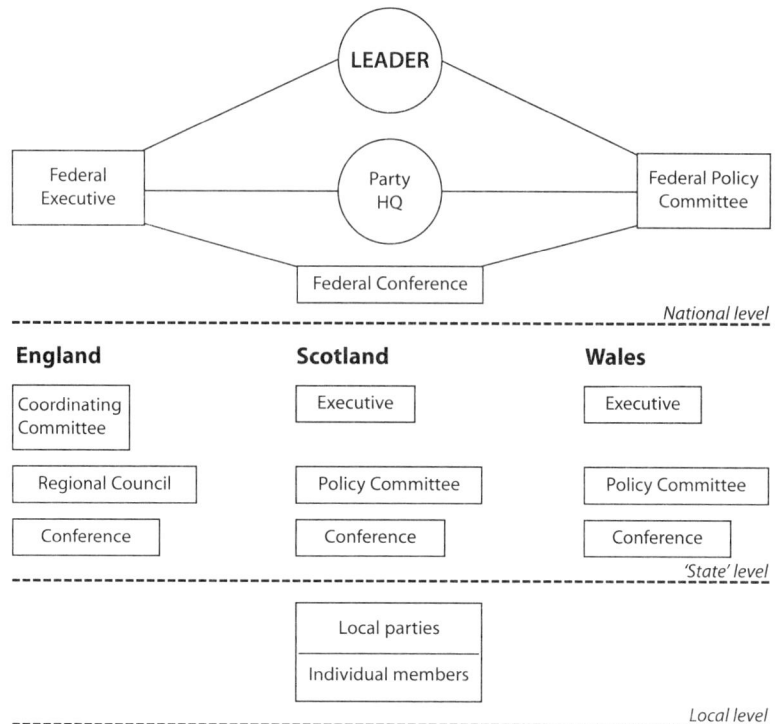

The Federal Policy Committee
1. Is responsible for the formulation of policy.
2. Is composed of the leader, the President of the Party (like the party chairman in the Conservative Party), four MPs, one peer, three councillors, two Scottish and two Welsh representatives and thirteen elected members chosen at the bi-annual conference.
3. Is responsible for the drafting of the election manifesto, in consultation with the political party.

The Federal Executive Committee
1. Organises and is responsible for the national organisation.

2. Is composed of the leader, the president of the Party, three vice-presidents, two MPs, one peer, two councillors and fourteen members elected at Conference.

Leadership election
The leader must be an MP and is chosen by a ballot of all the members of the Party.

The nationalist parties

In the 1992 General Election the nationalist parties of Wales and Scotland suffered mixed fortunes. The Welsh nationalists, Plaid Cymru, increased their parliamentary representation to four MPs.

The Scottish National Party (SNP), despite encouraging growth
support during 1990–92, fell to three seats loosing Jim Sillars who
had entered Parliament through a rare by-election success for the
SNP in 1988.[26]

Both nationalist parties were formed before the Second World War
and both have socialist tendencies. They believe in the provision of
a welfare state, the redistribution of wealth in favour of the lower
classes and re-nationalisation. Moreover, at the core of their
ideology is independence for both Scotland and Wales. In Scotland
there is a higher level of sentiment in favour of this goal, but this
has so far failed to translate itself into electoral power for the SNP.
In Wales as a whole such an aim is weakly supported and Plaid
Cymru's electoral power is concentrated in the North
Wales/Cardigan Bay region. A solution to the lack of support which
Plaid Cymru suffers is to move the ultimate goal to independence
for Wales as an autonomous region within a Federal Europe. Both
parties have become members of the cross-Europe 'Rainbow
Alliance' with this aim in mind.

The high point in the support of both parties came in the second
half of the 1960s and during the 1970s when anti-Westminster
feeling developed within both regions. The English-dominated
Parliament was perceived as remote and hostile to the socio-
economic aspirations of the populations of Scotland and Wales. In
Wales this alienation with Westminster was driven by legislation
which heavily discriminated against Welsh language and culture.

In the middle of the 1970s the SNP had eleven seats and Plaid
Cymru had three. In the 1974–9 Parliament the Labour government
with its small majority strove to gain the support of both sets of
nationalists by agreeing to a devolution referendum in Wales and
Scotland.[27] Moreover, a Welsh Language Act was passed to further
secure Plaid Cymru support. Neither referendum proved successful.
In Wales only 11.8% and in Scotland only 32.5% of the population
voted in favour of devolution.

From 1979 the fortunes of both parties have hardly changed. In the
1979 election both lost the momentum which had previously
driven them to success. During the 1980s with the shift to the right
that occurred in the political landscape it is perhaps remarkable
that they both retained representatives in Westminster. However,
both parties developed better strategies in local government
elections which have resulted in their creating a fairly solid
foundation at a grass roots level. At the European level, however,
they have been unable to gain a seat in the European Parliament. In
recent years Plaid Cymru have benefited from the growing
popularity and importance in business of the medium of Welsh and
by having developed a strategy which identifies them as the 'Party
of Wales.'[28] Though this label has not fully removed their image as a

Welsh-speakers only organisation. Furthermore, they appear to have carved an electoral niche within North Wales based on popular, moderate characters and effective representation of the region. Their voting strength is concentrated in this corner which affords them four MPs on just over 160,000 votes. By comparison the SNP suffer from a wide dispersal of votes across Scotland – 660,000 in 1992 – which resulted in only three MPs in Westminster.

In parliamentary terms since 1992 Plaid Cymru and the SNP have been able to exact a number of concessions from John Major's small majority government. During the various stages of the Maastricht Bill they supported the Government on a number of occasions in the lobbies in return for the guarantee of places for their representatives on the Committee of the Regions, which it is hoped will increase their political profile as representatives of Scotland and Wales across Europe.[29] Other incentives have been offered, including a new Welsh Language Act, to secure their support for the Government at certain points in the first two years of this Parliament. Such practices have not been used by a government since the 1970s and both parties have received benefits.

Questions

1.   What do the Liberal Democrats believe in?
2.   What are the main beliefs of the nationalist parties?

4.6 | **The issue of party funding**

The Conservative Party has always been wealthier than the Labour Party. The majority of Conservative Party funds are donated by the business world and industry and smaller amounts are donated by constituency associations and individuals. The Labour Party relies on membership dues, trade union affiliation payments and private donations but they publish full public accounts. The Conservatives have always been shy to make public where the majority of their funds come from but in 1993, following the Nasir case, a public controversy developed about the secret nature of Conservative Party backers.[30] John Major refused to allow the names of the people who donate money to the party to be made public, but a debate developed in the press, which was fuelled by pressure from the Labour Party about the nature and size of Conservative funding and whether those individuals who allegedly donated over £17 million before the 1992 General Election were hoping to gain something other than just a Tory victory.[31]

The controversy over the funding of the Conservative Party came at the same time in 1993 when in Italy the ruling Socialist Party and numerous leading Italian industrialists were facing criminal charges over alleged corruption linked to political donations.[32] Efforts in this country to cast some light on the relationship between the ruling party and its financial backers remain blocked by John Major. The British debate became part of a European-wide debate about political parties. It has led to calls for greater state funding of political parties in Britain to avoid corruption criticisms. In Britain public money is given to parties for secretarial and research expenses according to the amount of seats the party has in the House of Commons. But this is very limited form of state funding. On the Continent state funding of political parties has existed for some time – in Germany since 1954, Finland since 1967, Italy since 1974 and in Spain since 1977. There are a number of different systems. Lump sums may be given to national parties for their day-to-day organisational expenses, the amount determined by a mix of parliamentary seats and electoral votes. This is one of the sources of funds in Italy. Since 1987 political parties in Spain have received annual funds only if they are represented in the Chamber of Deputies. Other systems reimburse election expenses, as in Germany and the amount is determined in part by the seats won and in part by votes received. In the United States presidential campaign donations are matched by federal funds.[33]

The House of Commons Select Committee on Home Affairs investigated political funding and produced two reports in April 1994. Unusually the Committee split along party lines with the Conservative majority producing the main report and the Labour membership publishing a minority report. The Conservative majority report saw no reason to recommend any changes in the way parties in Britain raise funds, and ruled out curbs on secret donations, gifts from foreigners, or choice for shareholders on political funding. The report rejected any new state funding and proposed a code of practice for political parties but do not go so far as to suggest any form of statutory controls.

The Labour report identified a number of areas of 'potential corruption' and recommended that an electoral commission should be created to oversee parties' financial and election procedures. [34]

Modern political parties now have a voracious appetite for money. The debate over greater state funding of political parties in Britain has abated but on the Continent, with party memberships continuing to fall and corruption scandals often breaking, the debate will continue.

Questions

1. What are the different means of party funding?
2. How are parties funded in Britain?

4.7 | The debate over the two-party system

During the late 1970s and for most of the 1980s political scientists discussed whether the two-party system, which had existed since 1945, was threatened by the electoral successes of third parties. The debate centred around the voting figures in the elections since 1970 which showed an increase in the proportion of the vote for third parties and a decline in support for the two major parties. In the five elections from February 1974 to 1987 the two major parties averaged 74.8% of the vote whereas in 1951 they held 96.8% of the popular vote. The arguments both in favour of a decline and against are set out below.

Arguments in favour of the existence of a three-party system

1. The decline in the popular vote for the two major parties. Between 1945 and 1966 the major parties gained on average 87.5% of the popular vote. In 1992 Labour and the Conservatives again gained only 76.3% of the popular vote.[35]
2. The decline in electoral support for the Labour Party. Since 1979 Labour's proportion of the vote has fallen and remained low: 1983 – 29%, 1987 – 31% and 1992 – 34.4%.

Labour's natural foundation for electoral success in the 1950s, 1960s and 1970s, the working classes, have placed their support elsewhere. In order to form a majority government Labour needs to attract some of these voters back into its fold, especially in the south-east of England, but in this area of the country it is the Liberal Democrats who are coming second behind the Tories in general elections, rather than Labour. As a result of the 1992 General Election, forty-four Conservative seats are vulnerable to an electoral swing to the Liberal Democrats.[36] Since 1992 it has been the Liberal Democrats and not Labour who have gained seats in by-elections, most notably in Christchurch and Newbury. This level of support for the Liberal Democrats places them in a better position than Labour to win Conservative southern seats. Essentially the general vote against the Conservatives is split between these two parties and critics argue that unless Labour improves its electoral position in the south they will be unable to gain an majority of seats in the House of Commons.

3. The electoral support for third parties in local government and European elections.

Further evidence for the existence of the three-party system is found in the results of local government elections and European Elections.

In local government elections the Liberal Democrats have become a third force across the country. In May 1994 they gained 388 seats, nine councils and achieved 27% of the vote.[37] In June 1994 in the European parliamentary elections the Liberal Democrats gained two seats in the south west and 17% of the vote. Although their proportion of the vote was down compared to the previous month according to one commentator, had their vote been 1.5% higher the Conservatives would have only had eight Euro-seats rather than eighteen.[38]

4.   The decline of class-based politics (*see Chapter 13*)

This means that prior to the 1979 General Election there was a tendency for people to vote and support political parties according to their class, e.g. the majority of unskilled and skilled manual workers voted Labour. Since 1979 there has been a class de-alignment which has resulted in Labour losing their traditional support from the working classes and the Conservatives loosing a proportion of the middle-class vote. This has meant that the Liberal Democrats have gained electoral support from both the working classes and from a proportion of the middle classes, disaffected with the Conservatives but unwilling to vote Labour. This is evidenced in the voting figures in the south-west of England where the Liberal Democrats gained 31.4% of the vote in 1992 compared to Labour's 19.2% and in the south-east where they gained 23.3% to 20.8%.[39]

Arguments for the existence of the two-party system

1.   In the last two general elections third parties did not make the breakthrough that had been predicted: in 1992, Labour and the Conservatives battled it out and only if there had been a hung Parliament would any of the third parties have been able to wield power. The battle for power in the next election will see Labour in a position to convincingly challenge forty-three Conservative seats out of a total of seventy vulnerable to Labour. Equally, however, Labour has fifty-nine seats vulnerable to the Conservatives. Proponents of the two-party system argue that these figures show that a two-party system exists. It is in seats such as these and between the two major parties that the battle for power will always be won or lost.[40]
2.   Those who support the idea of the two-party system argue that by-elections are futile indicators of third-party support because they are opportunities for the electorate to register protest votes, which in general elections return to one of the main parties. In 1992 all the by-election seats won by the Liberal Democrats between 1987 and 1992 returned to the Conservatives. Moreover, local government and European parliamentary elections are contests between the Conservative and Labour parties who both possess the majority of seats between them.

3. Supporters of the idea of a two-party system argue that the Labour Party is regaining some of the electoral ground it lost during the 1980s.

In the 1980s the formation of the Social Democratic Party (SDP) and the subsequent formation of the SDP–Liberal Alliance affected the level of Labour's electoral support. In 1983 Labour gained only 27.6% of the vote (8.4 million votes) but the Alliance gained 25.4% (7.7 million votes). During this period proponents of the three-party system claimed that disaffected voters from both major parties were casting their votes for the Alliance and that these figures demonstrated the early stages of an evolution towards a three-party system.[41]

However, in 1992 Labour regained much of the electoral support that it had lost in the 1980s achieving 11.5 million votes, i.e. 34.4% of the popular vote. By comparison the Liberal Democrats did poorly when compared to 1983 receiving only 5.9 million votes, or 17.8% of the popular vote. Supporters of the two-party system claim that these figures demonstrate the re-emergence of that system and point to the fact that in 1992 Labour gained a 4.4% swing compared to a decline the Liberal Democrat's vote of –4.7%.[42]

4. Since 1990 both political parties appear to have regained some elements of the post-war consensus. John Major's premiership has seen the Conservatives attempting to put some distance between the 1990s and 1980s broadcasting a new message and doctrine for the new decade. The Kinnock–Smith–Blair leadership of the Labour Party has seen Labour's policies move onto the middle ground and towards the Conservative agenda. Proponents of the two-party system argue that the emergence of a new consensus between the major parties is re-attracting voters who previously supported the Liberal Democrats or 1980s Alliance, thus reducing the electoral impact of third parties in favour of the two-party system.[43]

Essay questions

1. 'Of all the major parties, the Liberal Democrats have the widest concept of citizenship and the most radical commitment to it.' Discuss.
2. To what extent does Britain have a two party system?
3. What is the role of political parties in Britain today?
4. 'The Conservative leader is stronger but the Labour leader is more secure.' Discuss.

Essay planning

2. To what extent does Britain have a two-party system?

This question asks the student to use the material in section 4.7 'The debate over the two party system', and Chapters 12 and 13 to argue:

(a) the extent to which Britain has a two-party system;
(b) that the two-party system has been replaced by a three-party system.
(c) in your conclusion you should argue that the two-party system is qualified by the success of third parties in by elections, local government elections and European parliamentary elections.

   Example:
   Liberal Democrats won nine councils and 388 seats in 1994 and two seats in the 1994 European Parliamentary Elections.

(d) In general elections since 1987 more Liberal Democrat Candidates come second in southern Conservative, held seats than Labour candidates. You may argue that this gives Britain a three-party system in many respects.
(e) But you can argue that in general elections, third parties are squeezed between the two major parties. Use material contained in *Chapters 12 and 13* to supplement this conclusion.

Notes and references

1. See Hancock, D. et al. *Politics in Western Europe* (London, 1993). pp. 95–258 and Hall, P. et al. *Developments in French Politics* (London, 1990) pp. 15–54.

2. McKie, D. *The Guardian Political Almanac, 1993/94* (London 1993), pp. 331–2.

3. *The Best future for Britain: The Conservative Manifesto 1992*, p. 47.

4. Anderson, B. *John Major: The Making of the Prime Minister* (London, 1991), p. 292.

5. See Kavanagh, D. *The Thatcher Effect* (Oxford, 1989), chs 5 and 18, and Kavanagh, D. *Thatcherism and British Politics* (Oxford, 1990), chs 1, 8 and 9.

6. *The Guardian*, 29.11.90.

7. *The Guardian*, 10.01.94.

8. *The Sunday Times*, 09.01.94 and 16.01.94.

9. *The Guardian*, 25.07.94 and 24.06.94.

10. *The Sunday Telegraph*, 24.07.94.

11. Derbyshire, J.D. *The Business of Government* (London, 1987).

12. BBC Television, 'The Downing Street Years', No. 4.

13. *The Guardian*, 07.05.94.

14. *The Daily Telegraph* 09.10.93 and *The Sunday Times*, 10.10.93.

15. *The Economist*, 11.04.92. and *New Statesman Society*, 24.04.92.

16. *The Guardian*, 13.05.94.

17. *The Times*, 30.09.93

18. *The Guardian*, 13.12.94.

19. *The Labour Party: Conference Arrangements Committee Report*, 1993 (London, 1993).

20. *The Guardian*, 13.05.94.

21. Derbyshire, J. D. *The Business of Government* (1987).

22. *The Daily Telegraph*, 11.04.92.

23. *Changing Britain for Good: The Liberal Democrat Manifesto, 1992*.

24. Derbyshire, J. D. *The Business of Government* (1987).

25. McKie, D. *The Guardian Political Almanaci* (1993), p. 283.

26. Whitehead, P. *The Writing on the Wall* (London 1986), pp.293–302.

27. *TUAG AT 2000/TOWARDS 2000: Plaid Cymru's Programme for Wales in Europe* (Cardiff, 1993).

28. Interview with Plaid Cymru officials, 14.08.94.

29. *The Guardian*, 14.04.94.

30. *The Guardian*, 03.07.93.

31. Ibid., p. 11.

32. Ibid.

33. *The Times* and *The Guardian*, 14.04.94.

34. Crew, I. 'Voting and the Electorate', in Dunleavy, P. et al. *Developments in British Politics*, Vol. 4, p. 95.

35. McKie, D. *The Guardian Political Almanac* (1993), p. 327.

36. *The Times*, 07.05.94.

37. *The Guardian*, 14.06.94, p. 15.

38. McKie, D. *The Guardian Political Almanac* (1993), p. 284.

39. Ibid., pp. 326–9.

40. McKie, D. *The Election: A Voter's Guide* (London 1992), p. 276.

41. *The Daily Telegraph*, 14.04.92 and McKie, D. *The Guardian Political Almanac* (1993), p. 284.

42. *The Sunday Telegraph*, 14.07.94.

Further reading

Drucker, H. and Gamble, A. 'The Party System', in Drucker, H. et al. *Developments in British Politics*, Vol. 3 (London, 1990).

Heywood, A. 'The Dominant Party System', *Talking Politics*, Vol, 5. No. 2, 1993.

Heywood, A. 'A New Political Consensus?', *Talking Politics*, Vol. 4, No. 2, 1991/2.

Ingle, S. *The British Party System* (Oxford, 1987).

Ingle, S. 'Political Parties in the 1990s', *Talking Politics*, Vol. 6, No. 1, 1993.

Kavanagh, D. *Thatcherism and British Politics*, 2nd edn (Oxford, 1990).

Kelly, R. N. *Conservative Party Conferences* (Manchester, 1989).

Mair, P. *The Western European Party System* (Oxford, 1990).

Minkin, L. *The Labour Party Conference* (Manchester,1980).

Moran, M. The Future of the Labour Party, *Talking Politics*, Vol. 5, No. 3, 1993.

Rose, R. *Do Parties Make a Difference?* (London, 1984).

CHAPTER 5

Pressure groups in the UK

Pressure groups exist in most modern democracies. In Britain, over the past thirty years, the number of pressure groups that operate in the UK political system has increased, paralleling the change in the size and influence of British government. Pressure groups have existed since the nineteenth century, when ideas of 'group interest' were forged, resulting in the formation of, for example, trade unions, to protect and represent the interests of workers against those of capitalists. During this period commercial and trading groups put pressure on government to advance and protect their interests, and social and economic changes produced by the Industrial Revolution led to the creation of pressure groups that aimed to represent the poor and the weak in society. Over time the diversity and size of 'group interests' in society has increased. Today there are thousands of pressure groups representing a huge array of interests all attempting to exert pressure to influence those who hold power.

This chapter will include :

5.1   Definitions of pressure groups.

5.2   Classifications in the British system.

5.3   How pressure groups work.

5.4   The theoretical models of pressure group activity.

5.5   The benefits and criticisms of pressure groups.

5.1 | Definitions of pressure groups

A pressure group may be defined as:

> 'an organised group which has as one of its purposes the exercise of influence or pure pressure on political institutions for the purpose of securing favourable decisions or preventing unfavourable ones.'

Or as:

> 'a range of organised groups possessing both formal structure and common interests. As part of their activities they seek to

influence government at the national, local and international level without seeking election to representative bodies.'[1]

Characteristics of pressure groups

1. Pressure groups seek to influence those in power.
2. They are organised and use a variety of different tactics to highlight their cause. They campaign to bring pressure to bear on politicians, e.g. by lobbying.
3. They do not seek elected office, rather they seek to influence those in power. In the United States some pressure groups provide financial and electoral support for those candidates who support their cause.
4. Their range of concern is narrower than those of political parties.
5. They recruit members who provide human resources and finances for the group to succeed.
6. They may be large or small.
7. They are **extra-parliamentary** organisations, meaning that they exist outside of Parliament but have a high degree of constructive interaction with Parliament. By comparison anti-parliamentary refers to those who are against the parliamentary system, such as extreme political organisations, including the IRA.

Example:
The Confederation of British Industry (CBI), which has a very large membership, is a pressure group, but the Chesterton Residents Against Rubbish Dumps is also a pressure group even though it has a small membership of no more than 100 people and smaller financial resources. Both seek to influence government, national and local.

These characteristics may vary: the range of concern of a pressure group may be as wide as a political party.

Questions

1. What is a pressure group?
2. Define 'pressure' and 'influence'.
3. What characteristics distinguish pressure groups from political parties?
4. What is the difference between extra-parliamentary and anti-parliamentary activity?

Key term: lobbying

This is usually defined as those activities by which group pressures are brought to bear upon legislative bodies and the legislative process, e.g. writing letters, meeting with those in power and presenting the administration with the pressure group points of view, thereby persuading those in power to make regulations favouring the group's particular interests. Lobbying often takes place in legislative bodies, and it often has important effects there, but it can also be directed at administrative agencies and even the courts.

Key term: a lobbyist

This is someone who is paid by a company or group of people to represent their views using lobbying tactics. Lobbyists have a sound knowledge of the workings of Parliament and rely on access to a wide range of political contacts in all the political parties and persuasion, to represent their clients views and interests effectively.

Key concept: pressure

Pressure constitutes all those means other than force or law by which government and people can influence each other politically. The application of pressure may take a variety of forms, e.g. letters, petitions, public protest, suggesting a continuous exercise until an aim has been achieved. Moreover, pressure suggests that a variety of sanctions may be used to accomplish success.

5.2 | Classifications of pressure groups

In Britain there are two types of pressure groups: promotional or *cause*, and protective or *sectional* groups. It is best to use the latter name in both cases.

Cause groups

These promote some particular cause or objective or express the attitudes and beliefs of their members. Cause groups:

1. vary in size and aims
2. can be temporary, disbanding when their cause is achieved or irreversibly lost
3. have an almost limitless range.

Example:
Shelter represent the homeless, while other groups express moral and social attitudes. The National Viewers and Listeners Association acts as a watchdog against sexually explicit or violent television programmes.

Sectional groups

These protect and represent the interests of their members, particularly their economic interests.

1. They are usually well organised.
2. They are often consulted by government officials and organisations.
3. They sometimes apply sanctions in dealings with government bodies.

Example:
Trade unions have strong sanction powers, as demonstrated in the Miners' Strike of 1973 which was influential in the events which led to the general election in February 1974. This election ended the Conservative Government of Sir Edward Heath.[2]

4. They are usually better funded than cause groups.
5. They are often permanent, which allows them to build up an expertise and size that means they are more often consulted by government.
6. They tend to have closer links with the two main political parties. There are very strong institutional links between the Labour Party and trade unions, and close non-institutionalised links exist between the Conservative Party and business-orientated pressure groups including the CBI and the Institute of Directors.
7. Some have special status and powers. These are known as official or semi-official pressure groups, which have rights of

access to certain government bodies, sometimes classified as 'quangos' (*see Chapter 3*). Quangos include OFTEL, which is the official watchdog of British Telecom.

Example:
Other examples of sectional pressure groups are the Law Society, the Bar Council, the British Medical Association, the Campaign Against Racial Discrimination and the National Farmers Union.

This distinction between the two different types of pressure group in Britain is not clear cut. It must be treated with some caution because some groups exist which cannot be so neatly categorised. Another form of classification distinguishing groups might be:

- *Insider groups*, which are regarded as legitimate by government and are consulted on a regular basis.

- *Outsider groups*, which either do not wish to become part of the policy-making process perhaps because of ideological differences with the Government of the day, or are unable to gain official recognition.[3]

These two categories can be further subdivided.

Insider groups consist of:

1. Prisoner groups which find it hard to break away from the Government because they depend on it for some form of assistance, e.g. financial, or because they are part of the public sector. Many of the newly created privatised industry watchdogs would fall into this category.
2. Low profile groups which tend to concentrate on 'behind the scenes' relations with government and avoid contact with the mass media.

   Example:
   The Automobile Association (AA).

3. High profile groups which cultivate public opinion by using the mass media to reinforce their role and links with the Government.

   Example: *The Terrence Higgins Trust or Shelter.*

Outsider groups consist of:

1. Potential insider groups. These are outsider groups and would like to become insider groups but have yet to become accepted. These groups adopt responsible and conventional tactics which may lead to their being taken into the realms of the insiders.

   Example: *The League Against Cruel Sports.*

2. Outsider groups which may also wish to become insider groups but lack the political knowledge to gain recognition. Their tactics may be classified as extreme by government bodies.

Example: The Anti-Racist Alliance.

3.   Ideological outsider groups which do not seek change through the existing political system, and whose aims and methods do not win widespread popular approval.

Example: The Animal Liberation Front.

Pressure groups exist in most liberal democracies. In the United States, Australia, Germany and France they represent a variety of interests and seek to influence governments and legislatures. In other countries pressure groups are sometimes labelled **interest groups**. Although different words are used students should note that their classification is similar to the British system.

France and the United States

By way of comparison, in France there are a large number of freely organised interest groups which play a significant role in French political life. There are both sectional and cause pressure groups representing, on a national level, every conceivable sector and interest: labour, business, agriculture, teachers, environmentalists, anti-nuclear groups and women's rights groups.[4]

Interest groups in France participate in the political process in a similar way to their counterparts in Britain and the USA. They **lobby** members of the legislature, help elect candidates who sympathise with their views to political office, and attempt to influence the higher civil service and government ministers. By comparison, the French have more of a tradition of direct action – blocking ports or roads. Many French pressure groups have formed an ideological and political linkage with certain political parties. In parallel with Britain, employers and business organisations are linked to the French right-wing parties, while labour interests are linked to French left-wing parties.[5]

In the United States pressure groups fulfil a similar function, organising and transmitting to the Government and politicians the views of particular sections of society. There are both sectional and cause pressure groups in the United States, although they are organised along slightly different lines to those in Europe.

Questions

1.   What is the difference between cause and sectional pressure groups?
2.   What are insider and outsider groups?
3.   What are the similarities and differences between pressure groups in Britain and France?

5.3 | **How pressure groups work**

There are a variety of methods which pressure groups use to achieve their aims, but primarily pressure groups use seven channels of access. These are:

1.   the executive and civil service
2.   the Legislative Assembly: the UK Parliament
3.   the European Union
4.   political Parties in the UK
5.   local Government in the UK
6.   the Courts
7.   the media and public.

The size and resources of the pressure group, as well as experience and whether they are insider or outsider groups, can determine whether they use all of these avenues or just a few.

The executive and civil service

In any country this is the most important and effective target on which pressure groups concentrate. It is within the confines of the Government that policy decisions are made and pressure groups aim to persuade the Government to take their views, opinions and interests into account when framing legislation and deciding policy.

In a unitary state, pressure groups are more likely to concentrate on the centre from which power emanates.

In a federal system, like the United States, a strict separation of powers exists and power is divided between the organs of the Federal State and the political institutions of each state. For this reason interest groups are more selective depending on the issues and their aims.

This is a two-way process, serving the interests of the group and those of the government. The executive branch encourages contact with some groups because it can provide useful information. Some groups become part of the process of government, closely involved in policy-making.

Governments seek contact with pressure groups for the following reasons:

1.   the supply of external expert information;
2.   to gauge the opinion of pressure groups about policy ideas, prior to finalisation and publication;
3.   to foster the notion of 'government by consent'. In most liberal pluralist democracies governments wish to be seen to be listening to the opinions of others (*see Chapter 1 and in this chapter, page 121*).

There is a well-established system of formal and informal contacts between pressure groups in the UK and Ministers and civil servants in Whitehall. These include the following:

1. Royal Commissions and advisory committees.
    These usually interview representatives from various pressure groups to gain information and opinion. Advisory committees are established to provide alternative advice to the Government which it can either choose to use or to ignore. There are a great many advisory committees and by serving on them pressure groups gain status and influence.

    Example:
    The Health Education Council or the now-defunct Milk Marketing Board.

2. Contacts between pressure groups and government are generally handled by civil servants.

During meetings both sides seek consultation and alternative information. These meetings can not and should not be described as negotiations. Pressure groups use them to get their message across and gain valuable insights into government thinking.

3. Some pressure groups receive financial help from the Government, demonstrating the interrelationship between pressure groups and Whitehall.

    Example:
    The Keep Britain Tidy Campaign receives an annual grant from the Department of the Environment as does the Terrence Higgins Trust from the Department of Health.

4. The theory of 'incorporation'.
    This means that certain pressure groups are incorporated into the policy process allowing governments to claim that they are governing by consent and consultation. Groups are incorporated into the policy-making process because they make a valuable contribution to policy formulation. They include the Howard League for Penal Reform, which has a special relationship with the Home Office. The Automobile Association and the Royal Automobile Club are also 'incorporated'.

The Legislative Assembly – Parliament in the UK

In the UK most MPs have links with pressure groups. Those pressure groups which are unable to forge a working relationship with civil servants or Ministers concentrate on Parliament to further their cause. Thus:

1. MPs provide a channel to gain government, media and ultimately public attention for a pressure group.

Key term: Royal Commissions

These are committees of inquiry created to make an in-depth examination of a problem and submit a wide-ranging series of recommendations in their final reports. They can normally sit for up to two years and are given considerable terms of reference to interview and consult a wide range of people, organisations and groups who play a role in the subject area under investigation. John Major appointed a Royal Commission to examine the criminal justice system in Britain, which reported in 1993.[6]

2.   Some MPs approach pressure groups which represent issues of interest to them rather than waiting to see who approaches them. A vast range of pressure groups have MPs to speak for them, usually because an MP sympathises with their cause. However, in some cases these MPs are paid spokesmen.

There are a five main ways in which pressure groups influence Parliament :

1.   **Sponsoring MPs**

Instead of putting up their own candidates, pressure groups participate in parliamentary elections by sponsoring candidates. A number of Labour MPs are sponsored by trade unions. MPs who are sponsored are expected to press the interests of the sponsoring organisation in Parliament, but are not regarded as delegates of the sponsoring body. MPs will normally follow party policy in preference to union policy on issues where the two conflict.

2.   **Engaging MPs as parliamentary consultants or parliamentary agents**

This means that an MP may become an adviser on Parliamentary matters to a pressure group, business organisation or public relations company. Agreements between MPs and these institutions can range from informal liaisons to the payment of fees. Some pressure groups use professional lobbyists who are sometimes called **parliamentary agents**. They act as intermediaries between pressure groups and Parliament.

The relationships between MPs and private lobbyists have raised awkward questions concerning an MP's divided loyalties. Constitutionally an MP is elected to represent a constituency and a party. If he or she is then paid by another organisation to represent their interests a conflict of loyalty can arise where the interests of the constituents and the interests of the organisation that pays the MP a fee are incompatible. In 1975 a voluntary register of MPs' interests was established to publicise their other roles. However, the register has been ineffective as shown by a variety of incidents in the 1980s and, more recently, in 1994 through the 'questions for money' scandals. This has given rise to fears about the relationship between MPs and the new and growing phenomenon of professional lobbying. It is possible that in the next few years a much tougher regulatory system will be introduced to govern their relations.[7]

3.   **Personal interest**

Many individuals who become MPs arrive in Westminster with a collection of their own interests and subsequently work for pressure groups which represent those issues. In some cases an MP will develop a close personal involvement with a pressure group and often take on honorary roles with organisations.

4. **Appearances before Departmental Select Committees**

Since 1979, when the Departmental Select Committee system was created, pressure groups have been appearing before these committees to give evidence. Prior to 1979 those Select Committees which existed did invite pressure group participation, but since 1979 this participation has grown considerably. Pressure groups can provide the committee with expert information, briefings and opinions. Pressure groups now regard an appearance before Select Committees as a great opportunity to 'get their message across' especially since the House of Commons has been televised. Pressure groups are now 'incorporated' into the system of scrutiny of the executive via Select Committees, because most committee inquiries usually ask relevant pressure groups to give evidence.

5. **Lobbying**

This is where direct persuasion is used on MPs and Lords, either individually or collectively. Members of pressure groups meet with MPs to express their groups' views and persuade the MPs to put pressure on their leaders (or Ministers if in power) to adopt policies in line with the aims of the pressure groups. Sometimes a pressure group may persuade an MP to introduce a Private Member's Bill on their behalf. Many Private Member's Bills originated in the offices of pressure groups. Sometimes there is a mass lobby of Parliament. This means that the pressure group tries to mobilise the majority of their members to come to London and meet with their constituency MPs in Parliament. Traditionally, it meant that a constituent would wait in the central lobby area of the Palace of Westminster and request that their MP come to talk to them there. These mass lobbies often attract a great deal of media attention and are effective in placing an issue on the news agenda.

During the 1980s members of the Lords became more of a target for pressure groups. As the House of Lords has become a more critical reviser of government legislation it has been the target of more and more pressure groups. Some Lords now act as consultants or lobbyists for single-issue pressure groups such as Shelter and Help the Aged.

It should be remembered that most policy decisions are taken in Whitehall and that Westminster has a restricted role in policy making. The 1992 Baggott survey confirmed that Parliament was ranked by most pressure groups below Ministers, civil servants and the media in terms of its influence on public policy. Nevertheless, the influence which pressure groups seek to exert upon MPs serves as an indirect and at times complementary means of influencing the decision-making process of the executive.

In the United States pressure groups use similar methods to influence the Congress. The Congress has greater powers and a more independent role than the British Parliament because, by comparison, the US party system is weak. The structures and traditions of party discipline are weaker in the United States compared to the rigid, highly-disciplined system that exists in Britain. Congressmen are ideal targets for interest groups and professional lobbyists, many of whom exert substantial influence over individual members of Congress. Large financial contributions to members' or candidates' election expenses give these bodies an important access point to members of the Congress who have to raise vast sums of money in order to seek re-election. In addition to contributing to the election funds of members, lobbyists in the USA use similar tactics to those employed in Britain; providing briefings, information, arranging meetings, testifying before Congressional Committees (similar to Select Committees), etc.

Example:
The power of United States interest groups was clearly demonstrated in the case of the Clinton Crime Bill which included provisions to limit the availability of certain weapons. The National Rifle Association succeeded in persuading enough members of Congress to vote against the first version of the Bill in August 1994.[8]*An amended version was passed later in the month.*[9]

The European Union

The institutions of the European Union (EU) are now an important area for pressure group activity. In particular the European Parliament in recent years has become a new lobbying target for pressure groups in Britain. With the implementation of the Maastricht Treaty, which will increase the legislative role of the European Parliament, there will be a growth in the significance and importance of the Parliament to pressure groups across the EU.

The EU has welcomed the influence of pressure groups, especially if organised on a European-wide basis. The corporatist attitude of the EU provides for potentially greater influence for pressure groups than perhaps the strict pluralist models of democracy in Britain.

Methods employed
1. Pressure groups work at a national level to influence national governments on EU policy. They use their existing contacts with Ministers and civil servants to suggest whether EU policies should be adopted or resisted. Pressure groups have found that a new element exists within this supra-national arena, where diplomacy plays a vital role, often meaning an interest will be sacrificed in the pursuit of higher goals and diplomatic co-operation. Pressure groups attempt to put

pressure on Ministers to accept or reject European proposals, often seeking meetings with Ministers and civil servants before they depart to Brussels to attend a Council of Ministers meeting to decide policy.

Example:
One of the most active groups in this area is the National Union of Farmers (NUF) because much of EU legislation relates to agriculture.

2. Pressure groups work through European-level federations of national pressure groups. Federations of pressure groups have developed during the 1980s as the significance of the EU has increased. This is likely to grow even more during the 1990s. They are known as 'Euro-groups' and they seek to represent the interests of their sector or cause at the EU level. Their policy interests naturally reflect the policy concerns of the EU. This is most obviously seen in the size of the agriculture lobby where over 150 Euro-groups can be identified.
3. Pressure groups make direct representations to Brussels. National pressure groups can take a direct approach to Brussels in an attempt to directly influence the institutions of the EU. Some major British pressure groups have established offices in Brussels for this purpose. These include the CBI and the NUF.

The European policy-making process is complicated and unpredictable. However, in Brussels there exists an ethos of co-operation with pressure groups to a much greater extent than in Britain, certainly during the Thatcherite 1980s. This has seen a growth in the attention which British pressure groups are now showing towards the EU. However, Pan-European Euro-groups will only become more effective as the need for greater co-operation increases and national interests decrease in reaction to an expansion in the powers and roles of the post Maastricht Union Institutions (*see Chapter 9*).

Political parties in the UK

Theoretically, pressure groups should maintain a political neutrality which allows them to influence whichever party is in office, but over the past thirty years this theory has deteriorated because of changes in the practices of pressure groups. Some groups have shown active sympathy and interest in particular political parties or sections of parties.

Example:
The Hunt Saboteurs Association has aligned itself with the radical left. By comparison, the British Field Sports Society is aligned with the right.

Moreover, political parties have sought to use the services of some pressure groups to make their own campaigns more successful.

During the passage of the legislation to privatise the Water Industry, the Labour Party allied itself with a number of environmental pressure groups who were against privatisation. This identifiable link between some pressure groups and the major political parties in Britain has grown as a result of the breakdown of the post-war consensus. Similarly in the United States particular pressure groups have sought to establish links with either the Republican Party or the Democratic Party.

Example:
Many conservative religious groups are closely associated with the Republican Party in the US.

In Britain some pressure groups have had a long association with political parties. The Labour Party has an institutionalised link with trade unions. However, most pressure groups in Britain still seek to steer an apolitical course through Westminster. Links between pressure groups and political parties in the UK remain weak. The danger of becoming too closely associated with one party can mean the loss of influence when that party is not in office. Equally pressure groups target members of a party either collectively or individually, and not necessarily the institution itself. Therefore most pressure groups are keen to maintain congenial relations with all the major political parties.

Local government

Pressure group activity in relation to this area of government takes the form of smaller locally-based pressure groups, but some national pressure groups do target local authorities.

Example:
The charity organisation Shelter is as active locally as it is nationally.

Most groups are concerned with the provision of local services and most have a short life, disappearing once the issue is resolved either favourably or unfavourably.

At a local level these pressure groups can establish close relations with councillors and officials. They use similar tactics to national pressure groups, meeting with officials and councillors, providing information, petitions, public protests and mass lobbies of council committees or the full council.

The courts

In the UK pressure groups make less use of the courts than in the United States. Britain's constitutional arrangements are different to those in the United States which means that decisions made by the executive cannot easily be challenged in the British system. Moreover, because Parliament is sovereign the Government can overturn a court decision which it dislikes by using Parliament to pass new legislation which changes the law. However, such legislation cannot be retrospective and the Government must act within the existing law. Despite these restrictions, some pressure groups have sought to use the powers of the courts, employing the procedure known as 'judicial review' to bring pressure to bear in an attempt to achieve their aims.

Example:
During the early 1990s a number of environmental pressure groups sought to prevent a number of road building schemes by pursuing action through the courts. Many of these cases used the judicial review procedure to prevent such schemes from going ahead.

Action through the courts is long and costly in Britain. It is also rare. However, in the United States the courts are part of the political process because of the power of judicial review, and judges make decisions concerning aspects of political, social, and economic life which in other countries would be the responsibility of elected officials. Judicial practice and ethics prevent interest groups from using many of their mainstream tactics, but pressure groups in the United States have sponsored test cases through the courts. In the United States there is both a constitutional and cultural difference from Britain which encourages interest group activity via the judiciary.

Example:
In the 1950s the Black Civil Rights pressure group, the National Association for the Advancement of Colored People sponsored a series of cases to reform the racial segregation that existed in the United States education system.[10]

Finally, pressure groups may give evidence to public or judicial inquiries established to examine a particular social problem or issue.

Example:
The 1991–3 Royal Commission on Criminal Justice is an example of a judicial inquiry where penal reform pressure groups gave evidence.

The media and public

The media can be a useful tool for a pressure group in any country to carry its message and recruit support from the public. In Britain in the 1970s and 1980s pressure groups moved away from low profile campaigning, with discreet contacts in Whitehall, to a high-profile method of campaigning with greater use of media-orientated campaigns. Larger and well-resourced pressure groups now run regular campaigns via advertising in newspapers and cinemas. Some even stretch their budgets to include television commercials.

In the 1990s it is not unusual to see pressure group advertisements in newspapers. The RSPCA, Greenpeace, Respect for Animals and the Home of Rest for Horses have all used such strategies.

Public campaigns can be used to promote the image of the group, or to mobilise public support to achieve a quick result.

Questions

1. How do pressure groups seek to influence (a) the European Union and (b) local government?
2. How do pressure groups seek to influence the executive in Britain?
3. What is meant by the terms 'lobbying', 'sponsoring' and 'incorporation'?

5.4 | The theoretical models of pressure group activity

There are a range of different theories about our political system which can be used to explain the need for pressure group activity and enable us to assess the benefits and criticisms of pressure group activity in modern liberal democracies. These political theories are *pluralism, corporatism* and *neo-liberalism.*

Pluralism

Pluralism suggests that power in society is fragmented and dispersed between a large number of different groups. Although power may be dispersed unevenly, those that are powerful in one area are not necessarily powerful in others. Pluralist theory suggests that an equilibrium exists because one group will balance another.

Critique: There is a great deal of inequality between pressure groups in relation to funds, organisation and access to and influence upon decision makers. Some groups have greater influence and power than others.

Corporatism

Corporatism, as explained earlier, is the tendency for the institutions of a state to work closely with a variety of groups in the making of public policy. Corporatism envisages a social partnership between the institutions of the state and interested groups. It developed as the state became more interventionist in economic and social areas. Producer groups became increasingly involved in policy making, implementing and sharing responsibility with the government. According to this theory pressure groups become incorporated into the policy-making process.

Critique: In Britain the extent of incorporation of a small number of pressure groups into the policy-making process has been overstated. The 1960s and 1970s are usually cited as examples of a time when Britain came closest to the definition of a corporatist state, but Britain has never resembled a corporatist state except in the special conditions of wartime. By the end of the 1970s, Margaret Thatcher's Governments had moved away from any corporatist tendencies.

The neo-liberal view

The neo-liberal view lays stress not on the activities of special interests in the pursuit of the 'public good' but on a system of parliamentary representation in which representatives consider national rather than sectional interests. This view sees Parliament as the body which protects the national interest and the welfare of the people against sectional interests, acting as a control on executive power.

When considering these three approaches it is important to realise that there is no right or wrong answer in respect of any one theory. Britain, the United States, France and Germany are all pluralist democracies. Yet there are certain characteristics within their political systems which at different times, incorporate both corporatist and neo-liberal thinking. Pressure groups are not the villains that neo-liberalism considers them to be. Pressure groups allow for minorities to express themselves in the crowded political arena. There are rich and poor pressure groups and often it is the richer groups that are more influential.

Questions

1. What are 'neo-liberalism' and 'pluralism'?
2. Outline the differences between the neo-liberal and pluralist models of interest group activity.

5.5 | The benefits and criticisms of pressure groups

The benefits of pressure groups

1. Participation
- They encourage ordinary citizens to take an interest in an area of political activity.

- They act as a substitute to political parties, allowing citizens the opportunity of expressing their interests in a particular issue.

- Single-issue campaigns allow the 'man in the street' to understand the political system more clearly and give the individual a real sense of commitment.

2.   Protecting minorities

In most political systems pressure groups allow minority interests to be expressed and represented.

Example:
In both Britain and the USA a variety of lesbian and gay rights pressure groups have represented this minority very effectively, placing gay rights on the political agenda. In the 1992 presidential election in the United States, Bill Clinton actively wooed the gay vote to help him win the election.[11]

3.   Legitimising function

Pressure groups help to legitimise the functions of government. They are very successful at drawing people into the political process, encouraging interest and providing an alternative channel for people with grievances to use, complementing the traditional representative of the citizens an MP. Through 'incorporation' they are involved in a policy-making process which benefits the French, United States, German and British democracies.

4.   Critics of government

Pressure groups are often severe critics of government policies because of their specialism, experience, and devotion. Unlike many MPs, who tend to be generalists, pressure groups are highly motivated specialists. They enhance 'democracy' by providing alternative views and interpretations of government policy and raising issues which do not occupy the political centre stage.

Example:
In 1991 the Asylum Rights Campaign campaigned against the Government's new asylum policy for refugees, claiming that it would limit refugees' rights and deny many refugees asylum in Britain.[12]

5.   Maintaining freedoms

Pressure groups are desirable because fundamental freedoms, such as freedom of speech and association, can be furthered and maintained by pressure group action. Pressure groups can promote strong campaigns about particular issues, creating widespread public support, which sometimes governments cannot easily ignore.

Example:
The size and passion of the public outcry against the October 1992 mine closure plan was successfully used by the National Union of Miners to force the Government to re-think its proposals to close thirty-one pits.

Criticisms of pressure groups

1.   Undermining parliamentary democracy

Critics of pressure groups and those who believe in neo-liberalism argue that pressure groups distort the democratic process. MPs should be the arbiters of the national interest and are in the best position to judge what the national interest should be. Pressure groups are self-interested organisations which interfere with the democratic process, diverting attention from Parliament. They are not accountable to the electorate and are undemocratic.

2.   The power of some pressure groups

Concerns are expressed over the power and influence of large pressure groups compared to smaller ones. The richer and stronger a group is, the greater its influence on government. Particular concerns have been expressed over some sectional groups, primarily those with economic interests. The trade unions when Labour was in power and the CBI under the Conservatives have been criticised for wielding too much influence.

3.   Lack of democratic characteristics

Most pressure groups do not have a democratic structure and their leaders are not elected. Many are appointed and are not representative of the group's membership.

There may be an appearance of balance between competing groups, but those with good financial resources are able to mount better campaigns and create more influence than those with fewer resources. The Brewing and Tobacco Industries are able to supply greater funding to their lobby groups than those in the Health Lobby can hope to provide.

4.   Self-interest

Pressure groups are criticised for being self-interested organisations, often not concerned with the national good. Critics argue that both sides of the industrial lobby, employers and trade unions have pursued self-interested goals which have damaged the long-term national interest.

5.   Secrecy

Most pressure groups do not normally operate in full public view. Some, such as the Institute of Directors, jealously guard and hide links with Ministers. However, given the secret nature of the British system of government it is hardly surprising that pressure groups adopt these tactics if they are to gain influence.

Question

What in your view are the two most important benefits of pressure groups? Explain.

Essay questions

1. To what extent has the influence of pressure groups changed in recent years?
2. To what extent is the role of pressure groups in British policy changing?
3. Why is Parliament subjected to so much lobbying by pressure groups?
4. Discuss the view that pressure groups have more influence than Parliament on the making of government policy.

Essay planning

5. Discuss the view that pressure groups have more influence than Parliament on the making of government policy.

This essay is asking you to :

(a) Explain how pressure groups seek to influence the executive, using material from *section 5.3*, 'How pressure groups work'.

(b) Analyse the relationship between pressure groups and the executive and compare it with the influence which Parliament has on the making of policy.
   (i) Pressure groups are included in the policy-making process to a greater extent than MPs.
   (ii) The theory of 'incorporation' allows pressure groups greater influence.
   (iii) Parliament is usually presented with finalised policies, although through Green and White Papers and General consultative documents they are given opportunities to influence the policy-making process.
   (iv) Even on important policies MPs have limited access to Whitehall compared to many pressure groups.

   Example:
   The Budget. The brewers' lobby normally have a meeting with the Chancellor while the Budget is being composed to persuade him not to increase excise duties.

   (v) Depending upon the party in office some pressure groups have greater influence.

(c) Using materials from *section 5.5*, 'The benefits and criticisms of pressure groups', you can suggest whether the influence that pressure groups appear to have upon the executive is good or bad.

(d) You may wish to argue that in a pluralist democracy it is beneficial for the nature of that democracy that pressure groups are 'incorporated' into the policy-making process and alternatively, that the pureness of this democracy is undermined if sectional interests have greater influence than the elected legislative chamber.

Notes and references

1. Grant, W. *Pressure Groups: Politics and Democracy in Britain* (London, 1989), p. 9.

2. Whitehead, P. *The Writing on the Wall* (London, 1986), p. 110.

3. Grant, W. *Pressure Groups* (1989), p. 14 and 'Insider and Outsider Pressure Groups', in *Social Studies Review*, Vol. 5, No. 3, 1990.

4. Ibid., pp. 150–7.

5. Hancock, D. et al. *Politics in Western Europe* (London, 1992), p. 152.

6. *The Guardian*, 07.07.93.

7. *The Guardian*, 12.07.94. See 'Vote of Confidence for MPs', *PR Weekly*, 10.03.94.

8. *The Times*, 13.08.94.

9. *The Times*, 23.08.94.

10. McClenaghan, W.A. *Magruder's American Government* (Cambridge, Mass., 1988) pp. 157–9.

11. *The Guardian*, 13.09.92.

12. ARC Leaflet, 1992.

Further reading

Alderman, G. (ed.) *Pressure Groups and British Government* (London, 1984).

Barr, G. 'The Anti-Poll Tax Movement: An insider's view of an Outsider Group', *Talking Politics*, Vol. 4, No. 3, 1992.

Baggott, R. 'Pressure Groups and the British Political System: change and decline?', in Jones, B. and Robbins, L. (eds), *Two Decades in British Politics* (Manchester, 1992).

Grant, W. *Pressure Groups, Politics and Democracy in Britain* (London, 1989).

The Economist, 'A Nation of Groupies,' 13.08.94.

CHAPTER 6

The office and powers of the Prime Minister

This is probably the most interesting topic within the whole arena of British politics and together with the Cabinet it is one of the few areas of study with which students can easily identify. The powers of the Prime Minister are the subject of a continuing debate which has raged for over thirty years. The essence of this debate is whether the office of Prime Minister has invested within it so much power that the holder can attain near presidential status within a parliamentary system of government. Critics of the current system argue that Britain has Prime Ministerial government rather than Cabinet government *(see section 7.6)*.

The British Prime Minister is one of the most powerful heads of executive positions in the Western world. But the person holding this position is not as powerful as the United States President because of the USA's military and economic strengths and because there all executive power is embodied within one office.

This chapter will discuss the following:

6.1 The powers of the Prime Minister.

6.2 The constraints on a Prime Minister's power.

6.3 The Thatcher and the Major styles of leadership.

Key term: presidential government

This term refers to an executive arrangement where all power is concentrated into one office, the holder of which is normally called a President. The President appoints staff to a vast range of political posts in his or her government: Ministers, civil servants and private advisers. The decision-making process is dominated by the President and characterised by bi-lateral meetings between a President and his close advisers who may or may not be members of the Cabinet. The executive branch of government in the United States fits this model.

6.1 | The powers of the Prime Minister

The constitutional theory of executive power in Britain suggests that the Prime Minister is *primus inter pares* – first among equals, with his or her Cabinet colleagues. This theory says that Britain has Cabinet government, meaning that the powers of the executive are exercised by a group of ministers who reach their decisions through collective decision-making processes creating an executive consensus. The Cabinet discusses matters of policy and reaches agreement through internal debate. The debate concerning the extent of the powers of the office of Prime Minister began publicly when a former Labour Cabinet Minister, Richard Crossman, wrote in the introduction to the new edition of *The English Constitution* by W. Bagehot in 1963,[1] that Cabinet government had given way to government by the Prime Minister. Crossman suggested that the term *primus inter pares* had become redundant as a description of the nature of the relationship between the Prime Minister and his Cabinet colleagues. The Crossman thesis suggested that the powers wielded by the Prime Minister had created in the post-1945 period a 'quasi-president' or elected monarch who dominated the decision-making process of Cabinet. This idea was supported by a number of leading academics and began a continuing debate. Opponents of the Crossman thesis included the former Prime Ministers Harold Wilson, Edward Heath and James Callaghan, who argued that all Prime Ministers were subjected to a range of checks upon their powers which would prevent 'an elective dictatorship' – a phrase used to describe the executive dominance of the parliamentary system by Lord Hailsham in 1977 – from arising. The Thatcher premiership added fuel to the fire.

The Prime Minister is appointed by the Queen, who asks the party leader with the largest number of seats in the House of Commons to form a new government. The Prime Minister is head of the British executive/government and head of the largest party in the House of Commons. These positions afford the office holder a range of powers which stretch across the British political system including the Cabinet and the central administration, the Party system and Parliament. The primary powers of the Prime Minister rest within the institution of the Cabinet and his or her role as head of that body and therefore the Government. The powers which are exercised are called royal prerogatives, which have been transferred through the course of our history from the Crown to the Prime Minister. These include the power to appoint and dismiss Ministers, chair Cabinet meetings and request a dissolution of Parliament and a general election.

Powers of the office of Prime Minister

1.   It appoints the Cabinet

When a Prime Minister takes office, his or her first job is to appoint a Cabinet. The Cabinet is a committee which performs a range of executive and political functions. It is composed of twenty to twenty-four senior members of the party who normally head a Department of State, although one or two Cabinet members may not actually head a department.

Example:
The Chief Secretary to the Treasury is a member of the Cabinet but is only second in rank to the Chancellor of the Exchequer, who is the Cabinet Minister responsible for the Treasury. The importance of the Treasury and economic policy is emphasised by the fact that the British Cabinet contains two members of the Ministerial team responsible for the Treasury.

Technically, the Prime Minister has complete freedom regarding who is appointed to which portfolio. However, a number of constraints exist which limit this freedom of choice. These are discussed below. Prime Ministers often put their keenest supporters into those Cabinet positions which they view as important for the strategy of their government.

Example:
Throughout her Premiership, Margaret Thatcher attempted to ensure that the key economic posts in the Cabinet, the Chancellorship, the Chief Secretary to the Treasury and the Secretary of State for Trade and Industry, were held by those who shared her economic views.

Equally Prime Ministers may choose to give difficult assignments to those whom they do not care for, in order to lessen their standing in the Party and therefore their power to oppose.

2. It appoints the other members of the Government team

In addition to the Cabinet, the Prime Minister is responsible for appointing the other staff of the government, junior Ministers from both the House of Commons and the House of Lords and other government positions, e.g. the Parliamentary Private Secretary. The total number of personnel which the Prime Minister appoints to staff the executive positions in Whitehall now totals over 100.

In appointing these junior posts the Prime Minister seeks to advance the careers of the ablest MPs on the back benches, appoint those who are loyal supporters, and introduce fresh blood into the Government.

Example:
During the 1980s Margaret Thatcher chose to advance the careers of MPs John Major, Nigel Lawson and Peter Lilley, who advanced from the back-benches to the Cabinet table.

3. It dismisses, demotes and transfers any member of the Cabinet or government members

The Prime Minister has the right to change the membership of his or her Cabinet and government at any time. This is often described as a 'reshuffle'. Prime Ministers may use these occasions to elevate junior Ministers into Cabinet positions, replacing Cabinet members who have been ineffective in their positions or disloyal. They are infrequent and when they do occur are often opportunities for Prime Ministers to reinvigorate the public image of the Government. In theory reshuffles allow Prime Ministers the opportunity to strengthen their position in the Cabinet by appointing MPs who are supporters of their policies and by dismissing opponents.

Example:
After her election victory in 1979 Margaret Thatcher waited until 1981, when she felt that she was established as Prime Minister, before she reshuffled her first Cabinet. She removed from this first Cabinet a number of Ministers who were against her radical policies, including Sir Ian Gilmour, and promoted a number of supporters. This strengthened her hold over the Cabinet. In later reshuffles she removed other less enthusiastic supporters, including senior members of the Conservative Party such as Francis Pym and John Biffen. However, sometimes a reshuffle can weaken rather than enhance the position of a Prime Minister as it did in 1963 when the Prime Minister Harold Macmillan dismissed seven Cabinet Ministers.

Key terms: a reshuffle

This term is used to describe the process through which a Prime Minister transfers or dismisses members of his or her Cabinet and government team. Often 'reshuffles' occur when a member of the Cabinet resigns or a Prime Minister feels that the Cabinet team needs new members in order to boost its image and effectiveness.

Example:

As Prime Minister, John Major organised a significant reshuffle in July 1994 to restore his own control over the Cabinet, reinvigorate his government team in the hope of freshening up the Government's performance and bring fresh talent into the Cabinet. A total of four Cabinet Ministers were dropped and four new members were brought into the Cabinet, including Jonathan Aitken and Stephen Dorrell.[2]

4.   It summons and chairs Cabinet meetings, controls the agenda and sums up the conclusions of the Cabinet

These functions allow the Prime Minister to wield considerable power. It allows the Prime Minister to control the business of the Cabinet. He or she can frame the context of a meeting and lead the Cabinet to reach decisions on policy which he or she wants and limit Cabinet discussion. The exercise of these powers depends very much on the personality of the Prime Minister and issues involved. If a Prime Minister wishes to prevent a matter from being discussed by the Cabinet they can do so (e.g. Margaret Thatcher and the Westland Affair of 1986).

Similarly, if a Prime Minister wishes to place his or her own interpretations on the Cabinet discussion, this can be done by drawing the discussion to a close and saying, for the official minutes of the meeting, 'I believe that we have decided that ...' Margaret Thatcher often used this tactic. By comparison, John Major is known to seek the active consensus of his colleagues when concluding Cabinet discussions. The Prime Minister, however, has supreme control over the business of government if he or she chooses to exercise it.

5.   Exercises a major influence on policy

Through the powers of command that the Prime Minister has over the Cabinet he or she is able to be a major influence on the construction and implementation of policy.

6.   Determines size and composition of the Cabinet

A Prime Minister has the power to create a larger or smaller Cabinet and to decide which departments should have Cabinet representation. Conventional wisdom suggests that the Cabinet should be composed of between twenty and twenty-four members, although some Prime Ministers have taken office vowing to reduce this number.

The Prime Minister has the power to create, amalgamate or abolish government departments and say which departments should have Cabinet representation. During the post-war period the membership of the Cabinet has changed in accordance with the changing significance of the various departments, and new ones have been created. In the 1950s, the Ministers of Housing and Local Government were members of the Cabinet. Their Cabinet seats are now occupied by the Secretary of State for the Environment who now has responsibility for these areas.

Example:
In 1992, John Major created a new department with Cabinet status, the Department of National Heritage, and the Office of Public Services and Science headed by a Cabinet Member.

7.   Appoints Cabinet committees

Cabinet committees have assumed an increased importance in the machinery of British Government over the past fifty years but only recently has their number, role and importance become fully appreciated.

The Prime Minister has complete authority over the Cabinet committee system. He or she decides the numbers, roles and composition of all the Cabinet committees and appoints the chairpeople of each committee. The most important committees – Defence, Foreign Affairs and the Treasury – are often chaired by the Prime Minister and it is natural that he or she will chair other committees which are to deal with the most crucial matters. They are important because in these small forums the Prime Minister may exert further concentrated influence on government policy.

Comment

It is clear that as the size and responsibilities of British Government have grown considerably in the post-war period, the full Cabinet meeting for two hours a week cannot possibly fulfil its role of determining policy, and of co-ordinating both the implementation of government policy and the actions of the administrative machine. Therefore it seems only sensible that small sub-committees of the full Cabinet should perform these roles with greater effectiveness – although this inevitably enhances the powers of the Prime Minister. John Major has created a new practice of giving one senior member of the Cabinet the responsibility for chairing many Cabinet committees and the responsibility for the smooth operation of the Cabinet machine. This person is in close liaison with the Prime Minister and responsible to him for ensuring that his wishes are represented on these committees, and that conclusions in line with the Prime Minister's thinking are reached. This individual has taken on the unofficial title of the Prime Minister's Chief of Staff. Between 1992 and 1994 this position was held by Lord Wakeham who was replaced in the 1994 reshuffle by David Hunt.[3]

Key term: Cabinet committees

A Cabinet committee is a subcommittee of the full Cabinet. There are two forms of Cabinet committee – standing (permanent) and *ad hoc* (temporary). As the size and role of government has increased, more and more government business is referred to these small committees of Cabinet members. They are efficient and effective tools for discussing and recommending policy to the full Cabinet. There are Standing Committees for every Department of State, including Defence, Home Office and the Treasury.

Evidence suggests that Cabinet committees have been used by various Prime Ministers to reach decisions whose full discussion in Cabinet is stifled by the Prime Minister exercising one of his or her other powers to ensure the decision of the Cabinet committee prevails. Margaret Thatcher was believed to have done this in the 1980s but events in the early 1990s have shown that John Major has used Cabinet committees to take decisions without a full Cabinet discussion taking place.

Example:
The decision to end trade union membership at the Government Communication Headquarters, GCHQ, in Cheltenham in the mid-1980s was made by a Cabinet committee and was not brought before the full Cabinet.

8.   The dissolution of Parliament

'The right of recommending a dissolution rests solely with the Prime Minister' – Sir Winston Churchill.

Through the exercise of the royal prerogatives the Prime Minister may, at any time within five years of the last general election, go to the monarch and request a dissolution of Parliament and a general election. This is a unique power, which allows a Prime Minister to decide in many ways his or her own fate by affording him or her the opportunity to choose the most favourable time to 'go to the country' and seek re-election. Thus the Government has a distinct advantage over the opposition parties. During the Thatcher years, the Conservative Governments were able to time the General Elections of 1983 and 1987 to their best advantage, when they were ahead of their rivals in the opinion polls. In both cases the party in power was able to prepare its party machine weeks ahead of the election knowing more accurately than the other parties when the election would be called.

Key term: fixed-term elections

This term means that elections are fixed by law to be held at regular periods. In the case of the European Parliament elections to the Parliament are held every five years. In the case of the United States, presidential elections are held every four years. By comparison, in the British system, according to the Representation of the Peoples Act 1949, general elections have to be held within five years of the last general election, but the Prime Minister can decide the timing of this election.

This is perhaps the greatest power that the Prime Minister has and critics fear that it could be abused. They urge that Britain adopt a fixed-term system for its general elections rather like the fixed-term election for the European Parliament or the United States Congress and Presidency.

Proponents of the Prime Ministerial government thesis argue that the Prime Minister has an almost dictatorial status because he or she can, to a great extent, decide his or her own fate and ensure continued governance. A wise Prime Minister will implement the most unpopular policies early in the lifetime of a Parliament (at the earliest part in the five years of a Parliament), and then pursue more popular policies which should improve his or her own – and the party's – popularity and call a general election when he or she consider it is their best opportunity to retain power. Equally, some Prime Ministers have taken office with small majorities which they have sought to increase by requesting a dissolution to increase their majority in the House of Commons. However, opinion polls are fickle things and some recent Prime Ministers have got it wrong.

Example:

In 1964 Labour won the general election with a very small majority of five seats. Subsequently Harold Wilson, the Labour Prime Minister, requested a dissolution of Parliament and a general election in 1966 with the aim of increasing the Labour majority. His strategy was successful and Labour won the General Election with an increased majority of ninety-seven seats.

However, in 1970 Harold Wilson called a General Election ahead of time because he thought that he could win again. This time the opinion polls turned and the Conservatives won the election with a majority of thirty-one seats in the House of Commons.

9.   Other prerogative powers

The Prime Minister uses a number of other prerogative powers which can enhance his or her influence. These include:

(a)   recommending those who should receive honours to the Queen;

(b)   recommending who should be the Archbishop of Canterbury, and other Bishops;

(c)   recommending the appointment of the chairmen of various public bodies, agencies and quangos including the Chairman of the BBC.

These roles are described as the powers of patronage because they give a Prime Minister very wide discretionary powers on a whole range of appointments and preferments which have very little to do with the business of government. They have arisen through the long-term and constant expansion of government business. Tony Benn has suggested that power is of greater significance that many of the other more concrete powers of the Prime Minister. Such critics argue that the exercise of these powers has never been well scrutinised or studied. It is fair to suggest that a Prime Minister who was driven by ideology could use these powers to ensure that like-minded people were installed in all the posts open to their influence, to ensure that government policy in every area of activity was implemented without opposition. Some commentators have suggested that vast numbers of Conservative supporters now occupy all the most important chairmanships of quangos and other public bodies across Britain because of the regular exercise of this power by both John Major and Margaret Thatcher. Clearly, if a Prime Minister wished actively to achieve this through the exercise of the power of patronage he or she could do so. These powers are not easy to quantify, but the arguments suggest the extent of the influence which a Prime Minister may chose to exercise.[4]

Example:
In the late 1980s, when a new Archbishop of Canterbury had to be chosen proponents of the presidential thesis voiced concerns that Margaret Thatcher would seek to influence the choice of a new Archbishop to a greater extent than would otherwise have been the case, because the Church under Archbishop Runcie had been a constant critic of her government. Rumours abounded that she was keen to appoint a less politically active Archbishop.

10. Inner Cabinets

Inner Cabinets are a close team of senior Cabinet colleagues and selected advisers forming an inner group within the Cabinet structure whom the Prime Minister consults to discuss policy. They help him or her take decisions which may or may not be referred to the full Cabinet. It is normal for a Prime Minister to rely on colleagues for advice and it seems that most post-war Prime Ministers have created an Inner Cabinet in one form or another. The importance these bodies was revealed in the Crossman diaries published in the 1970s which identified an Inner Cabinet that existed under Harold Wilson. This was composed of a few selected colleagues, both Cabinet and non-Cabinet members, and met in the kitchen in the Prime Minister's flat at the top of No. 10 Downing Street. It was called the 'Kitchen Cabinet' and was responsible for a number of major decisions which were then passed through the full Cabinet without demur.

It was not until Margaret Thatcher had established herself in the position of Prime Minister that she began to use a form of Inner Cabinet. She sometimes relied on a small group of Cabinet colleagues to deal with important policy decisions and strategies, although through her term in office the composition of her Inner Cabinets, of those she considered 'one of us', varied.

During the Major premiership the practice of using Inner Cabinets continued, despite the fact that during the earlier years of the Major Government the Cabinet's role as the main collective decision-making body appeared to have been restored. From 1992 onwards it appears that John Major used Inner Cabinets to take some of the most important policy decisions.

Example:
The 1992 Coal Mine Closure Plan, the Back to Basics Policy Agenda and the European Parliamentary Election Manifesto.

It seems probable that John Major's use of Inner Cabinets may have increased as divisions with his Cabinet became more and more public over European policy. It is reported that by the Summer of 1994 he was relying more and more on the advice of a few Cabinet members and a select group of advisers.

The importance of Inner Cabinets:

1.   They remove some decision-making power from Cabinet and place it in the hands of a small, selected group who share the Prime Minister's views.
2.   They increase the Prime Minister's decision-making control, by enabling him or her to divert major decision-taking to a group who share his or her approach and beliefs.
3.   Their existence weakens the collective decision-making role of Cabinet. They are another tool for a Prime Minister to use to usurp Cabinet government.

All of these powers combined create a very powerful head of government. Perhaps the three most important powers are the appointment/dismissal power over the 100 government posts, the appointment of Cabinet committees and the exercise of the dissolution power. However, the Prime Minister receives additional power from other sources, including the party, Parliament, the administration and the media.

The party and Parliament

As leader of the party the Prime Minister owes his or her position to this institution. The party is any Prime Minister's power base. The Prime Minister must maintain its backing and support both in Parliament and throughout the country. A Prime Minister must maintain the loyalty of the party and pursue policies which are popular within it, but as leader he or she can use the powers of the Prime Minister to ensure party support. The control of appointments, the powers of patronage, the use of the whips, good performances in the House of Commons in debates and at Question Time all ensure that 'the troops' remain loyal and morale is kept high, especially at times of adversity. By using these powers and events Prime Ministers can assure their positions and enhance their power. However, the events surrounding the resignation of Margaret Thatcher in 1990 showed that Prime Ministers or leaders must do one other thing to retain the loyalty and power base of the party: they must remain in touch with their supporters on the back benches and elsewhere.

The administration

As head of the Government the Prime Minister is responsible for all aspects of government business and appointments. This is shown by the additional title of First Lord of the Treasury which is bestowed on a Prime Minister. Thus a Prime Minister:

1.   Appoints the head of the Home Civil Service and the other civil service heads of departments. Usually this is left to the

Civil Service Commission but the Prime Minister can take an active interest.

2. Can establish additional administrative machinery to provide additional resources and powers over the whole Whitehall machine. The Prime Minister is given additional support via the Cabinet Secretariat in the Cabinet Office and the Prime Minister's Office, which is composed of a Private Office, a Political Office, a Policy Unit and a Press Office.

Harold Wilson suggested that the Cabinet Secretariat could be used to enhance the strength of a Prime Minister. Wilson said that although the Cabinet Secretariat was designed to serve the Cabinet a Prime Minister could use it to his advantage as an additional private resource. To illustrate this point Wilson suggested that the Cabinet Secretary was both responsible to the Cabinet and to the Prime Minister 'as an adviser on Cabinet affairs, Cabinet committees and the general running of government'. Crossman went further to suggest that there was almost a conspiracy between the Prime Minister and the Cabinet Secretary to produce minutes of Cabinet meetings which reflected the views of the Prime Minister thereby limiting the power of the Cabinet.

The Prime Minister's Office

The Press Office

The Press Office co-ordinates the relationship between the Prime Minister and the press and television. The Press Secretary, a civil servant, heads the press office and is responsible for briefing journalists who report on political affairs and are known as the 'press lobby'. These briefings are unattributable and are often described in the newspapers as 'sources close to the Prime Minister'. The job of the Press Secretary is one of the highest-profile and most politically-charged jobs in public life. The role of the Press Secretary came to high prominence during the 1980s through the activities of Margaret Thatcher's Press Secretary, Sir Bernard Ingham.

The Policy Unit

The Policy Unit was established in 1974 by Harold Wilson. It is designed to advise the Prime Minister on policy matters and provide him with briefings on prospective policy ideas. It has a small, specialised staff and a number of part-time special advisers appointed personally by the Prime Minister. The Policy Unit is also responsible for monitoring the implementation of various policies and providing the Prime Minister with an alternative source of advice across the whole range of public policy.

The media

The Prime Minister is the personification of the Government and so receives more media attention than any other politician in the country. This can enhance a Prime Minister's image, power and authority but this can equally work in the opposite direction when the policies of the Government are unpopular.

From all of the above one could easily believe that Britain has an elected dictator. In any essay that concerns itself with the issue of *primus inter pares* all of the above 'powers' can be used to show that the Prime Minister is more than merely first among equals. Clearly it can be shown that the powers of the office elevate him or her far above other Cabinet members. In any discussion students can add weight to their arguments by drawing on the experiences of the Thatcher premiership.

However, there is another side to this argument, because a range of constraints exist which redress some of the balance. These constraints suggest that we do not have a Prime Ministerial government, rather that our system of Cabinet government within parliamentary democracy is alive and resilient. These counter-arguments have been revived by the experiences of the Major years and by a slowly evolving reassessment of the true nature of the Thatcher premiership.

Questions

1. Define the term *'primus inter pares'.*
2. What is the role and importance of the Prime Minister's office?
3. What are Inner Cabinets?

6.2 | The constraints on a Prime Minister's power

Appointing the Cabinet

(a) Prime Ministers have to appoint people to the Cabinet who may not be their natural supporters, because they are senior members of the party. If senior members are left out of the Cabinet they can attract support on the back benches and become a nuisance by expressing their opinions, criticisms of government policy and of the Prime Minister's leadership.

(b) A Prime Minister has to accommodate all wings of the Party within the Cabinet so that they are represented in Cabinet, again preventing unwanted criticism and rivary. This policy means that the party does not become internally split between its different wings and internal rivalry does not develop between those in Cabinet and those dispossessed of power.

These constraints limit the freedom of choice which a Prime Minister has regarding his Cabinet. All of these factors must be considered and a Prime Minister must find the right balance.

Limits on the power of dismissal

A Prime Minister cannot act as a dictator and dismiss from his or her government all those who do not agree with every policy or fill their Cabinets with 'Yes men'. The power to dismiss can be a double-edged sword for a Prime Minister, and must be used sparingly and with great thought for the possible consequences.

Examples:
Margaret Thatcher dismissed more Ministers than any other Prime Minister, but she was careful not to dismiss any potential rivals until the threat had passed.

John Major dismissed Kenneth Baker after the 1992 General Election because he believed that Baker would not be a threat to his authority on the back benches.

Reshuffles can be caused by:

1. The need to improve the public image of the Government.
2. The resignation of a Minister for professional or private reasons.
3. The death of a Minister.

Reshuffles can result in the dismissal of Ministers or their resignation because they are not happy with being demoted. This can weaken a Prime Minister because convention allows Ministers who resign to make a resignation speech, which can sometimes prove very damaging.

Example:
Perhaps the best example is the resignation of Sir Geoffrey (now Lord) Howe in November 1990, which mortally wounded Margaret Thatcher as Prime Minister. Sir Geoffrey resigned from her Cabinet because he did not agree with her attitude towards the European Union.

Control of the agenda and Cabinet business

The Prime Minister's control over the business of the Cabinet is limited by the practicalities of politics. If a member of the Cabinet wishes to discuss a matter it can prove very difficult for a Prime Minister to keep this off the agenda. The Westland affair showed what can result if freedom of choice within the Cabinet structure is severely curtailed.

The Crossman thesis suggests that a Prime Minister can persuade the Cabinet to agree with him or her on decisions most of the time. However, we know that Prime Ministers do not always get their own way either in Cabinet or in Cabinet committees.

Examples:
Margaret Thatcher was defeated in Cabinet during the first years of her government on the extent of public expenditure cuts, and she was forced in 1990 by members of a Cabinet committee to agree to Britain's membership of the Exchange Rate Mechanism (ERM).[5]

Cabinet committees

Crossman suggested that the Cabinet committee system enhanced the powers of a Prime Minister but although the Prime Minister exercises much control over Cabinet committees the sheer scale of government activity mean that this control is limited by the practicality that they cannot lead/chair/attend every meeting and that some decisions must be taken by these committees and accepted at full Cabinet which may not be fully in accord with the thinking of the Prime Minister.

Cabinet support

A Prime Minister must have the confidence and support of his senior colleagues in (primarily) the Cabinet and (secondly) within the wider parliamentary party. Without this a Prime Minister will find his or her position untenable. During the 1980s it seemed that Britain was led by a Prime Minister who commanded the support of a Cabinet by intimidation and domination. This was an overstatement: Margaret Thatcher was a dominant personality but we now know that the Cabinet did function during these years as a collective decision-making body. There were many occasions when the Cabinet followed the lead of the Prime Minister and others where it chose to take an alternative course. Personality looms large here. Any explanation of the nature of British government during the Thatcher years must not overstress her domination: power rested upon the personalities of her Cabinet as well as the premier herself. The different personalities that occupied seats around the Cabinet table during her eleven years in office affected her power and command over the Cabinet.

What is clear is that she commanded the support of her Cabinets, whether grudgingly or willingly. From about 1989 onwards, Margaret Thatcher encountered increasing problems with a Cabinet that was not truly Thatcherite. She became isolated and increasingly relied upon the advice of a small group of Cabinet Ministers, former Cabinet members and other advisers. No. 10 was frequently referred to as the 'No. 10 bunker' in the press, and the

Prime Minister appeared to become increasingly isolated and unpopular within the Parliamentary Party and in the country. In 1990 she clearly was on the point of losing the support of the majority of Conservative MPs, but it was the loss of the support of her Cabinet that forced her resignation. This was the exercise of the ultimate check upon the powers of the Prime Minister, and heralded a revival of Cabinet government in Britain.

The party and Parliament

1. The loyalty of the party is responsible for securing the position of the Prime Minister. A Prime Minister must avoid policy splits within the party keeping it united behind him or her. Furthermore, a Prime Minister must pursue policies and project a personal image which keep the party electorally popular, ensuring his or her own security by enjoying the majority of support from the party in Parliament and in the country. Post-war political history suggests that Conservative Prime Ministers are perhaps more vulnerable than Labour leaders. If the Conservative Party fears that the Prime Minister or leader cannot deliver electoral success it has shown itself to be ruthless.

   Example:
   Both in the case of Sir Anthony Eden in 1957 and Harold Macmillan in 1963 the Prime Minister resigned for health reasons. However history has implied that these resignations were forced upon both men by the senior men of the Party.

2. As a member of Parliament the Prime Minister must command the support of Parliament. Performances at the dispatch box can boost the fortunes of a Prime Minister and the morale of his back benchers. Equally poor performances can have the opposite effect and increase the possibilities for a leadership change. The restraints that Parliament can impose rest upon these performances and the ability of a Prime Minister to command the loyalty of his or her troops. Frequent meetings with many back-benchers are impossible for Prime Ministers to fit into their schedule. However, 1990 showed that a Prime Minister must be seen around Westminster maintaining even the semblance of contact with ordinary back benchers.

3. A vote of 'no confidence' in the Government is a motion placed before the House of Commons which can either remove a Prime Minister from office, or the entire Government and lead to a general election. They are very rare, the last one being in 1979 which was successfully carried against James Callaghan's Labour administration and resulted in the general election which brought the Conservatives to power. They are an ultimate sanction that Parliament can use against a Prime Minister.

Parliament does impose restraints on the power of the Prime Minister because constant bad performances at Question Time and in debates can lead to discontent on the back-benches and this can lead to discontent within the party at large. Ultimately a Prime Minister cannot continue in office without party support.

Conclusions

1. As Sir William Harcourt noted, 'In practice the thing depends very much upon the character of the man. The office of the Prime Minister is whatever the holder chooses and is able to make of it.'

2. The Prime Minister is a political being but there are limits. Many commentators in the 1980s felt that the Crossman thesis had come true, but from the perspective of 1995 it is clear that the unwritten constitution provides for balances to exert themselves on even the most strong-willed and ardent Prime Minister.

3. Party loyalty and Cabinet support are necessary for a Prime Minister to continue in office. When these are in question the influence and power of a premier is weakened.

4. The sheer size of the Government machine means that one person, even if they are at the apex of the structure, cannot possibly exert full control over the entire organisation.

5. The personality and style factor is important in determining the power that a Prime Minister is able to yield. David Lloyd George (Prime Minister, 1916–22) was viewed as a powerful Prime Minister because he treated his Cabinet in a cavalier manner. Equally Margaret Thatcher was powerful by the way she dominated her Cabinet through her feminine qualities, the projection of her personality and the effective use of many of the powers in the office. By comparison John Major does not have a powerful image similar to Margaret Thatcher. His style of Government has been described as 'consensual or collegiate', meaning that he seeks the agreement of his colleagues in the Cabinet. Moreover, the powers of the Prime Minister are balanced by the personalities of his Cabinet.

Questions

1. Explain two powers of the Prime Minister and assess the constraints that exist upon those powers.

2. What is the significance of Cabinet reshuffles?

6.3 | **The Thatcher and Major styles of leadership**

The Thatcher style

Margaret Thatcher was seen to be the archetypal presidential-style Prime Minister, dominant over her Cabinet to the extent of being almost authoritarian. A comment in the Soviet Press in the mid-1970s proved to be prophetic when it branded her 'The Iron Lady'. Even then she was seen to possess commanding qualities.

1. Margaret Thatcher portrayed an image of confidence and self-assuredness over her Cabinet. This is demonstrated by comments expressed in the memoirs of one member of her Cabinet. Cecil (now Lord) Parkinson, records:

    'she did not seem on occasions to be aware of how intimidating she could be to people who felt inhibited about arguing with a Prime Minister . . . What was combativeness to her was rudeness to a lot of people.'[6]

2. She successfully used Cabinet reshuffles to replace dissenters with supporters.
3. She used fewer Cabinet meetings to simply endorse decisions which had been made elsewhere, i.e. Cabinet committees.
4. According to Peter Hennessy, Margaret Thatcher:
(a) developed a tendency to avoid or by-pass Cabinet for certain decisions instead relying on Cabinet committees, or bilateral meetings between herself, the departmental Minister and her advisers, or interdepartmental task forces of able civil servants reporting directly to No. 10.[7]
(b) relied on the advice of private advisers, Sir Charles Powell, in her private office on foreign affairs, Sir Alan Walters on economic affairs. This reliance was fuelled by a suspicion of the civil service, who she saw as responsible for running the country down after she heard a senior official once claim that the job of the Civil Service was, 'to manage the decline of the Country'. This suspicion was most militantly directed towards the advice proffered by the great departments of state, the Treasury and the Foreign Office.
(c) interfered in departments' affairs, following policy discussions with a department with a keen interest and interfered in the promotion of senior civil servants across Whitehall.

However, with the publication of her own memoirs and those of other former Cabinet members this image has been clarified. Margaret Thatcher's domination over the Cabinet depended upon the composition and personalities contained within it. Only after

1987 could the Cabinet be seen to be purely Thatcherite. During 1983 to 1987 the image of domination developed. By comparison in the early years in office Margaret Thatcher's Government was divided between the 'wets' and the 'drys', and her style of leadership took some time to evolve.[8]

The powers which Margaret Thatcher used have always existed within the confines of the office, but she used them more effectively than any other modern Prime Minister. She was a conviction politician, an advocate of the (neo-liberalist) New Right who used her drive, enthusiasm and energy to do the job and implement her policies.[9]

These qualities created a hard, abrasive and dominant image of the Prime Minister, which at first won favour with an electorate in search of a strong leader but later became a negative factor in Margaret Thatcher's public image. [10]

Figure 15 Margaret Thatcher and John Major with their spouses.

The Major Style

John Major's style is very different to Margaret Thatcher's. The following points have been made on his early period in office:

1. His style of leadership is less conflictual and more consensual. He consults with and seeks the agreement of his colleagues. He has sought to create a collegiate Cabinet. He has shown a preference for devolving more responsibility to his colleagues than Margaret Thatcher.
2. Supporters claim that unlike Margaret Thatcher, John Major has a gentle and affable manner and yet has the power to inspire those around him.[11]
3. His political message is different to Margaret Thatcher, although some aspects of Thatcherite policy has continued, mainly anti-inflationary economic policies and privatisation. John Major has attempted to construct his own political message. Very early on in his premiership he spoke of creating a classless society; a truly open society where everyone was able to enjoy the same opportunities. This was accompanied by a

Key terms: collegiate Cabinet

A Cabinet working together through the free and open expression of views and agreement and consensus. After his first Cabinet meeting one member of the new Cabinet privately claimed that for the first time in his entire career as a Cabinet member he had been able to express his true opinions.

pledge to improve Britain's public services via his Citizens' Charter initiative, launched in the first year of his premiership and designed to improve the provision, quality and delivery of public services in Britain, e.g. health and transport[12] (*see Chapter 8*). His new message was expanded in 1993 through 'Back to Basics' programme, that was subsequently dropped in the Spring of 1994.

4.   During the Gulf War his leadership was not rousingly patriotic unlike Margaret Thatcher in 1982, but firm and assuring.

5.   In December 1991 he triumphantly returned from the European Council meeting at Maastricht, praised for his negotiating style and the personal chemistry he had deployed to reach agreement with his continental colleagues.

6.   John Major's style has however been criticised since the 1992 General Election for being weak and indecisive as his Government has fallen foul of one crisis after another. These have included the Coal Mine Closure Plan in October 1992, the ERM crisis, and the troubled, lengthy and vicious Maastricht ratification process which finally ended with the Prime Minister threatening to call a general election if his own MPs did not back him.

Criticism of John Major has been compounded by a range of other policy U-turns and his low popularity ratings in the opinion polls during the parliamentary session 1993–94, which saw 'Back to Basics' his new policy agenda, collapse amid scenes of Cabinet in-fighting, ministerial impropriety, and indecisive leadership from the Prime Minister.[13]

Critics now argue that his style has created the image, in contrast to Margaret Thatcher, of a weak and indecisive Prime Minister overly concerned with his media image, lacking any long-term perspective and unable to control his divided party. Consequently, since early 1994 a question mark has periodically hung over his position within the Conservative Party. In July 1994 he reshuffled his Cabinet team in an attempt to restore his own standing within the Conservative Party and the country. This has had some positive effects, creating an image of a Prime Minister who is prepared to wield the knife where necessary and is concerned to maintain the support and unity of his MPs.

Questions

1.   How would you describe Margaret Thatcher's style of leadership?
2.   Why did Margaret Thatcher's style of leadership give rise to an image of a presidential leader?
3.   Describe John Major's style of leadership.
4.   What significant changes in style exist between the premiership of Margaret Thatcher and that of John Major?

Essay questions

1. What constraints exist upon the powers of a Prime Minister?
2. What are the factors which are likely to influence a Prime Minister in his choice of Cabinet members?
3. (a) What is meant by the term 'presidential powers'?
   (b) Does the Prime Minister have presidential powers?
4. Discuss the relationship between the office of the Prime Minister and Parliament.

Essay planning

1. What constraints exist upon the powers of a Prime Minister?

This question asks you to discuss the controls that exist upon the powers of a Prime Minister. Students should explain:

(a) The nature of the power invested in the office of Prime Minister. You may wish to set the question within the context of the debate, which has arisen in recent years about the existence of Prime Ministerial government.
(b) The constraints that exist upon the Prime Minister using the material in *section 6.2*.
(c) During a description of these constraints a student should analyse which are the most effective constraints upon the powers of the Prime Minister.
(e) If this essay has been set within the context of the 'Prime Ministerial debate', you may conclude by arguing that these constraints suggest that Prime ministerial government does not exist.

Notes and references

1. See Bagehot, W. *The English Constitution* (London, 1963).

2. *The Guardian*, 22.07.94.

3. *The Guardian*, 21.07.94.

4. See Chapter 3 and 'Indirect Government: Quangoland', in Robbins, L. *Politics Pal, 1994* (Leicester, 1994), p. 10.

5. Thatcher, M. *The Downing Street Years* (1993) pp. 721–4.

6. *The Guardian*, 1.20.93.

7. Hennessy, P. *The Cabinet* (1986) p. 103. Students should read Chapter 3, this volume.

8. *The Downing Street Years*, BBC Documentary, 1994.

9. Anderson, B. *John Major: The Making of the Prime Minister* (London, 1991), p. 292.

10. *The Guardian*, 1.10.93.

11. BBC, *On the Record*, 17.02.91.

12. Anderson, B. *John Major* (1991) pp. 292–303.

13. *The Guardian*, 08.04.94.

Further reading

Baker, K. *The Turbulent Years* (London, 1993).

Donoughue, B. *Prime Minister* (London, 1987).

Gilmour, I. *Dancing with Dogma* (London, 1993).

Hennessy, P. *The Cabinet* (London, 1986).

Hennessy P. *Whitehall* (London, 1990).

Kavanagh, D. *Thatcherism and British Politics* (Oxford, 1990)

King, A.[ed.] *The British Prime Minister* (London, 1985).

Lawson, N. *The View from No.11* (London, 1992).

Letwin, S. R. *The Anatomy of Thatcherism* (London, 1993)

Norton, P. 'Prime Ministerial Power', *Social Studies Review*, January 1988.

Thatcher, M. *The Downing Street Years* (London, 1993).

CHAPTER 7

The Cabinet

This chapter links directly to the previous one on Prime Ministerial office and powers. The Cabinet is the committee of the most senior ministers appointed by the Prime Minister, which is responsible for co-ordinating the actions of the various Departments of State, deciding and implementing government policy. The Cabinet is a powerful institution, being the place where all the major decisions are made. Bagehot called it 'a combining committee – a hyphen which joins, a buckle which fastens the legislative part of the state to the executive part of the state.' By this Bagehot meant that the Cabinet is responsible for organising government, providing collective leadership and, via the fact that its members are drawn from both Houses of Parliament, that it is accountable to the legislature. Traditionally, the Cabinet is seen as the supreme decision-making body in central government. This view is central to the entire topic because in modern times, this role has been questioned.

There is a considerable controversy about the precise nature and role of the Cabinet within our system of government; is the Cabinet still the supreme decision-making body or has it been usurped by the Prime Minister? This thesis was first aired by Richard Crossman who claimed that the idea of Cabinet Government was 'passing away'. Writers such as Peter Hennessy have pointed out the weaknesses in the powers of the modern Cabinet, suggesting that what the Cabinet is and does depends on a mixture of personalities and situations: 'Cabinet Government remains a putty-like concept. A Prime Minister can make of it very largely what he or she will, provided colleagues do not balk at their treatment.'[1]

The whole of this topic is interwoven with the chapter on the Prime Minister and students should study the two together, treating them as interdependent. In this chapter we will discuss the role and powers of the Cabinet and assess whether Cabinet is still the supreme decision-making body.

This chapter will discuss:

7.1   The role of the Cabinet.

7.2   The composition of the Cabinet.

7.3   The role of Cabinet committees.

7.4   Collective and individual ministerial responsibility.

7.5   The role of the Cabinet office.

7.6   The debate over the existence of Cabinet government or Prime Ministerial government.

7.1 | The role of the Cabinet

Many executives in a number of Western countries use the Cabinet system. France, Germany and the United States have Cabinets which fit our definition. This enables each government to co-ordinate its policies and activities and to control its bureaucratic administration. However, the conventions of collective and individual ministerial responsibility do not apply to all executives. There is no collective responsibility in the United States government. The President appoints a Cabinet, but it is not a particularly important body. The United States Cabinet is composed of the ministerial heads of the Federal Government departments, Treasury, Department of Defense, etc., who are responsible to the President for their actions. The United States executive is dominated by the President, in whom all decision-making power is invested, and there is no concept of collective decision making. Hence open disagreements between the different federal departments often occur. Presidents rely on bilateral meetings with individual departmental heads or with their own large team of appointed advisers in the White House rather than their Cabinet for policy advice and discussion. In recent years observers of the British system have suggested that it has evolved into a form of presidential government, namely Prime Ministerial rather than Cabinet government. This problem lies at the heart of any discussion of the nature of government in Britain today.

The roles of the British Cabinet

1.   The British Cabinet implements the policy plans contained in a party manifesto. This means that individual Cabinet members take responsibility for implementing aspects of the party's election manifesto. Normally this means that the Secretary of State will present his legislative proposals to the Cabinet before they are put before Parliament. Once Cabinet has approved the legislative package, i.e. the Bill and the parliamentary timetable which it should follow, the Bill will be presented to Parliament.

Example:

Kenneth Clarke was Secretary of State for Heath in 1989 and was responsible for introducing a variety of Health Service reforms both to the Cabinet for their agreement and then to Parliament for their approval. Kenneth Clarke was responsible for leading the parliamentary debates on these reforms and for seeing that they were successfully approved.

2. Cabinet co-ordinates the activities of government and the administration. Cabinet theory suggests that the Cabinet co-ordinates the activities of the government and manages the administration, i.e. the civil servants in Whitehall. The weekly meeting affords Ministers the opportunity to discuss what each department is doing and the direction which the Government is taking, and to discuss the Government's overall strategy. Although this may have been the case when the responsibility of government was small, in modern Britain Cabinet is no longer the effective co-ordinator of all government activity. The sheer scale of the Whitehall bureaucracy means that the Cabinet simply does not have the time to perform the task of co-ordination effectively or efficiently.

Each Secretary of State is responsible for his or her department, managing and organising its activities, defining its policies and priorities, and acting as the chief spokesperson for the Department in Parliament, in Cabinet and to the public. Given these responsibilities, Cabinet Ministers are unable to read the many Cabinet papers which are produced on matters outside their departmental interests. Co-ordination is now provided in other ways, such as:

*   informal meetings between Ministers from different departments;
*   formal inter-departmental meetings between senior civil servants and Ministers.

Both provide opportunities to discuss policy and co-ordinate the activities of departments.

Better co-ordination is also achieved:

*   through the activities of the Cabinet office which circulates Cabinet papers and follows up Cabinet decisions;
*   through the use of Cabinet committees, which are a more effective tool for managing the co-ordination of Government activities.

It may be concluded that the Cabinet, as a single body is not an effective co-ordinator of all government activity or controller of the central administration. However, as a many-faceted institution, Cabinet provides a number of opportunities for this function to be performed, at a lower level than the full Cabinet, perhaps most importantly through Cabinet committees.

3.   Cabinet discusses budgetary estimates. It is responsible for discussing and deciding a range of budgetary matters. The members of the Cabinet represent the interests of their departments and when discussion begins over the annual budget, each member usually presents to the Chancellor of the Exchequer and the full Cabinet an estimate of the amount of money which he or she believes that his or her department should receive in the new Budget. Often Ministers press the case for their department to have more money.

     If the Cabinet cannot reach agreement on each departmental estimate, or other particular aspects of the budget, the outstanding matters are often referred to a Cabinet committee, specially selected to adjudicate on these disputes. It is often chaired by a very senior member of the Cabinet. This committee has been labelled by the media as 'the Star Chamber'.

     The final budget is presented to the Cabinet on budget day and many of its technical aspects are often not brought to the attention of the Cabinet until budget day itself.

4.   Cabinet decides policy and spending priorities.

     This is linked to point 1, but the primary function of Cabinet is to decide policy, prioritising that which has to be implemented first when the new Cabinet takes office and determining policy throughout the whole of its term of office.

     Example:
     In 1979 the first Thatcher Cabinet decided to prioritise its commitment to introduce legislation to allow people to buy their council houses, and to reform the powers of the trade unions. The 1980 Housing Act and the series of 1980s Trade Union Acts fulfilled these aims.

     The perceived wisdom until recent times was that Cabinet was responsible for the final determination of policy to be submitted to Parliament. However, with the growth in the size of modern government, the massive breadth of responsibilities which a modern Cabinet member now has, the growth of Cabinet committees and the growth in the power of the Prime Minister, this function has been superseded. Much policy is now decided elsewhere and sometimes it has been the case that not even the most important decisions are brought to the Cabinet for discussion and decision. Cabinet is now the final arbiter of disputes which have arisen in Cabinet committees, or sometimes simply a rubber stamp, endorsing decisions taken elsewhere.

The very size of government today means that a committee of twenty people meeting once a week for, on average, two hours cannot deal with everything that, in principle, they should. This is one of the prime reasons for the existence of Cabinet committees, which are better suited to dealing with policy matters more comprehensively.

Examples:

The 1994 Heseltine De-Regulation Act was discussed in full Cabinet, but the scope and form of the Bill was decided in the Department of Trade and Industry and discussed by the Cabinet Committee responsible for legislation before it was presented to the full Cabinet.

On the other hand, the 1992 Coal Mine Closure Plan was decided by a small Cabinet committee and was not brought before the Cabinet. Similarly, the 1984 decision to end trade union membership at the Government Communications Headquarters in Cheltenham (GCHQ) was not discussed by the full Cabinet.

Since the late 1940s very little foreign policy has been discussed at Cabinet level, only at times of crisis have foreign affairs been brought to the Cabinet for discussion, e.g. Suez 1956, the Falkland Island 1982. Most discussion of British foreign policy takes place in discussions between the Prime Minister and the Foreign Secretary, and the Foreign Affairs Cabinet Committee.

Today the Cabinet deals with only a small percentage of government affairs and policy; but much policy consideration remains within the exclusive orbit of the responsible department.

Example:

The 1993, 'Back to Basics' policy was multi-faceted, incorporating policies on law and order and education, which meant that it was discussed in Cabinet in a variety of forms, either collectively or individually.

5. Cabinet takes emergency decisions.

   When emergencies occur the Cabinet, or those members of the Cabinet in London, will have an unscheduled meeting to address the emergency and decide how to deal with the problem.

   Example:

   In 1982 when Argentina invaded the Falkland Islands there were a number of emergency Cabinets called by Margaret Thatcher to decide the British response to the invasion.

Questions

1. What is the Star Chamber?
2. List and explain two roles of the Cabinet.
3. What is the difference between Cabinet and government?

7.2 | **The composition of the Cabinet**

In the twentieth century the size of the Cabinet has grown in parallel with the growth of the British bureaucracy, and the variety of ministries which enjoyed Cabinet membership has altered as the importance of each department has grown or declined.

The modern Cabinet normally consists of between twenty and twenty-four members. The decision about the composition and size of the Cabinet rests with the Prime Minister. On taking office some Prime Ministers have sought to reduce or increase the size of the Cabinet by creating new departments or amalgamating a number of departments into one huge Department of State. Prime Ministers are able to tinker with the Whitehall system, elevating or diminishing some functions of government according to their perceptions, ideas and aims.

Example:
As Prime Minister, John Major created a new Department of State, the National Heritage Department. This has been called the 'Ministry of Fun' because it is responsible for arts, heritage and entertainment. It was responsible for organising the D-Day commemorations in 1994, and is responsible for the process of renewal of the BBC Charter.

Some Prime Ministers have attempted to reduce the size of the Cabinet in order to make it more efficient. This is best exemplified by Edward Heath, who on taking office in 1970 sought to create a number of 'super departments'. Heath created the Department of the Environment, which has responsibility for housing, environmental policy, and local government. These were all previously separate Ministries.

Factors outside the control of even the most powerful Prime Minister effect the composition of the Cabinet. Therefore as the roles and responsibilities of government have changed membership of the Cabinet has been altered accordingly. We no longer have a Colonial Secretary, a Secretary of State for War or a Secretary of State for India.

The permanent membership of the Cabinet is supplemented from time to time by other government Ministers who sit in on Cabinet meetings on a temporary basis, depending upon the agenda.

It is worth remembering that the choice of the Cabinet depends on the Prime Minister. Senior colleagues have to be included, all wings of the party need to be represented and talented young MPs have to be elevated.

Membership of the Cabinet depends on a variety of factors aside from patronage of the Prime Minister. Cabinet members have generally been members of the House of Commons for some time, although there are exceptions to this. Usually Ministers have held a variety of junior posts in which they have proved their administrative competence, political skills and debating qualities. Those members of the Cabinet who sit in the House of Lords have to show similar qualities.

Example:
Margaret Thatcher's first Cabinet included Lord Carrington as Foreign Secretary. In later Cabinets she included Lord Young of Graffham as Secretary of State for Employment (1985–87) and Secretary of State for Trade and Industry (1987–89).

The Cabinet may also include members who may have a specific and important role to play, but do not head a Department of State.

7.3 | The role of Cabinet committees

Having considered the role and membership of Cabinet it should now be clear that the Cabinet as a single entity is unable to co-ordinate the activities of government and decide policy. The majority of these roles are performed in other ways, most importantly through the activities of Cabinet committees, where ideas and policies are thrashed out in small groupings of Cabinet members and a high degree of co-ordination over the activities of the Government is achieved.

From 1945 the Cabinet committee system expanded to cover all aspects of government and become a permanent feature of Cabinet government. Until recently, their numbers and work have been shrouded in a veil of intense secrecy. However, under John Major's 'Open Government' initiative, the numbers, membership and responsibility of the various committees has been made public.

There are three types of Committee:

1. *Standing*: These are permanent and deal with a particular subject area of government. Many shadow the activity and responsibility of the various Departments of State rather like Select Committees of the House of Commons.

    Example:
    EDE – the environment Cabinet committee which is designed to 'consider questions of environmental policy'.

2. *Ad Hoc*: These are temporary and are usually established to deal with a particular problem or issue.

    Example:
    During the Miners' Strike 1984/5 an ad hoc Cabinet Committee was established to co-ordinate the Government's response to the

strike called MISC. 57. The 'Star Chamber' is another example of a temporary ad hoc *Cabinet committee as are the War Cabinets established during both the Falklands and Gulf Wars.*

3. *Official Committees:* These consist of senior civil servants and are designed to operate in parallel with committees of Ministers.

The chairmen of Cabinet committees are appointed by the Prime Minister, and often the most important committees are chaired either by the Prime Minister him or herself or by loyal senior colleagues. This gives the Prime Minister greater influence and control over the most important areas of government activity.

When a new Prime Minister takes office the committee system undergoes a revision and a range of new committees are often established depending upon the priorities of the new Prime Minister.

These committees:

1. discuss issues and ideas and construct policy blueprints which are then submitted to full Cabinet for approval;
2. streamline the work of the Cabinet and the Government;
3. carry out the role of co-ordination across the whole range of government activities, allowing ministers to meet in small groups to discuss inter-departmental affairs;
4. are more effective in assessing options and reaching decisions because they are compact. It is always easier to debate a problem and decide a course of action to take when only a small number of people are involved. Therefore the committee system allows Cabinet members the opportunity of in-depth discussions and the chance to formulate policy which can then be recommended to the full Cabinet in a compact form, with a degree of agreement which would otherwise be hard to reach.
5. hammer out disagreements in advance and make recommendations to the full Cabinet.

If every single issue or policy which needs to be addressed by the Cabinet was dealt with by the full Cabinet it would probably have to sit twelve hours a day, seven days a week. This devolved decision-making system ensures the Cabinet fulfils its roles efficiently and effectively. It reduces the (a) quantity of decisions and (b) the debate time, which the Cabinet needs to undertake on weekly basis.

However, this system has been criticised:

1. It allows the Prime Minister to by-pass the full Cabinet and expand his or her own power. A number of policy decisions made by the Thatcher Government were not addressed by the

full Cabinet including the GCHQ union decision and policies relating to unemployment.

2. Further, the Prime Minister's power to establish the committees and write his or her terms of reference, appoint the chairman and members, increases Prime Ministerial influence over the Cabinet policy machine.

3. Issues and policies have been kept off the full Cabinet agenda, which has suggested the demise of Cabinet government and added authority to the argument concerning the rise of Prime Ministerial government.

4. The main general criticism of the Cabinet committee system is that decision-making power has been transferred from the full Cabinet to the committees, and although a Minister may appeal against a committee's conclusion to the full Cabinet this may only occur with the consent of the committee chairman. The role of Cabinet as the place where the important decisions of government are taken has been subverted by the existence of these committees. During Margaret Thatcher's tenure many important decisions were taken at committee level.

Example:
The decision to replace the British nuclear deterrent Polaris with the United States Trident Missile in 1980 was taken by an ad hoc committee consisting of the five most senior Ministers of Margaret Thatcher's Cabinet. Because of the nature of this committee, when the decision was brought to the attention of the full Cabinet it is unlikely that anyone really questioned it.

However, Margaret Thatcher reduced the numbers of Cabinet committees when she became Prime Minister. During her premiership she developed a preference for bilateral meetings between her office and the departmental Ministers and civil servants, and small 'working parties' of advisers, officials and ministers to decide policy.

Under John Major similar important decisions have been taken which have not even been referred to the full Cabinet, e.g. the 1992 Coal Mine Closure Plan.

In conclusion one can see that the system of committees is a necessary tool which enables the institution of the Cabinet to complete its roles. Decision-making power is inevitably transferred in pursuit of this goal from the full Cabinet. The significance of the committees has grown in recent decades and there will continue to be much controversy about whether they are a valuable aid to the system, taking the load off the Cabinet and allowing it to concentrate on the essentials, 'the major topic decisions' or whether they are a device for by-passing the full Cabinet.

Questions

1. What factors influence the composition of the Cabinet?
2. Account for the differences between the three types of Cabinet Committees.
3. What is the role of Cabinet committees?
4. What criticisms have been levelled at the Cabinet committee system?

7.4 | # Collective and individual ministerial responsibility

Central to the mechanics of the British executive are the two conventions of collective and individual ministerial responsibility. They lie at the heart of the notion of responsible government because all members of the government are responsible to Parliament, as the elected assembly of the people, for their actions.

Collective responsibility

Collective responsibility means that all members of the Government are collectively responsible for the decisions of the Government and must be seen publicly to support and defend them, even if they have private doubts. If they are unable to do this, they must resign their office.

This is a widely accepted doctrine which extends from the very top down to the very bottom level of the Government, e.g. from Cabinet Ministers to parliamentary private secretaries. In this way the Government presents a united front to Parliament and to the electorate. Policy is presented in a unified manner and the loyalty of the parliamentary party to government policy is ensured.

The operation of this doctrine has been weakened in modern times. Since the 1960s there has been a tendency of some members of a government to break the united front and express dissent.

Example:
Perhaps the first example of this breakdown was in Harold Wilson's Government in 1966, when Frank Cousins, while Minister of Technology, expressed support for criticisms of the Government's incomes and pricing policies and shortly afterwards resigned.[2]

Collective responsibility has continued to break down since then. As the size of government has grown unity has been harder to preserve and the diversion of decision-making power to Cabinet committees, upon which few ministers sit and by which policy is imposed upon the members of the Government, has increased opportunities for dissent.

These factors have led to the phenomenon known as 'leaks'. A leak is the passing on of confidential or secret government information to the press by a Minister. During the 1970s and 1980s leaks were commonly described by the media as 'sources close to the Cabinet'. These break the convention and allow members of the government to express concerns over the policies being adopted.

During the Thatcher years leaks were a common occurrence. Moreover, some Ministers who were not part of the inner circle made carefully worded speeches to make their real views known.

Example:
Peter Walker made a number of carefully coded speeches which revealed that he was at variance with his colleagues on a number of aspects of economic and social policy.

This is not to suggest that the doctrine of collective responsibility is dead. In 1986 Michael Heseltine resigned because he disagreed with the Prime Minister over the Westland Helicopters sale. In 1990, Sir Geoffrey (now Lord) Howe resigned from the Cabinet because he disagreed with the direction of the Government's policy towards the EU. This resignation contributed to the fall of Margaret Thatcher.

In the post-1992 General Election period the Major Government has been beset with problems over breaches in this doctrine over the European issue. In 1993 a number of the 'Euro-sceptic' members of the Cabinet reportedly threatened to resign if John Major embraced the Social Chapter. This would have been correct according to the doctrine of collective responsibility but the leaking of this story confirmed the deep division which exist within the Cabinet over the future direction of the EU.

At certain times the convention has been suspended to allow a greater public debate to occur. This happened in 1975 when Harold Wilson allowed Ministers to express their views during the European referendum campaign, thereby avoiding a very damaging party split.[3]

The practice of the convention of collective responsibility in the past thirty years has resulted in a debate over its necessity. Politicians such as Tony Benn, who was no great observer of the doctrine, have suggested that the convention should be abandoned because it is unrealistic and only gives 'a spurious air of unanimity to Government policies'. Others have argued that the public would have greater confidence in their government if they know that Ministers do disagree and that the public have 'a right to know' more about the processes of government and the factors which affect policy decisions.

However, if the doctrine was rescinded it would have dire consequences on the operation of the party system in Parliament. Collective responsibility maintains cohesion in government and helps to ensure the existence of responsible government within the UK.

Individual ministerial responsibility

Individual ministerial responsibility means that all Ministers are individually responsible to the Prime Minister, Parliament and the public for their own behaviour and conduct, the actions of their department and its civil servants. This convention applies most particularly to the most senior members of the Government, i.e. every Secretary of State is responsible and accountable to Parliament for the actions and policies of his or her department. Thus the civil servants who provide advice are shielded from political controversy, ensuring their neutrality.

Sometimes a Minister will resign if the errors committed by their Department either warrant a 'scapegoat' or public pressure demands it. In 1982, Lord Carrington resigned as Foreign Secretary over the Argentine invasion of the Falkland Islands because he felt that his department had failed. That he should resign was felt to be the honourable thing to do. This deflected criticism from the whole government.[4]

Personal misconduct often warrants a resignation because it receives so much public attention. This was very much the case in 1963 when John Profumo, the War Minister, resigned because he had lied to Parliament over his relationship with Christine Keeler. Similarly in 1984 Cecil (now Lord) Parkinson resigned from Margaret Thatcher's Cabinet because of his affair with his secretary.

If a Minister receives the support of his or her colleagues, especially the Prime Minister, it is often the case that resignation is not required. However, recent events have shown that if public pressure is strong enough not even this can save a Minister's 'bacon'.

Example:
In 1967 James (now Lord) Callaghan did not resign as Chancellor of the Exchequer after his economic policy seemingly failed and he was forced to devalue the pound. The Prime Minister, Harold Wilson, continued to support him but moved him sideways to Home Secretary, deflating the crisis which could have forced Callaghan to resign.[5]

In the early 1990s the convention of individual responsibility has become the subject of much debate because it seemed that it was not working. A number of Ministers from John Major's Government have refused to go after either the failure of policy or personal misconduct. In 1992 David Mellor, the National Heritage Secretary, refused to resign over his extra-marital affair because he

Figure 16 David Mellor, who was forced to resign as National Heritage Secretary in 1992.

continued to enjoy the support of the Prime Minister. However, the media refused to let the issue drop, citing past instances where sexual impropriety had warranted resignations. Subsequently, David Mellor was forced to resign. Again in October 1992 the media called for the resignation of the then Chancellor of the Exchequer, Norman Lamont, because of the failure of the Government's economic policy on 'Black Wednesday', when Britain was forced to withdraw its currency from the Exchange Rate Mechanism (ERM). Norman Lamont survived this storm until a reshuffle in the summer of 1993.

Questions

1. Define collective ministerial responsibility.
2. Define individual ministerial responsibility.
3. How does individual ministerial responsibility work in practice?

7.5 | The role of the Cabinet office

The Cabinet office was established in 1916 to serve the Cabinet and today lies at the very heart of British government. It consists of a secretariat and a historical section. The secretariat consists of six smaller secretariats which service the Cabinet and its committees.

Figure 17 The Cabinet secretariat.[6]

The Cabinet secretariat
1. **The economic secretariat** – this is responsible for economic, industrial and energy policies.
2. **The overseas and defence secretariat** – this is responsible for co-ordinating information on defence and overseas policy for the Cabinet.
3. **The European secretariat** – this is responsible for dealing with EU business and is probably the machine that John Major employed to conduct an audit of EU legislation in 1994.
4. **The Home Affairs secretariat** – this is responsible for covering social policy, law and order issues, environment, education, housing and local government. This secretariat is responsible for co-ordinating the government's legislative programme.
5. **The Science and Technology secretariat** – deals with science and technology policy.
6. **The Security and Intelligence secretariat.**

The functions of the Cabinet Secretariat are:
1.   the preparation of Cabinet and Cabinet committee agendas;
2.   recording the decisions of Cabinet and its committees;
3.   the summoning of members to Cabinet meetings and other meetings when necessary;
4.   the circulation of all Cabinet papers, reports, briefs, circulars and minutes across Whitehall;
5.   following up the decisions of Cabinet.

The office is staffed by civil servants and is headed by the most senior civil servant in Whitehall, the Cabinet Secretary, who is the Prime Minister's chief administrative adviser and attends all full Cabinet meetings. In recent years, two main changes have occurred in the practices of the Cabinet office. First, outside advisers have been brought into the Cabinet office. In 1970 Edward Heath created the Central Policy Review Staff (CPRS), known as the 'Think Tank', which was a group of about fifteen to twenty outsiders, academics and business people. The CPRS was designed to undertake independent studies of particular problems for the Cabinet, with a longer-term perspective, free from departmental interference. The CPRS encountered some civil service hostility and had a far from successful career. In 1983 it was abolished by Margaret Thatcher. Second, there have been a number of accusations that the Cabinet office has fallen under the influence of the Prime Minister to an extent where charges were made during the Thatcher premiership that it was little more than a tool of the Prime Minister. This criticism, however, has proved less valid during the Major premiership.

Questions

1.   Describe the structure of the Cabinet office.
2.   What is the role of the Cabinet office?

7.6 | The debate over the existence of Cabinet government or Prime Ministerial government

This debate lies at the heart of the British system of government. It has raged since the writings of Richard Crossman were first published. Clearly the office of the Prime Minister has a concentration of power which qualifies it for comparison with the powers of a President. These comparisons have drawn on the fact that all executive power, as with a President, is concentrated in the hands of the Prime Minister, and using the recent history of the office proponents of the idea suggest that Prime Ministerial government exists.

The case for the existence of Prime Ministerial government

The term 'Prime Ministerial Government' means that

'the wide range of powers at present exercised by a British Prime Minister, both in that capacity and as Party Leader, are now so great as to ... undermine the essential role of Parliament [and] usurp some of the functions of collective Cabinet decision making ... leading to a centralisation of power into the hands of one person ... and amounting to a system of personal rule at the very heart of our parliamentary democracy.'[7]

1. There is a large body of academic opinion which believes that Prime Ministerial government exists. The accusations made by Richard Crossman head this body and present-day supporters include Tony Benn and Martin Burch.[8] These writers argue that the powers of the office elevate the Prime Minister above his colleagues. The power of appointment, dismissal, setting Cabinet agendas, chairing Cabinet and Cabinet committees, etc., all afford the Prime Minister complete, near-presidential control over the executive branch of government. Even more convincing is the recent practice of Prime Ministers who have used these powers in a presidential manner, from Harold Wilson to Margaret Thatcher.

    Example:
    Margaret Thatcher's preference for meetings with small groups of advisers from which policy would evolve is a characteristic of Presidential and not Cabinet Government. With this reliance upon small bilateral meetings to decide policy, and her command over the Cabinet system, commentators in the 1980s increasingly drew comparisons between her style of government and the characteristics of presidential government. Comments by some members of Margaret Thatcher's Cabinet increased the belief that Britain had moved to a presidential style of government.[9]

2. The Prime Minister has the absolute power to encourage policies he or she favours and kill policies he or she dislikes. The famous comment by Margaret Thatcher to Sir Geoffrey Howe at one Cabinet meeting which killed off any Cabinet discussion provides evidence for this point: 'Geoffrey, I know what you are going to recommend. And the answer is "No".'[10]

3. The marked increase in the use of private advisers and the increasing importance of the Prime Minister's Office has strengthened the Prime Minister's command over the Cabinet machine and the policy-making process. In recent years there have been examples where Cabinet Ministers have resigned as a result of the activities of these private advisers.

    Example:
    Nigel Lawson, The Chancellor of the Exchequer, in 1989.

4. As leader of the majority party in the Commons the Prime Minister is able to exercise legislative power, controlling the parliamentary agenda and the parliamentary party through the whips.
5. The power to chose the date of a general election gives Prime Ministers the power, up to a point, to decide their own fate and that of the majority of MPs. This can be used as a controlling device over each Prime Minister's own back-benchers, as John Major found in 1993 (*see Chapter 9*).
6. The sheer scale of government business has allowed Prime Ministers the opportunity of diverting decision making from a Cabinet which sits for two hours a week to a range of sub-committees where his influence over policy has increased.

The Thatcher premiership added great weight to many of these arguments especially in relation to Margaret Thacher's style, but the manner of her demise suggests that the existence of Prime Ministerial government was not as concrete as perceived (*see Chapter 6*).

The case for the existence of Cabinet government

1. There are a number of restraints on the powers of the Prime Minister which former Prime Ministers and political commentators, such as Patrick Gordon Walker,[11] believe restrain the holders of the office. These include:

(a) *Strictures of the party*: the existence of competing factions, potential rival leaders, and the Prime Minister's political performance all contribute to limit his or her exercise of power. Prime Ministers must maintain the support of their MPs to remain in office, as the events of 1990 showed.
(b) *Cabinet restraints*: He or she cannot restrict posts to certain wings of the party or ignore the younger generation. Furthermore, the power to control the Cabinet agenda has its limits, e.g. the effects of external events and the persuasive power of senior members of the Cabinet. On occasions during the Thatcher premiership the Prime Minister was forced to accept collective Cabinet decision making.

2. Peter Hennessy, in his book *Cabinet*, argues that Cabinet government is 'a putty-like concept', possessing such flexibility that 'a Prime Minister can make of it very largely what he or she will, provided colleagues do not balk at their treatment.'[12]
3. Hennessy suggests that the traditional model of Cabinet is unable to fulfil the roles that it was designed for given the modern scale of government activity. Full Cabinet cannot discuss every possible policy, every issue, or idea. Therefore in-depth discussion has been devolved to a smaller system of committees staffed by the Prime Minister and a range of Cabinet members. This is where decisions are made.

Full Cabinet considers matters of great importance and normally endorses the recommendations of its committees. Hennessy argues that we do not therefore have Prime Ministerial government, rather that we have government by formal Cabinet committees and by informal cliques of key Ministers. One may argue that this form of Cabinet government exists because Cabinet members still discuss and implement policy and co-ordinate the activities of their departments in committees.

4. The sheer size of government, which is a limiting factor on the powers of the Cabinet, is an equal restraint on the power of the Prime Minister. All Premiers must delegate simply because they cannot oversee all the work of all the government departments. Harold Wilson suggested that Prime Ministers were in a relatively weak position compared to their Secretaries of State responsible for the biggest departments. Prime Ministers cannot control every decision made in Whitehall. They can influence the major decisions but the scope of their control is, in reality, limited.

5. The Prime Minister's power varies with political events. After a general election they are strong but after a by-election defeat they are weakened. Equally their power rests on their personality. If people respect and fear you then you are more powerful. If they consider you weak they (party and Cabinet) are more likely to oppose you.

6. One of the major arguments against the existence of Prime Ministerial government is the absence of either a Prime Ministers' Department or anything comparable to the United States President's Executive Office, which is the President's own personally appointed team of advisers and specialists. The British Prime Minister only possesses a small private staff, not comparable with this large office. However moves are being made in this direction. In July 1994 John Major appointed David Hunt as a quasi-chief of staff responsible for progress chasing, enforcing order within the Cabinet machine and chairing some of the most important Cabinet Committees. This could be seen as a step towards the creation of a Prime Minister's Executive Office but such a development appears to remain some way off at the present time.[13]

One can suggest that although Margaret Thatcher's practices as Prime Minister gave rise to ideas of the death of Cabinet government, a British Prime Minister with a large majority is in a very strong position only as long as his or her party have confidence in the leadership. When this confidence disappears the Cabinet can become pre-eminent in convincing a Prime Minister that he or she should resign: 1990 showed that even an all powerful, near-presidential Prime Minister can be dismissed by the party and Cabinet. It showed that the idea of Prime Ministerial government in Britain has its limits.

But there is enough evidence on both sides of this debate to demonstrate either that Cabinet government still exists or that Prime Ministerial government has replaced it.

Evidence that Prime Ministerial government exists

1. Increased use of smaller *ad hoc* groups to discuss and decide policy – Margaret Thatcher.
2. Decline in the number of full cabinet meetings in 1980s suggesting that it was not used as the main decision-making tool – Margaret Thatcher.
3. Use of 'kitchen Cabinets' – Harold Wilson.
4. Use of Cabinet committees to decide policy, sometimes referred to full Cabinet at other times not – Margaret Thatcher and John Major.
5. Use of Prime Minister's position to control agendas, minutes and discussions – Margaret Thatcher.

   Example:
   1984 January – The Cabinet Overseas and Defence committee: The subject to be discussed was the possibility of an attempt to normalise relations with Argentina. Sir Geoffrey (now Lord) Howe is four minutes into the Foreign Office paper on the need to open exploratory talks with the Alfonsin Government. Margaret Thatcher cuts in, 'Geoffrey I know what you're going to recommend. And the answer is "No!" ' End of item : nobody argues with the boss.[14]

Evidence that Cabinet government exists

1. Cabinet was used during the 1980s to discuss major policy decisions, especially during the early part of the Thatcher premiership;
2. In 1980s Cabinet committees were used but they are part of Cabinet structure and members of the Cabinet were involved in these policy discussions.
3. Examples of where Margaret Thatcher was pressured by Cabinet colleagues to make decisions which she disliked: in 1990 over economic policy and joining the ERM.
4. The end of the Thatcher premiership saw Cabinet power exercised to remove a Prime Minister.
5. The nature of Cabinet decision-making under John Major:

- Prime Minister listens to the views of colleagues;
- an emphasis on collegiate Cabinet;
- Cabinet discussions longer;
- more frequent meetings and greater involvement in policy discussions.

Example:
The full Cabinet met on a number of occasions to prepare the Prime Minister's negotiating position before the Maastricht Summit in 1991.

Questions

1. Define Prime Ministerial and Cabinet Government.
2. What are the main differences between these two descriptions?

Essay questions

1. 'Cabinet co-ordinates and decides.' Is this still a true description of the role of the British Cabinet?
2. Assess the importance of the Cabinet committee system.
3. Is the Cabinet 'the hyphen which joins, a buckle which fastens the legislative part of the state to the executive part of the state?'
4. Does Britain have Prime Ministerial government or Cabinet government?

Essay planning

1. 'Cabinet co-ordinates and decides.' Is this still a true description of the role of the British Cabinet?

   In this essay you are being asked to discuss the role of the Cabinet as a decision maker and co-ordinator of government activity, and assess whether the Cabinet still fully performs these roles, using material contained in *sections 7.1, 7.3* and *7.6*.
   (a) Define the Cabinet.
   (b) Explain the main roles of the Cabinet, pointing out that co-ordination and decision making, are two of a series of roles.
   (c) Argue why co-ordination and decision making are so important.
   (d) Analyse whether the Cabinet still performs these roles by suggesting that the recent practices in the Executive Branch of Government have usurped these roles:
       (i) the increased use of Cabinet committees;
       (ii) the existence of Inner Cabinets;
       (iii) the use of Prime Ministerial power to reduce powers of Cabinet;
       (iv) the size of modern government versus the size of Cabinet.
   (e) You may wish to conclude by suggesting that the Cabinet remains a powerful institution, co-ordinating and deciding policy but not in the traditional sense, rather a new modern diversified and devolved way through committees, subcommittees, etc. It still sits at the pinnacle of British government and politics.

Notes and references

1. Hennessy, P. *Cabinet* (Oxford, 1986), p. 4.

2. Pimlott, B. *Harold Wilson* (London, 1992), p. 409.

3. Ibid., p. 656.

4. Thatcher, M. *The Downing Street Years* (London, 1993), pp. 185–6.

5. Pimlott, B. *Harold Wilson* (1992), p. 485.

6. Hennessy, P. *Cabinet* (London, 1986), pp. 390–2.

7. Benn. T. 'The Case for a Constitutional Premiership', *Parliamentary Affairs*, 33 (1), Winter 1980, p. 7.

8. Ibid. Benn, T.

9. Hennessy P. *Cabinet* (1986), p. 99. Students should read Ch.3, pp. 94–122.

10. Hennessy, P. *Cabinet* (1986), p. 99.

11. See Walker, P.G. *The Cabinet* (London, 1972) and a collection of new articles in King, A. *The British Prime Minister* (London, 1986)

12. Ibid. p. 4.

13. *The Guardian*, 21.07.94. See also Hennessy, P. *Whitehall* (London, 1989), p. 387.

14. Hennessy, P. *Cabinet* (1986), p. 99.

Further reading

Burch, M. 'The Demise of Cabinet Government', *Teaching Politics*, Vol. 3, No. 3, 1985.

Hennessy, P. *Cabinet* (Oxford, 1986).

Hennessy, P. 'The Secret World of Cabinet Committees', *Social Studies Review*, Vol. 1, No. 2, 1985.

Howard, A. (ed.) *The Crossman Diaries* (Hamilton, 1979).

Jones, A. 'Crichel Down Revisited', *Talking Politics*, Vol. 5, No. 3, 1993.

King, A. *The British Prime Minister* (London, 1985).

Norton, P. *Constitution in Flux* (Oxford, 1982).

Pyper, R. 'Why Ministers Resign', *Talking Politics*, Vol. 5, No. 2, 1993.

Rush, M. *The Cabinet and Policy Formulation* (London, 1984).

The Benn Tapes, BBC Radio Collection, 1994.

CHAPTER 8

The civil service

This topic is perhaps one of the most straightforward to understand and learn. Generally examination questions concern themselves with the role of the civil service and its political neutrality. However, during the 1980s a reform process began which is still continuing. These reforms have seen the civil service restructured and re-organised, so new questions will no doubt be asked which address these changes.

The civil service is one governmental system. A civil service is the body of public servants who organise and administer the state, usually appointed independently of political considerations. It serves the government of the day, implementing their policies.

Civil services exist in every state, administering the state organs and serving the government. Organising the modern state is a massive task which requires skill, experience and expertise and it is civil servants or bureaucrats who supply this. The function and powers of each country's civil service varies, but in the Western world, the bureaucracies and their officials are very powerful. In the United States the top tiers of the Federal Bureaucracy are political appointees, meaning that every time a new president takes office all the senior officials in each Department of State are replaced with his team. This can amount to over 2,000 appointments.[1] To indicate the size of the Federal Bureaucracy in the United States there is now one civil servant for every fifteen Americans.

In this chapter we shall examine:

8.1 The role of civil servants and the structure of the civil service.

8.2 Methods of recruitment.

8.3 The traditional principles of the civil service.

8.4 Post-war criticisms of the civil service and the Fulton Committee.

8.5 The debate over the neutrality of the British civil service.

8.1 | **The role of civil servants and the structure of the civil service**

The roles of civil servants throughout the world are similar, the function varying depending on the size and structure of the State.

1. Civil servants advise Ministers. In France, the United States and Britain these public servants provide Ministers with advice by sifting through all the sources of information which a bureaucracy has at its disposal, to suggest ways of implementing the Minister's policies and ideas. A modern bureaucracy has a variety of different sources of information including: planning reports, advice from planning papers, the bureaucratic experience, surveys, intelligence reports and business and foreign contacts.

2. In most countries the civil servants have been in their job for a longer period than most Ministers, and they are able to offer this experience to an inexperienced Minister. In the United States, Cabinet Ministers tend to take office with a team around them which they have chosen themselves. This includes friends and colleagues who they think will enable them to do the best possible job.

3. In addition to advising Ministers, civil servants implement the decisions and policies of Governments. In Britain, if the Government wishes to introduce a new transport policy it is the civil service who discuss the options and present them to Ministers. Once this Minister has chosen the policy option the civil servants go about implementing the decision.

4. Civil servants plan for every eventuality. When considering policies they make a whole variety of plans covering every possible option. They are planning animals. In every sphere of activity – education, economics and even foreign affairs – teams of civil servants discuss options and plan.

    Example:
    In the late 1940s and again in the late 1950s a team of Foreign Office officials reviewed the UK's worldwide position and planned a number of different foreign policy options for the UK to follow depending on how the Cold War developed.[2]

5. The British civil servants are bound by an Official Secrets Act so that they cannot discuss their work outside the office. This ensures that confidential and highly secret matters are not given out to the public, the press or to foreign powers who may use the information to the detriment of the UK's national security. Sometimes Civil Servants leak without authorisation confidential information to the press and public. If the information is covered by the Official Secrets Act action will be

taken to discover the source of the leak. This can mean that sometimes the civil servants responsible are found and prosecuted under the Official Secrets Act.

Example: *The Ponting case*
Clive Ponting, an Assistant Secretary at the Ministry of Defence, was prosecuted under Section 2 of the Official Secrets Act in 1984 for leaking classified information about the sinking of the Argentine battleship, the Belgrano *during the Falklands War, to the Labour MP, Tam Dalyell.*[3]

6. They ensure the smooth running of the bureaucratic machine.

The structure of the civil service

The civil service numbers 565,000 employees divided into administrative, executive and clerical grades,[4] and a range of specialist posts including scientists, lawyers and accountants. When one discusses the civil service, it is the highest levels of the administrative grade that are the centre of attention. This class of civil servants are described as 'Mandarins'. The administrative class is involved in the formulation of policy, the co-ordination and improvement of Government machinery and with general administration and the control of the departments of the public service.

Above the Assistant Secretary level some 3,000 higher civil servants have direct dealings with Ministers. It is they who advise and implement the policies of Ministers and it is claimed in some quarters that they make political decisions. Throughout the remainder of this chapter it is the activities of this group that we will discuss.

Questions

1. Define a civil servant.
2. What is the major role of the civil service? (Longer answer required.)

8.2 | Methods of recruitment

In Western democracies the method of recruitment differs. In most countries the civil service is unified, recruiting through standardised procedures and controlled by a single system of rules and regulations. In France most senior civil servants are graduates of the Ecole Nationale d'Administration. In the UK recruitment for the civil service is organised by the Civil Service Commission. This body is responsible for recruitment at two levels: normal entry and fast-stream entry. Qualification requirements vary from GCSEs for the lower grades to degrees for higher grades and the fast stream. The Commission is also responsible for pay and promotion.

In the Netherlands there is no national civil service. Each department has its own recruitment procedure and is distinct from other departments. In the United States public service is held in low esteem and it does not attract the most able candidates, as is the case in Britain and other parts of Europe.[5]

8.3 | **The traditional principles of the civil service**

Key term: political impartiality

This means that the civil service will serve whichever political party is in office to the best of its ability. It will offer the best advice and implement the decisions of any Minister whether he is Conservative or Labour. When the Labour Party lost the 1979 General Election the same civil servants who had served them immediately began to work with the new Conservative administration on the morning after the election.

In Britain, the civil service can be divided into three groupings: the senior administrative civil servants based in Whitehall who are responsible for the formulation of policy and have direct contact with Ministers and number approximately 3,000; the executive category who execute policy under the direction of more senior grades, and the clerical category. It is the senior category which we shall concentrate on.

This top class of civil servants have been widely admired for its competence, dedication and **political impartiality**.

Traditional principles

1. *Civil servants are permanent.* Governments and Ministers come and go but a senior civil servant may work in the same department for twenty to thirty years. They advise successive governments of different political parties and implement their decisions. The senior posts are not discretionary appointments, so ministers may not appoint people who are known to share their views as is common practice in the United States.
2. *Civil servants are politically neutral.* In theory civil servants are supposed to provide impartial advice to Ministers, outlining all the problems and objections to the policy, and providing the Minister with all the available information. Ministers then take the decisions and once the choice has been made civil servants are meant to actively promote the Minister's policies.
3. *Civil servants do not reveal their own political opinions.* This is to ensure that they have the confidence of politicians of all parties and can serve successive political masters. There are regulations prohibiting them from participating in politics or even expressing political opinions publicly.

4. Civil servants are anonymous. This is to ensure that they are not identified with particular policies, otherwise this would undermine public confidence in the civil service.

5. The doctrine of ministerial responsibility means that, in theory, Ministers are responsible to Parliament for the activities of their departments and it is the Minister who resigns from office if the actions of his Department or civil servants are found to have acted wrongly, with negligence or failed to act properly. In such cases, civil servants do not resign because they are anonymous and permanent. Civil servants are, however, accountable to Parliament.

However, since the 1920s the civil service has been criticised regarding its role in British politics and since the 1950s criticisms have arisen concerning its quality as well. Critics argue that it is civil servants and not Ministers who now take decisions and that civil servants have always had a secret agenda to protect the status quo and implement only those decisions which they think best. Furthermore, critics now question the impartiality of the civil service after so many years of Conservative government.[6]

Questions

1. Why are civil servants described as impartial?
2. Explain each of the traditional principles of the British civil service.

8.4 | Post-war criticisms of the civil service and the Fulton Committee

Criticisms of the quality of the civil service centred on a growing unease in the 1950s that the institution was inefficient and unable to meet the demands placed on Britain's economic and strategic position in the post-war world. The upper echelons of the civil service were the targets of these criticisms being accused of having an 'elitist and amateur ethos'.

1. The administrative class was accused of coming from an exclusive background – mainly upper middle-class, public school and Oxford or Cambridge educated. Upper-class attitudes were favoured, which it was claimed, led to a determination to avoid radical changes in society and a preference for conservative policies.

2. The administrative class was also accused of incompetence. Critics argued that the civil service was full of generalists, who were accused of being 'amateurs'. The fact that HM Treasury was filled with 'humanities and classics graduates' allowed these civil servants to be blamed for Britain's poor economic performance relative to some of its rivals.

These accusations of elitism and incompetence reached a climax in the middle of the 1960s and in 1966 led the Prime Minister, Harold Wilson, to appoint a committee, chaired by Lord Fulton, to examine every aspect of the civil service.

The Fulton Committee, 1968

1. Fulton argued that 'the structure and practices of the civil service had not kept up with the changing tasks placed on it'.
2. The committee agreed with the critics of the civil service that it was too parochial and out of contact with the public it served.
3. Fulton reported that the civil service :
    (a)   was too rooted in the philosophy of the 'amateur';
    (b)   possessed an overcomplicated class structure;
    (c)   ignored specialists who were given a narrow role and limited responsibilities and opportunities;
    (d)   had too few skilled managers;
    (e)   had limited contact with the community it served;
    (f)   possessed poor personnel arrangements and career structures.

4. The Commission recommended a number of reforms:
    (a)   The creation of a Civil Service Department under the control of the Prime Minister which would have wide management functions, including size and deployment of manpower, personnel management and pay and conditions, etc. It was created in 1968 but abolished by Margaret Thatcher in 1981.
    (b)   The development of greater professionalism among administrators and specialists.
    (c)   More attention to training and career management.
    (d)   The encouragement of greater mobility between the civil service and other forms of employment.
    (e)   Reform of the civil service class structure by replacing it with a single unified grading structure.

The Fulton Report was very controversial.[7] It was accused of not addressing the central issue of how policy was made, and the problems which surrounded the relationship between Ministers and civil servants. By 1980, some commentators were claiming that all of the reforms to reduce the power of the mandarins instituted as a result of Fulton had been sabotaged. Fulton was only partially successful in reforming the civil service. More successful and far-reaching reforms were to occur under Margaret Thatcher (*see sections 8.6 and 8.7*). Further reforms have been instituted under John Major, which have radically altered the nature of the British administrative machine improving its competitiveness and introducing market forces into every echelon of Whitehall.[8]

8.5 | # The debate over the neutrality of the British civil service

The post-war criticisms of the civil service and the findings of the Fulton Committee gave rise to a debate over the neutrality of the civil service which has raged ever since. Below are the arguments ranged in favour of and against the proposition that the civil service is neutral.

Arguments that the civil service is no longer neutral

The relationship between Ministers and civil servants and the role of the civil service in policy making has long been an issue of controversy. The traditional theory is that Ministers make policy decisions and that civil servants advise the Minister. They may warn or even object to his policy but once the decision has been made they administer it without objection. However, this view has been criticised because it does not reflect the nature of the true relationship. Once a policy is made it is not a simple case of implementing the policy. Implementation involves a range of political considerations on how the policy is to be applied. It is at this stage in the administrative process that arguments are levied to suggest that the civil service is not politically neutral.

1. *The size of the civil service.* There are approximately 100 government Ministers. By contrast, there are approximately 565,000 civil servants, the majority of which play no role in policy making, but with such a small number of Ministers in each department it is difficult to see how they are able to control the activities of their group of administrative civil servants which heavily outweigh the ministerial team.

2. *The permanency of the civil service.* Ministers tend to last two or three years on average in their position before being moved on. During a ministerial career a Minister can move through four or five different departments and so they lack the depth of knowledge that civil servants possess, having spent twenty-five years moving through one department. Moreover, Ministers usually enter an office with a task to fulfil, a policy to implement which somewhat restricts their vision and interests. Therefore, in a great many ways, Secretaries of State rely on their civil servants to deal with many of the processes and functions of the department. The Scott Inquiry into the Matrix Churchill case has shown how Ministers are not made aware of every single decision taken by the civil servants in their department. This includes John Major, who claimed that while he was Foreign Secretary for three months in 1989, he was not told of policy changes by his senior civil servants.[9]

These revelations add weight to the opinion that civil servants are 'on top, not on tap' for Ministers.

3. *The role of official committees.* The senior administrative civil service have developed a system of departmental and inter-departmental committees which mirror the system of ministerial committees. These committees are designed to co-ordinate the activities of Whitehall and provide Ministers with sound advice and planning. Critics have suggested that these are policy-making committees which examine problems and make a series of recommendations to Ministers. They argue that these committees examine a wide range of possible policy options but present to Ministers a limited set of choices. Ministers have no part to play on these committees and are expected to make a decision on the limited information provided in short periods. Critics argue that inexperienced Ministers rely too heavily on the advice from these committees on which the civil servants indulge in political decision making.

4. *Secrecy and obstruction.* Ministers past and present have spoken of the obstructive techniques which civil servants have employed to prevent the Minister from implementing his policy as quickly as possible. This conflict stems from the fact that these two groups have two different agendas. Ministers have a short-term agenda to successfully implement reforms, e.g. Norman Tebbit and Trade Union Reform, Michael Heseltine and Inner City resurrection. Ministers look for speed and success whereas civil servants have a long-term perspective and wish to develop a programme of continuity. Critics argue that these two perspectives are incompatible and gives rise to conflicts between Ministers and civil servants.

Politicians and political commentators have also complained that the civil service is overly secret, with Britain being one of the most secretive states in the Western world, and it is claimed that civil servants have developed a high degree of secrecy for its own sake.

5. *Hostility of politicians.* Many senior politicians, some of whom had held high office, claim that they found the administrative grades of the civil service to be either hostile to government policies or determined to have their own policy implemented. Peter Shore, who served in the Labour Cabinets of the 1970s referred to civil servants as 'permanent politicians', and other members of Labour's Cabinets in the 1960s and 1970s, Richard Crossman and Barbara Castle, have claimed instances of deliberate civil service obstruction.

Hostility has not just come from the left wing; Conservatives have been known to criticise the civil service for obstruction. In 1973 Nicholas Ridley, a junior Minister at the Department of Trade and Industry, accused his civil servants of 'procrastination, inactivity and sabotage' in its response to a more commercial and independent role for the nationalised industries. Margaret Thatcher came into office suspicious of the civil service and contemptuous of the attitude, expressed by a senior civil servant, that its job was now 'simply to manage the orderly decline of Britain'.

6. *Civil service hostility to innovations in the machinery of government.* The civil service has been accused by a number of politicians of being hostile to any form of innovation by Prime Ministers and their colleagues. Innovation can take a variety of forms including the introduction of private advisers to reform of the service itself, e.g. Next Steps – see later in this chapter.

The civil service has jealously guarded its right to be the main adviser to politicians and it has shown itself hostile to the introduction of private advisers.

Relations between the senior civil servants based in No. 10 and the special advisors brought into No. 10 by successive Prime Ministers has also been a source of friction.

7. *The longevity of governments.* Recently, fears have been voiced by leading Labour politicians that civil service neutrality has been impaired by the longevity of Conservative government in Britain. Some suspect that were the Opposition to be the next government its members would encounter a hostile and difficult senior civil service in Whitehall. They believe that the senior civil service having served one political master for so long would have great difficulty dealing with the demands of a Labour Government.[10] This criticism is refuted by the civil service, who claim that even after long period of one-party government it is still able to serve a new political master equally well.

Critics have concluded that the senior ranks of the civil service have at their disposal a range of devices and techniques by which they can thwart the plans of Ministers. There is a feeling that they often have their own agenda which they wish to see implemented and are able to manoeuvre unsuspecting 'short termist' Ministers into their ways of thinking.

Arguments that the civil service continues to be neutral

The civil service has attempted to defend itself against the charges made that it is no longer politically neutral. There are many former Ministers, senior civil servants and Prime Ministers who believe that the case against their neutrality has been overstated. There are two arguments put forward which are used to claim continuing neutrality.

1. *Loyalty to the department and to the civil service itself.*
   Senior civil servants are regarded as loyal servants of the State. Their loyalty in the first instance is to the Crown and their profession. The civil service has a long history of impartial service which propagates itself. Many senior civil servants have been attached to one department for most of their working lives and a sense of loyalty can develop which is useful for Ministers. Moreover, their job is to offer the best advice and alternative ways of implementing policies.

2. *The ability of the civil service to serve different governments.*
   Supporters claim that the senior Civil Service has demonstrated throughout British post-war history its ability to serve Conservative and Labour governments without prejudice or bias. In 1979, it was the same civil servants who served Lord Callaghan who advised Margaret Thatcher when she became Prime Minister on the day after the General Election. Moreover, the civil service have implemented policies which have been the reverse of previous governments: privatisation has been carried out by the same civil servants who implemented nationalisation.

Conclusions

The arguments over the neutrality of the civil service rage on. During the late 1980s a number of civil servants who were members of Margaret Thatcher's No. 10 office demonstrated a loss of neutrality and provided ammunition for critics. Sir Bernard Ingham, Margaret Thatcher's Chief Press Secretary and Sir Charles Powell, Margaret Thatcher's Private Secretary both became ardent supporters of her regime and were accused of becoming 'politicised'.

There is no clear answer to the question of political bias. Evidence can be used to strengthen the arguments on both sides but one can suggest that ultimately the civil service is conservative with a small 'c', and to some extent the evidence for politicisation has always been slight. Rumour is far more potent in these arguments than fact.

Some critics of the present system argue that it may be better to replace the present top tier of civil servants with a team of appointed administrative experts and policy advisers. This would politicise the senior ranks of civil service in each department and be similar to the system that operates in the United States. Every time the government changed the top tier of the civil service would also change. The advantages of this system would be that these senior civil servants would have a better, closer, working relationship with Ministers, driven by the same philosophy as the politicians to implement the same agenda. However, the disadvantages include the blurring of the lines of executive responsibility to Parliament and the breakdown of the constitutional principle of ministerial responsibility.

Questions

1. (a) What recent changes have taken place in the practice of appointing senior civil servants?
   (b) What are the implications behind these changes?
2. Outline the case for the neutrality of the civil service.

Essay questions

1. Has the notion of a politically neutral career civil service come under threat?
2. Has the civil service been politicised?

Essay planning

2. Has the civil service been politicised?
   This essay is asking you to use the materials in section 8.5 to argue whether the civil service is politicised. The question does not specify a time from when 'politicisation' has taken place, so you must include reference to the origins of this debate in your introduction.

(a) Define the term 'politicised' and explain the traditional characteristics of the civil service.

(b) Present a summary of the arguments in favour of, and against, the idea that the civil service has been politicised.

Stress that this debate has become more topical because of the following factors:

(i) The influence of Margaret Thatcher on the appointment of senior civil servants.

(ii) The Conservative Government's reforms of the civil service.

(iii) The fears expressed by many opposition MPs that after so many years of Conservative Government the civil service has become too exposed to one master and has lost much of its political neutrality.

(c) You may conclude by suggesting that the neutrality of civil service has become tainted in the past few years, but that a question mark has existed over this neutrality for some time. Use the material from Hugo Young's book *No Minister,* to back up your argument.

Notes and references

1.   Burch, M. 'The Next Step for Britain's Civil Service', *Talking Politics*, Vol. 5, No. 3, 1993.

2.   Selby, I. 'The Permanent Under-Secretary's Committee and Foreign Policy Planning, 1949–1953.' M. Phil Thesis 1991, Cambridge University.

3.   McDonald, O. *The Future of Whitehall* (London, 1992), pp. 111–14 and Hennessy, P. *Whitehall* (London, 1989), pp. 344–5.

4.   *The Sunday Times*, 19.09.93.

5.   Hague, R. et al. *Comparative Government and Politics: An Introduction* (London, 1992), pp. 351–3.

6.   *The Sunday Telegraph*, 14.08.94.

7.   Ibid, pp. 190–9.

8.   Students should read Birch, M. 'The Civil Service Reforms', *Talking Politics*, Vol. 5, No. 3, 1993.

9.   *The Times*, 18.01.94.

10.   McDonald, O. *The Future of Whitehall* (1992), p. 87.

Further reading

Burch, M. 'The Civil Service Reforms', *Talking Politics*, Vol. 5, No. 3, 1993.

Dewry, C. and Butcher, T. *The Civil Service Today* (London, 1988).

Hennessy, P. *Whitehall* (London, 1989).

Kellner, P. and Crowther-Hunt, Lord *The Civil Servants* (London, 1980).

McDonald, O. *The Future of Whitehall* (London, 1992).

CHAPTER 9

Britain and the European Union

T
he European Union (EU) has become one of the most central and important topics in the domestic political agenda of the United Kingdom over the past twenty years. Since 1973 the influence which the EU exerts on the daily lives of every citizen of the UK has gradually increased. For example, EU legislation now regulates matters as diverse as the size of the apples we may buy and our freedom of movement across the Continent. The **sovereignty** (*see Chapter 1*) of every nation-state which has become a member of the EU has been reduced to varying degrees.

By signing the Treaty of Rome member governments have agreed that the institutions of the EU can make binding decisions for the whole EU. This means that some decision-making powers have been transferred from London, Madrid, Athens, and so on, to Brussels. Nation-states have agreed to a reduction of their sovereign power. But the problem for these states is that as the EU evolves and moves towards a system of greater integration and co-operation, more and more power is transferred from the periphery (i.e. member states) to the centre, Brussels. The problem of reduced sovereignty is the essence of this topic for examination purposes: to what extent has British sovereignty been reduced through membership of the EU?

This chapter will cover:

9.1   The history and development of the EU.

9.2   The institutions of the EU.

9.3   The British Parliament and the EU.

9.4   Britain and Europe in the 1980s.

9.5   Britain and Europe in the 1990s.

9.6   Conclusions: The future direction of the EU – Britain at the Heart of Europe?

Students should pay particular attention to the institutions of the EU and the major developments since 1973 because these are popular short answer questions on most examination papers.

9.1 | The history and development of the EU, 1957–73

Key concepts: supranationalism

This is power exercised by international institutions to make majority vote decisions that are binding upon all member states. It involves the transfer of decision-making authority in prescribed areas from member governments to a central body, e.g. Britain to Brussels. Members must accept supranational decisions or withdraw from the system. This idea in effect establishes a limited federal system with powers divided between two levels.

The present European Union began life as the European Economic Community (EEC) in 1957 with the signing of the Treaty of Rome by six continental European countries; the then Federal Republic of Germany, France, Italy, Belgium, the Netherlands and Luxemburg. In creating this union, these nation-states created a **supranational organisation**.

The reasons for the formation of the EEC were:

1. a desire for co-operation in order to achieve peace and economic prosperity after the ravages of the Second World War;
2. an attempt to keep the Federal Republic of Germany in the Western camp in the developing Cold War;
3. a widely held belief by the post-war leaders of Europe in the advantages of European co-operation as a result of the Marshall Plan of the late 1940s.

The primary consideration of politicians such as Robert Schuman, the French Foreign Minister in May 1950, was to reconstruct Europe in a form which would avoid the conditions which resulted in the Second World War. Economic and social co-operation and integration across the Continent were seen by both the Europeans and the Americans as a way of ensuring a peaceful future for Europe.[1]

The first step taken towards the formation of the European Union was the creation of the European Coal and Steel Union in 1952. This integrated Western Europe's coal and steel industries. At this time federalist ideas concerning the future of Europe became fashionable and the Schuman Plan was one of a series of schemes which were proposed in the early part of the 1950s.

The aims of the Treaty of Rome were:

1. The eventual creation of a 'common market' between the member states.
2. The elimination of trade barriers among community countries.
3. The ability for capital and persons to move freely within the community.

The idea of a federal Europe and the creation of a single market have their origins in the 1950s, and not the 1980s as it is often suggested today.

In the 1960s the six countries of the European Economic Community (EEC) underwent an economic boom. The success of

Key concepts: European Coal and Steel Union

The first of the original three communities which led to the establishment of the European Union. The Coal and Steel Union was created in 1951 with the signing of the Treaty of Paris and was designed to co-ordinate the policies of member states in the fields of coal and steel production, sales, etc.

the community proved to be an attractive draw to other European states such as Britain and Denmark, who wished to partake of this economic prosperity. British entry into the EEC in 1961 and 1967 failed because of French suspicions of Britain's commitment to the European idea and its special relationship with the United States. President de Gaulle was the architect of Britain's failure to gain entry and when he left office in 1969 the way was clear for Britain to apply again.[2] In 1972 Edward Heath, the Conservative Prime Minister, signed the Treaty of Accession and Parliament passed the European Communities Act later that year, allowing Britain to join on 1 January 1973.[3]

Questions

1. What were the aims of the Treaty of Rome?
2. What was the European Coal and Steel Union?

9.2 | The institutions of the EU

The EU is composed of four institutions, the European Commission, the Council of Ministers, the European Parliament and the European Court.

The European Commission

The European Commission is the civil service of the EU but it is a political institution and, unlike the UK home civil service, it makes political decisions.

Composition and role

1. The Commission is composed of twenty-one European Commissioners who are given specific policy areas to deal with in the same way that Cabinet Ministers in the UK are given responsibility for departments.
2. Each Commissioner is nominated to serve for a period of four years by the member state which they are to represent. On appointment they are expected to become enthusiastic Europeans and act independently of their home governments.
3. Each European Commissioner is responsible for a certain EU policy area, such as agriculture or trade.
4. A Commission President is chosen by the European Council and is responsible for co-ordinating the work of the Commissioners and for directing policy for the advancement of the EU.

5.   All Commissioners are subject to a veto vote by the European Parliament.

Functions

1.   The Commission prepares legislation and policy initiatives for the Union on a wide variety of topics ranging from the quality of Europe's drinking water to safety regulations on car ferries. Annually the Commission passes between 4,000 and 5,000 pieces of legislation.

     Example:
     The Clean Beaches Directive. This directive was designed to clean up Europe's bathing beaches. Those beaches which meet the criteria of the directive are given an award which acknowledges and publicises the cleanliness of the beach. A guide to the cleanest beaches in Europe is published annually by the Commission.[4]

2.   The Commission is able to propose to the Council of Ministers development policies for the Community's further expansion. These are considered by the Council of Ministers, which either approves, modifies or rejects its initiatives.

3.   The Commission manages the majority of funds and common policies which form the EU budget.

4.   The Commission ensures that EU rules and principles are followed and implemented by the member states. Where a rule is broken or not implemented, the Commission is responsible for addressing the matter with the member state. If the member state fails to comply with the Commission's request, the matter can be referred to the European Court. Any judgement from the European Court is binding on the member country and the whole EU.

     Example:
     Britain failed to import French UHT milk at the prescribed quantity in the early 1980s. The administrative procedures being used to delay importation were held by the European Court to be contrary to the ideas of a free market and free competition, contained in the Treaty of Rome. Therefore Britain was forced to allow UHT milk into the UK at the agreed rate.[5]

5.   A Commissioner can bring transgressions of EU rulings to the attention of the European Court.

6.   The Commission acts as a mediator between member states and as an external representative and negotiator between the EU and other nation-states.

     Example:
     The Commissioners responsible for agriculture and trade were the EU representatives and negotiators at the world trade talks known as the Uruguay round of GATT (General Agreements on Tariffs and Trade).

This system has worked well, with all commissioners leaving their national identity at home on becoming members of the European Commission. In Britain some commissioners have been seen by some Prime Ministers as 'going native'. This means that they have become too enthusiastic for the European idea; Margaret Thatcher believed this of Sir Leon Brittan after he took up his post.

The Commission in recent years has become the originator of ideas for the creation of a 'Federal Europe' and a large array of regulations, many of which have been castigated as trivial and absurd by the British press. Since the late 1980s, under its French President, Jacques Delors, the Commission has become unpopular with many of the citizens of Britain and other Union members because of its enthusiasm for federalism, and its trivial legislation.

Figure 18 Jacques Delors

Examples:
The classification of the British sausage as a non-sausage, and the rule that a carrot should be classified as a fruit. The Commission is launching a public relations exercise over the next few years in order to restore a credible public image.

The Council of Ministers

The Council of Ministers is the major decision-making organisation of the EU. The Council is composed of Ministers from each of the member countries.

Composition
This body is not a single institution, but a collection of different subject councils, e.g. agriculture, finance, employment, which the responsible Minister of each member state attends.

Example:
The British Secretary of State for Employment will attend a Council meeting of EU Employment Ministers.

Functions
1. It approves or rejects the ideas presented to it by the Commission. Directives and regulations for the whole EU are agreed upon in Council meetings.
2. The Council of Ministers has the power to revise the Commission's proposals.
3. Decisions of the Council depended upon unanimity until the Single European Act, 1986 came into force. This allowed individual members to veto any proposal which they considered was against their national interest.

The Single European Act, 1986 provided for majority decision making which means that decisions can now be decided by a majority of the Ministers present. Individual member states have thus lost further power to this European institution because it is now possible for Britain or Italy to be overruled in the Council.

Example:
*In May 1993, Britain was overruled in the Council meeting of
employment Ministers on the imposition throughout the EU of the
principle of a forty-eight-hour working week.*[6]

4. The Council is responsible for the further development and
    direction of the EU. It is a meeting place for Ministers to
    discuss concerns, differences, policy ideas and crises.
5. The President of the Council is provided in rotation by a
    different member country every six months. The Presidency of
    the Council allows each member country the opportunity of
    influencing the direction in which it would like to see the EU
    develop.

The European Council

This is the meeting of the heads of government/state of the
member countries, which convenes twice a year. They are often
presented as European 'Summit' meetings in the press and are the
forum where the most important decisions are made.

Example:
*The Maastricht Treaty was negotiated and signed at a European Council
Meeting in December 1991.*

These meetings tend to overshadow the normal Council meetings
between various Ministers, which are the workhorses of the EU
decision-making process.

The European Parliament

Composition

This Parliament consists of 567 members directly elected by the
peoples of Europe, every five years. The UK has eighty-seven Euro-
MPs.[7] The last election was held in 1994.

The European Parliament is not a legislative body in the same way
as the British Parliament. European legislation is prepared and
controlled by the Commission and the Council of Ministers has the
power to revise the Commission's proposals.

Functions and Powers

The functions and powers of the European Parliament are:

1. *Scrutiny:* The Parliament has eighteen standing committees
    which can examine the work of the Commission and the
    Council of Ministers. The Committees prepare reports which
    represent their views on the Commission's proposals to the
    Council of Ministers. These are called 'opinions'.
2. *Veto power:* It can accept or reject the EU budget. This means
    that the budget can be heavily scrutinised and if unpopular,

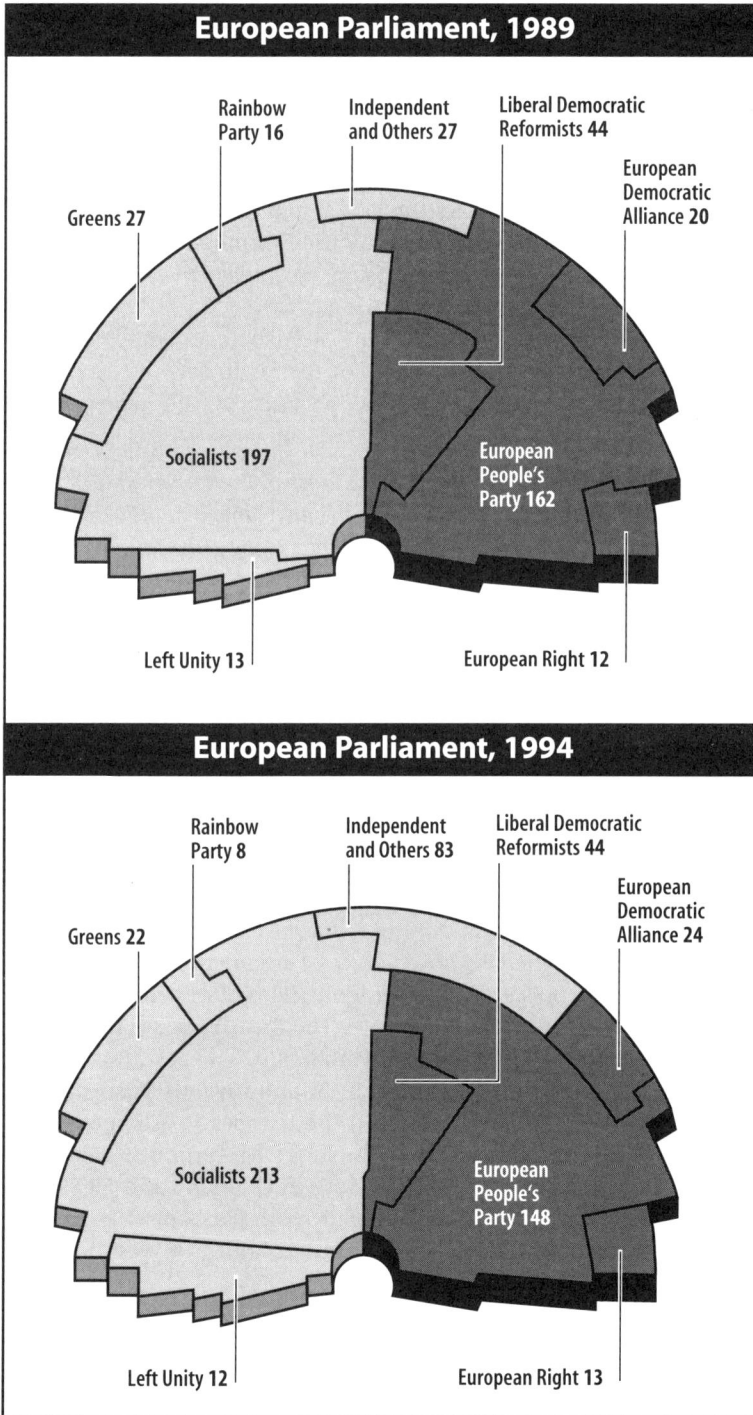

Figure 19 The European Parliament, 1989 and 1994.[8]

the Parliament can force the Commission to redraft its proposals. In the 1980s the Parliament began to assert its power and rejected the budget five times.

3. *Dismissive power:* The Parliament can dismiss the Commission by a two-thirds majority.

4. *'Co-operative procedure':* This was introduced through the Single European Act and allows the Parliament to offer amendments to drafts of legislation created by the Commission. In its first year of operation the Commission accepted 70% of the Parliament's suggestions.

5. *Debative function:* The Parliament can debate an issue, raising public awareness and the need for the EU to act.

    Example:
    A debate in June 1993 on nuclear waste dumping in Britain, was tabled by a British Member of the European Parliament (MEP), to highlight the risks associated with the large amounts of toxic waste imported into the UK, in the hope of provoking some form of EU action.

6. *Representative function:* The Parliament is composed of 567 members who represent the interests of their constituents in Brussels. MEPs like MPs speak on behalf of their constituents in the Parliament and elsewhere. They conduct surgeries and campaign on behalf of their constituents.

During the 1980s the Parliament was seen to be on the periphery of the European system. Its powers were limited and it was unable to define its role. However, since the Maastricht Treaty and with a new intake of MEPs after the parliamentary elections in 1994 it has become more active and is carving out a powerful role for itself within the EU.[9] In the UK, however, the Parliament has not been taken seriously. MEPs are unknown political figures who appear to wield little power in the public mind. The British press hardly ever report on debates in the European Parliament. The best illustration of the apathetic attitude that exists in Britain towards this institution is the very low turnout in the European parliamentary elections (36.5% in 1994).[10] This compares with turnouts elsewhere in these elections of 74.8% in Italy, 58% in Germany and 53.5% in France.[11] Many British MEPs see the European Parliament as a career stepping stone into 'the more serious power house' of Westminster.

Furthermore, the main political parties in Britain tend to use the European elections, which since 1979 have fallen conveniently between general elections, as indicators of their chances of winning a general election. It is only the smaller parties such as the SNP and Plaid Cymru which seem to regard the European elections as serious political opportunities. The Maastricht Treaty attempts to increase the role of the Parliament in the hope of correcting the public apathy that is directed towards it (*see section 9.3*).

The European Court

Composition

The European Court is composed of seventeen judges who are assisted by six advocates-general. These officials are appointed for six-year terms. The Court is the Community's supreme judicial authority and it is responsible for:

1. ensuring that each member observes Union law by interpreting the Treaties which created the EU and enforcing their legal obligations on the member states. The Court is responsible for deciding if a policy or action taken by a national government or the Commission/Council of Ministers is incompatible with EU law;
2. offering its clarification of EU law on request from a national court;
3. under the terms of the Maastricht Treaty the Court now has the power to fine member states who do not fulfil their legal obligations.

In relation to national sovereignty the Court is important because its decisions can override member states' domestic courts and legislatures. Over the past twenty-five years the Court has established the Community's legal order. Perhaps its most famous case is *Costa v. NEL, 1964*, where it ruled that no law unilaterally passed by a member state after joining could take precedence over Union legislation. Each individual member state's sovereignty is limited by this interpretation, which means that EU law is supreme over domestic law. Britain has suffered a number of times at the hands of the European Court for transgressions of EU rulings.

Questions

1. What is the role of the the European Commission?
2. What are the functions of the Council of Ministers?
3. What is the role of the EU Court?
4. (a) What are the powers of the European Parliament?
    (b) Does the European Parliament need reform?

9.3 | The UK Parliament and the EU

Through membership of the EU, Britain became subject to a vast amount of new legislation which did not need to be approved again by its Parliament. The volume of this legislation has grown and today thousands of pieces of legislation are created every year. The Westminster Parliament has attempted to scrutinise some of this legislation since 1973 via the Select Committee on European

Legislation. This committee categorises documents coming from the EU in terms of their political importance and recommends certain items for debate by the whole House of Commons. This Committee has limited powers and other Select Committees have proved far more effective in scrutinising EU affairs and legislation.

Example:
The Treasury and Civil Service Select Committee examined the results of British membership of the Exchange Rate Mechanism (ERM).

9.4 | Britain and Europe in the 1980s

Britain's relationship with the EU during the 1980s was dominated in the early part of the decade by rows over the UK's budgetary contribution and towards the end of the decade by the 'Federal' debate. Consequently Britain has been perceived by many on the Continent as a 'reluctant European'. The main creator of this image was Margaret Thatcher and her attitude towards the 'bureaucrats of Brussels'.[12]

Margaret Thatcher and the EU Budget

Margaret Thatcher came to power in 1979 with a mandate to reduce Britain's contribution to the EC budget. In 1979 the then EEC was an unfamiliar graft onto British political life; that year only 31.8% of the population voted in the European parliamentary elections, and Margaret Thatcher used this public suspicion of Europe to begin her attack on the EU.

In November 1979 at the European Council Summit in Dublin she told fellow heads of government that the UK budgetary contribution was too high and that she wanted a reduction of £1,000 million. The summit concluded by offering a reduction of £350 million but this was rejected by the British. During the Luxembourg summit in April 1980, the reduction offer was increased to £760 million but again she rejected it. At a meeting of the Council of Foreign Ministers later that year a substantial cut was agreed but Margaret Thatcher was not satisfied and the confrontation continued until the Fontainebleau Summit in June 1984, where the EU leaders agreed that Britain would receive a rebate on its budgetary contribution of 66%. This was the goal that Margaret Thatcher had aimed for, but this long campaign damaged Britain's position within the EU and convinced her that she could get her own way in Europe. These factors account for her strong resistance to moves towards greater European integration which began to surface in the mid-1980s.[13]

The Single European Act, 1986

The Single European Act was passed by the Westminster Parliament in 1986.

Its aim was:

1. to create a free internal market in the Union by the end of 1992. The member nations were committed to adapting or removing many distinct national regulations, e.g. immigration controls, with the objective of creating common competitive conditions throughout the EU;
2. to change the constitution of the Council of Ministers and introduce the principle of majority voting on a range of issues. This meant that any member may now be overruled on a proposal being unable to veto (as had previously been the case) a policy with which it disagreed.

   ### Example:
   In May 1993 the UK experienced the consequences of majority voting when the other members of the Council of Employment Ministers voted in favour of the introduction of a forty-eight-hour working week throughout the EU.

The Act's passage through Westminster was characterised by poorly attended debates. The consequences of the Act were not fully appreciated either by MPs or Margaret Thatcher. It was a serious attempt to revive ideas on economic and monetary union and in fulfilment of this, a step towards greater economic integration. These implications were not realised in Britain until Jacques Delors, the French President of the Commission, outlined a plan for the Community's future in April 1989.

The Delors Plan

This created a three-stage plan for progress towards *economic and monetary union*. Delors claimed that this flowed directly from the Single European Act.

- *Stage One* would break down the remaining barriers to opening up free trade and access to markets across the EU. All member countries would become members of the Exchange Rate Mechanism (ERM) of the European monetary system. This would mean that the exchange rates of member states would be sustained in a stable relationship creating fairer trading conditions.

- *Stage Two* demanded the creation and operation of a common monetary policy and a European economic planning machinery.

- *Stage Three* transferred even greater control of national budgets to Brussels, creating a single currency and a central bank to perform similar functions to those of the Bank of England for the whole of the Union.

During 1989 and 1990 there were EU-wide discussions on the economic and political union proposed by the Delors Plan. Margaret Thatcher responded unenthusiastically in 1988 at Bruges defending her vision of 'co-operation between independent sovereign states'. She expressed distaste for the concentration of power in Brussels, at the 'centre of a European conglomerate'. She viewed the creation of a **federal** structure in Europe as a hideous socialist idea. This speech established her as a leading Euro-sceptic and this position was one of the factors that eventually led to her downfall.

The discussions and summit meeting concerning greater integration, during the period 1988 to 1991, led to the signing of the Maastricht Treaty.[14]

The Exchange Rate Mechanism (ERM)

The exchange rate mechanism (ERM) is an attempt to create a stable system of currency exchange rates for the member countries. For the major Western trading countries it is important that they have a system of credible exchange rates, otherwise a lack of confidence in their currencies will undermine trading positions and damage the trading system.

The ERM is designed to give confidence, security and predictability to each member state's currency exchange rate. It was designed to end fluctuations and uncertainty in exchange rates which imposed increasing problems for the movement of goods and services within the EU. It requires that members keep their currencies with prescribed exchange value bands by using domestic interest rates as a means of controlling the value of the currency within each band. Currencies of approximate value are grouped into different bands giving the union a stable system of exchange rates for trading and other purposes. The British pound was placed in a band with the German Mark. The ERM was seen by many in Europe as part of a wider European Monetary System and as a staging post on the way to a fully fledged European **economic and monetary union**.

Margaret Thatcher was not in favour of the ERM but certain members of her Cabinet pushed for Britain to join in October 1990. John Major, then Chancellor of the Exchequer and Douglas Hurd, the Foreign Secretary, were hardly Euro-enthusiasts, but were prepared to let the process of integration evolve and to take a more constructive line in Europe than their leader. In 1989 Margaret Thatcher lost her 'unassailable' Chancellor, Nigel Lawson, and her

---

Key concepts: federalism

During the late 1980s and more recently in this decade many Conservative, and some Labour MPs have expressed concerns that the EU may become a federal structure. This would mean that the institutions of the EU would become responsible for major policy-making areas for the whole of the EU, e.g. defence and macro-economic policy. The British Treasury would not be responsible for organising the British budget, rather this would be done in Brussels. These MPs believed that the national institutions of each member state would have a greatly diminished role and that the EU would become an all-powerful bureaucracy. This anti-federalist sentiment was widely expressed during the debates over the Maastricht Treaty in the House of Commons. Critics believed that the provisions of this Treaty would take Europe a step further towards the creation of a federal government.

Key concepts: economic and monetary union

The eventual aim of the EU is to form from the member states a single economic bloc, with a single economic policy and common currency, administered from Brussels.

economic adviser Sir Alan Waters, in the damaging debate over Britain's membership of the ERM and, by implication, her attitude towards greater European integration.[15]

With Britain's entry into the ERM the European economic debate then turned to the issue of a single currency, the Ecu. Under Margaret Thatcher, Britain was opposed to any such move but John Major drew up a plan for an Ecu which might one day be introduced across the EU replacing national currencies, if the people of Europe wished it.

After the Rome Summit (European Council) in 1990, during which Margaret Thatcher followed the Cabinet line, she made a Cabinet-endorsed statement to the House of Commons. This was a neutral statement designed to contain the Prime Minister's own attitudes, but in response to questions on her statement Margaret Thatcher expressed her true feelings, revealing her complete distaste for a single currency with a resounding 'No, no, no'. This set in motion the events which led to the end of her premiership and the elevation of John Major into Number 10.[16]

Questions

1. (a) What are the aims of the Delors Plan?
   (b) What was Margaret Thatcher's attitude to the Delors Plan?
2. Describe the role of the ERM.
3. What is the Single European Act?

9.5 | Britain and Europe in the 1990s

John Major

Upon taking office John Major presented some of his ideas for the way in which he wanted to develop Britain while Prime Minister. On the issue of Europe he was cautious. The Conservative Party beneath the surface was then, and is now, split into two factions on Europe. He was mindful that he owed his position to this European problem. Major stated his aim of placing Britain at the 'heart of Europe'. This had different meanings to both sides of his party; to the Euro-sceptics it meant that Britain would be placed at the centre of the integration debate to delay and limit ideas on European Union, and to Euro-enthusiasts this statement meant that Britain would become an enthusiastic and committed member of the EU. When he attended the Maastricht summit in December 1991, John Major had to balance these two opinions to achieve a deal on the future of Europe that was acceptable to both wings of his party. He was far less committed to the project of economic, monetary and political union than either Neil Kinnock or Paddy Ashdown and the outcome was a treaty which accommodated British reservations.

John Major returned from this summit having deleted from the draft treaty all reference to a federal Europe, replacing this phrase with an expressed intention to move towards an 'ever closer union', and a series of fashionable opt-outs on some clauses. He heralded the deal as the best possible outcome for Britain and the EU.[17]

The Maastricht Treaty

The Maastricht Treaty was greeted by *The Economist* as,

'a step forward for the European Union on a par with the Treaty of Rome which created it 34 years ago. The treaty, one part covering economic and monetary union (EMU) and the other, political union – creates a so called European Union and sets its course for the years ahead.'[16]

The Treaty was the result of long-term discussions and negotiations, and two inter-governmental conferences, aimed at pushing the EU forward to meet the fresh challenges of Europe – i.e. the Single European Act and its results.

The Maastricht Treaty contains several important ideas:

1. It creates a European Union, with a common citizenship for all the peoples of member states.
2. It creates two more 'pillars' of activity for the EU which will be conducted on an inter-governmental basis, i.e. between governments, because not all members wanted to give the present institutions of the EU more power. These two new areas of activity are:
    (a)   a common foreign and security policy
    (b)   common home affairs and justice policy
3. It creates the principle of 'subsidiarity', which means that decisions are to be taken at the lowest level, compatible with efficiency and democracy. Only those decisions which are strictly necessary should be taken at the centre, i.e. Brussels. This returns to member states some decision-making power which they had previously lost to Brussels.
4. A new Committee of the Regions is to be created in response to the growing feeling in many member states that the regions of Europe should have a greater say in the EU's future. The Committee is designed to give the regions of Europe a new voice through which they can speak, and acknowledges the desire in some parts of the EU to give greater roles to the regions, e.g. Wales, and the Basque Region of Spain.
5. It lays down a timetable and a procedure for creating an economic and monetary union.

6. It establishes the idea of European citizenship with new, albeit limited, rights shared by all members of the EU.

The Treaty also:

1. gives new powers to the European Parliament to amend European legislation and even veto it, and the Parliament has increased financial scrutiny powers. These include:
    (a) the right to ask the Commission to give evidence regarding spending and financial control, with the Commission now being expected to act on the decisions and observations of the Parliament;
    (b) the Commission must now give financial assurances that new proposals which involve spending can be met within the existing budgets.
2. creates an **EU Ombudsman** to deal with maladministration, to whom citizens may complain.
3. creates new powers for the EU to enforce certain social rights and obligations, e.g. – the Social Charter. This was adopted in 1989 by all member states except the UK. It is an agreement to create a minimum right to employment, sexual equality, freedom of information and other social improvements throughout the EU. It was incorporated into the Maastricht Treaty in 1991 (Britain refused to accept this so it was put into a separate protocol signed by the eleven other members);
4. attempts to tighten up controls on Union finances by enhancing the role and powers of the European Court of Auditors to the status of a full institution of the EU.[18]

This next section will deal with the most important aspects of the Treaty in detail.

The aims of economic and monetary union and the timetable

The Maastricht Treaty aims to create a single usable currency which will be to the benefit of citizens and business by removing the uncertainty of exchange rate fluctuations. It suggests that a single currency will improve Europe's economic position, providing a stronger currency to compete with the Japanese yen and the United States dollar.

The timetable is divided into three stages:

Stage One

This began on 1 July 1990, with action being taken to improve co-operation and co-ordination between member states in economic and monetary fields. This means that individual governments had to begin putting into place programmes to achieve the **convergence** of all the economies of the member states. This stage was launched under existing EU powers.

Key concepts: regionalism

This suggests that national governments should allocate many of their roles and powers to smaller governing units based upon regional areas, e.g. Yorkshire or Cornwall, giving power back to the people. The concept also means that nations situated within a geographical area or sharing common concerns can co-operate with each other through a limited membership organisation to meet military, political or economic problems, e.g. NATO or the EU.

Key concepts: convergence

In the European context this is the policy which will lead to the progressive alignment of the economic policies of EU members with the intention of creating a set of similar and interdependent economies across Europe.

Example: Union members joining the ERM.

Stage Two

This began on 1 January 1994 with the establishment of the European Monetary Institute, which will:

1. promote co-ordination of member states' economic policies to bring about EMU;
2. strengthen co-operation between the national central banks.

Since 1994 each member should be following policies which will lead to greater economic convergence.

These criteria are:

1. price stability and a rate of inflation no more than 1.5% above the average three best performing member states;
2. interests rates should not be more than 2% above the average of the best performing member states over the previous twelve months;
3. there should be no excessive government deficit, no deficit should be above 3% of gross national product;
4. exchange rate and interest rate fluctuations in the European monetary system should not exceed their normal margins for at least two years.

Stage Three

This will begin on 31 December 1996 if the European Council takes a qualified majority decision that enough member states have met the convergence criteria to form a 'critical mass' to move forward to monetary union. This means that seven countries out of twelve, or six out of eleven, if Britain exercises its right to opt out at this stage, that meet the convergence criteria can form a monetary union, and the date for this union to occur would then be fixed.

If a date for union had not been fixed by the end of 1997, a slower path would be followed which involved the creation of a European System of Banks on 1 July 1998 whose function would be:

1. to maintain price stability;
2. to conduct European foreign exchange operations and;
3. hold and manage official currency exchange reserves.

This system would be responsible for creating conditions for convergence to occur.

Key concepts : the Ecu

This is the European currency unit. It exists in name only on the currency exchanges, but is to be put into a 'hard form', i.e. made into a coin or note to be used throughout the EU.

The Treaty states that Stage Three would begin automatically on 1 January 1999 with the **Ecu** becoming a currency in its own right.

All the participating states who fulfilled the convergence criteria would agree the conversion rates at which their currencies would be irrevocably fixed and exchanged for Ecus. From the first day of Stage Three the Treaty would create a *European Central Bank* which will:

1. be an independent bank, 'not taking instructions from anyone', whether EU institutions, governments or any other body;
2. exercise exclusive rights to issue the currency of the EU;
3. exercise all the functions of the EMI, which will be abolished.[19]

Britain and the opt-out

At Maastricht the UK negotiated an option to remove itself from these procedures. If it chooses to opt-in to Stage Three it would need to notify the European Council by 31 December 1996, or if the Union takes the longer, slower path, by 1 January 1998.[20]

These economic clauses are the main purpose of the Maastricht Treaty. However, some of the twelve member states will find it hard to get their economies into a position to join the stronger economies of France and Germany in the select band of countries which form Europe's monetary union. In the first instance, it seems likely that only the main economies of Europe will meet the criteria. The British economy was showing clear signs of the convergence necessary to give the UK the opportunity to opt-in if it wanted, until Black Wednesday (16 September 1992) when Britain left the Exchange Rate Mechanism.[21]

Subsidiarity

Subsidiarity means that the EU will only take action in areas which do not fall under its present jurisdiction if the desired objectives cannot be sufficiently achieved by the member states.

It is designed:

1. to limit interference from Brussels;
2. to ensure that the EU stays in touch with citizens' needs;
3. to attempt to 'roll back the Union', keeping its role and influence limited to areas where the issues are too large to be handled by the member state alone.

The concept of subsidiarity has yet to be clearly defined. At present it means one thing to Britain and something completely different to its continental colleagues. The Germans believe that the term is synonymous with federalism – distributing power between local communities, Bonn and Brussels. [22]

The Committee of the Regions

The role of the Committee of the Regions is vague (*see Figure 20*). Its powers are only advisory and it is far from clear whether it will have any real purpose. The Committee:

1. must be consulted by the Council and the Commission in all cases where they consider that it can make a valuable contribution to the policy discussion;
2. will have a membership which will be recommended by National Governments, composed of 189 members, twenty-four from the UK;
3. will have complete independence to make its own recommendations.

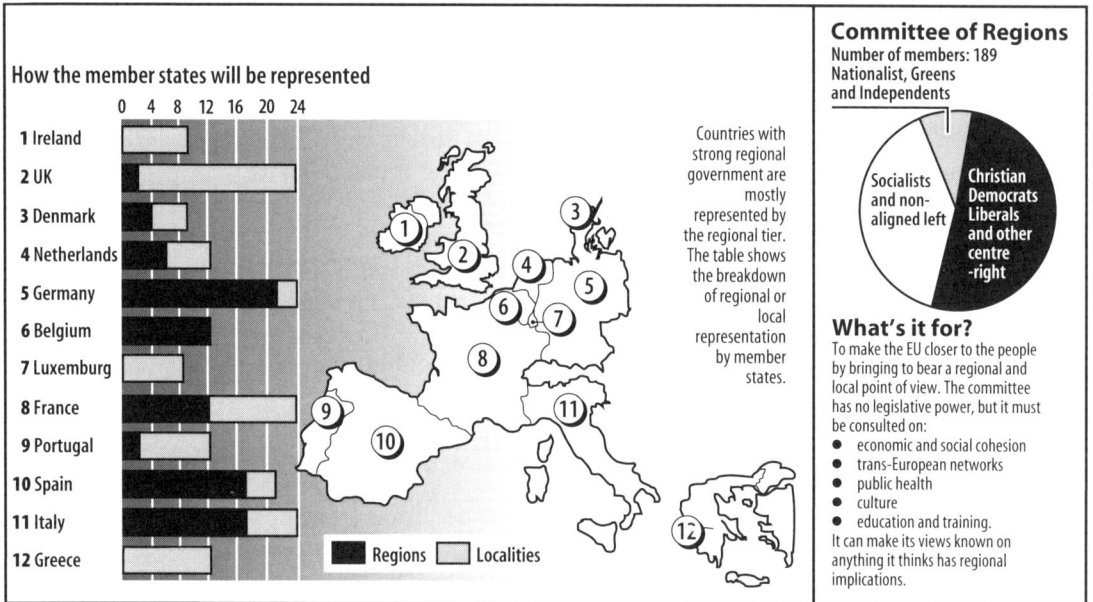

Figure 20 Europe of the regions: how the member states will be represented.[23]

The Committee's existence is recognition by the heads of government that the regions of Europe may assume increasing importance in the future, but it remains to be seen if this will be an effective forum for voicing the opinions of the regions. The nationalist parties in the UK supported the Government in the vote in the House of Commons on this section of the Maastricht Bill because they negotiated and guaranteed places on the Committee for their representatives. Plaid Cymru and the SNP hope that it will be an effective forum for discussing the needs of the regions and recommending to the Commission and Council what forms of social action, aid and investment should be taken in the regions of the EU.[23]

Other provisions of the Maastricht Treaty

Reform of existing institutions

The European Parliament is given new powers to remove what Germany saw as a democratic deficit at the heart of the EU.

1. it may propose amendments to legislation and it can veto legislation if a majority of MEPs agree;

Example:

In September 1993 the Parliament rejected a Commission proposal to ban the most powerful motorbikes from the roads of members.[24]

2. it can request on the basis of an overall majority of the Parliament that the Commission draws up new legislation;
3. it can set up a Committee of Inquiry to investigate contraventions or maladministration in the implementation of Union Law. This means that MEPs can now properly investigate constituents' complains;
4. it can draw up a set of proposals for a uniform election procedure for European parliamentary elections;
5. the European Parliament now has the power to veto the appointments of commissioners.

Example:

In July 1994 the European Parliament narrowly approved the appointment of Jacques Santer as next President of the European Commission. Furthermore, with the appointment of a new group of Commissioners, the Parliament has established a set of United States Senate-style hearings to investigate the suitability of member states' nominees to the Commission.[25]

Through these new powers the European Parliament has a co-decision-making role with the Council of Ministers. If the two institutions disagree on a proposal the Treaty creates a joint conciliation committee. The purpose of this committee is to establish a discussion process for both sides to reach agreement. However, if no agreement can be reached, the Parliament can reject the Council proposals by an overall majority. The Conciliation Committee is composed of representatives of the Council and the Parliament (50% from each body). This committee has a similar role in disputes between the Commission and the Parliament.

The other pillars of the EU

Common foreign and security policy

At present, no machinery exists to allow the members of the EU to co-ordinate their reactions in international crises. The Maastricht Treaty aims to encourage the Council of Ministers to take common positions on issues when they arise and decide whether or not there should be joint action. However it does not create a single set of policies. The Treaty expresses a readiness to develop a single policy structure on an intergovernmental basis rather than create a new institution to deal with such policies on a supranational basis. It is a system of 'joint action' where the twelve members can unanimously agree and implement a joint policy. The result would be a highly institutionalised system of EU foreign policy making. Britain, however, negotiated an opt-out where supreme national interest was at stake, and this new system has yet to be proved effective in relation to, e.g., the wars in the Balkans.

The Treaty seeks to create a common defence policy but again it is not precise on the means of achieving this. The **Western European Union** (WEU), a loose and rather insignificant grouping of states is singled out for a new, if ill-defined, role. The WEU is to 'elaborate and implement decisions and actions of the European Union which have defence implications'. Whether this makes the WEU complimentary to NATO or a rival remains to be seen. But the WEU is to move its secretariat to Brussels, set up a planning unit and invite all non-WEU EU members to join (including Greece, Denmark and Ireland)[26]

The third pillar: justice and home affairs

This aims to create greater intergovernmental co-operation and lists areas of common interest where joint positions may be formed. These include:

- asylum policy
- combating drug addiction
- customs co-operation
- immigration policy.

  Example:
  It is hoped that by the end of 1993 all members of the EU will have a common set of aims for their immigration policies.

The Treaty also creates a European police office providing a community-wide information exchange system on serious international crime.

The Treaty contains a set of other general provisions on a variety of policy areas including education, public health and environment. Most are designed to create better co-ordination and co-operation in these areas across the community.[27]

The Social Chapter

The Social Chapter was laid out in a separate protocol. Its provisions include:

1. the provision of proper social protection;
2. the promotion of dialogue between management and labour;
3. the reinforcement of EU rules on equal pay for men and women.

The extension of the EU's powers over social policy proved to be a divisive issue at Maastricht. The other eleven EU countries were keen to encourage community-wide legislation on improved living and working conditions, terms of employment, employee consultation and social security. Britain on the other hand, argued that these were policy areas where each nation-state should exercise legislative control and therefore the provisions were laid out in this separate protocol.[28] The remainder of the EU has pressed ahead with legislation under the terms of the social protocol including legislation designed to increase workers rights.[29]

Figure 21 'He who fights and runs away lives to fight another day' *The Guardian*.[30]

The Maastricht Treaty and the British Parliament

The Treaty was not able to come into force until it had been ratified by all twelve members of the EU. The method for ratification was not specified and has taken a variety of forms, from nationwide referendums, e.g. in France, Ireland and Denmark, to endorsement by national Parliaments.

In the UK, John Major has pressed the Treaty through the House of Commons. At times its passage seemed precarious and it has not emerged from the process unscathed. The inclusion of the Social Chapter was forced on the Government, after the débâcle of various Commons procedural motions. However in July, following the final damaging vote in favour of the Social Chapter (*see Figure 21*), the Maastricht debate turned into an issue of confidence for John Major's Government. Having lost the crucial vote on the Social Chapter on 22 July, the Prime Minister turned the whole issue into a motion of confidence in his Government's Maastricht policy the following day.[32]

This motion pulled all the Tory rebel MPs into line and concluded the Commons debates on the Social Chapter issue in favour of the Government. In this final debate on Maastricht and the Government's policy for opting out of the Social Chapter, the Government won by 339 votes to 301. This vote gave John Major final parliamentary authority to ratify Maastricht as he had signed it without the Social Chapter.[33] The Treaty passed through the House of Lords unscathed with the help of government backwoodsmen, who descended upon the chamber to prevent any last minute ambushes by Margaret Thatcher and her rebel band of former Ministers.[34] With the conclusion of the parliamentary process ratification of the Maastricht Treaty was delayed by an appeal for a judicial review, mounted by Lord Rees-Mogg, former editor of *The Times*, who claimed that British legislation to incorporate Maastricht into domestic law was legally and constitutionally flawed. In early August the High Court ruled that Parliament had acted within its powers by passing the Act incorporating the Treaty into British law. Lord Rees-Mogg announced on 2 August that he would not be appealing against this ruling and within hours the Government ratified the Treaty.[33] The Treaty came into effect on 1 November 1993 by which time all the member governments had ratified it.[34] Each state is now following policies to implement the provisions of Maastricht.

John Major won the day and forced his policy through Parliament but the cost has been high for him and for the country. In the end he was forced to threaten a general election in order to pull his MPs into line. The brutally extracted confidence motion and the threat of an election have badly damaged his authority.

Since December 1991 the whole debate on whether Maastricht is a move towards creating a federal United States of Europe has dominated British political life, in one form or another. The Conservative Party has torn itself in two over the issue. The 'Maastricht' domination of British politics has accounted for the policy stagnation of the Major Government from the summer of 1992 to the autumn of 1993. But there have been accompanying side issues:

Example:
Black Wednesday and the delayed arrival of 'the green shoots of recovery' have been blamed on membership of the ERM. These arguments have strengthened many Conservative and some Labour MPs' belief that greater and closer European integration will be bad for Britain. This debate will continue as the effects of the Maastricht Treaty in operation are felt.

The Treaty is designed to create a union. This union will inevitably mean that more and more British sovereignty is lost to the institutions of the EU. The Treaty itself moves yet more powers to Brussels from every member. Despite subsidiarity and opt-outs, British sovereignty has again been reduced. Reading between the lines, Maastricht is a step in the direction of the creation of a European super state. Once European monetary union (EMU) has been achieved it is hard to see the process ending there. However with the collapse of the ERM in the Summer of 1993 hopes of creating EMU within the Maastricht timescale appear to have faded.

In the UK the picture is more complicated. All the opposition parties remain more enthusiastic Europeans than many Conservatives but, as they are unlikely to have the opportunity to form a government before the next major summit on Europe's future, one has to look to John Major and the Conservative administration for an indication of Britain's further attitude towards Europe.

Britain's withdrawal from the ERM: 'Black Wednesday'

Britain remained in the ERM until Wednesday, 16 September 1992. In the last week of August the financial crisis began which led to the withdrawal of the pound. During this period, the pound slipped to the floor of the band which it occupied in the ERM, and in order to maintain its value the Bank of England spent vast amounts of currency reserves supporting it. Despite these efforts and statements from the Chancellor of the Exchequer, Norman Lamont, designed to restore confidence in the pound it remained very weak. Subsequently, the pound dropped through the bottom value of its band and continued to fall. The financial markets tested the Government's ability to keep the pound in its ERM band and won the fight of confidence. By withdrawing the pound from the ERM and allowing it to 'float', the UK currency was devalued.

Figure 22 Currency dealers distraught at the collapse of the pound on 'Black Wednesday'

The currency speculation which forced the devaluation of the pound affected other European currencies, even those not in the ERM. It showed that the system could not protect currencies against determined financial market speculation in spite of interest rate rises to protect currencies and interventions by central banks. Many commentators suggested that the ERM was fatally flawed and that Sir Alan Waters had been correct in his scepticism and contempt for the system. It is not clear when Britain will rejoin the ERM but since leaving it the economy has been able to recover from the recession. Euro-sceptics in both major parties believe that the ERM would have to be re-defined before the pound could re-enter to prevent a 'Black Wednesday' happening again. In July 1993 their claim that the ERM was fatally flawed was proved right.[35]

The failure of the ERM

With the exit of the pound in October 1992 it became clear that the ERM could not protect its member currencies from a speculative onslaught from the financial markets. In November 1992 the Spanish peseta and the Portuguese escudo were devalued and in January 1993 the Irish punt was forced to devalue after weeks of heavy speculation. At the end of 1992 financial analysts began to suggest that the French franc would be the next currency to suffer. In the Spring of 1993 the franc experienced its first bout of speculative pressure, but unlike the pound it survived. However, in July when the Germans failed to lower their key interest rate a financial crisis erupted resulting in the franc coming under sustained pressure on the financial markets. On 30 July European reaction to the German interest rate decision sent the foreign exchange markets into turmoil and pushed five ERM currencies to the bottom of their bands. On 31 July and 1 August Central Bank governors and finance ministers attempted to co-ordinate a response to the situation, but by 2 August no agreement had been reached, which effectively led to the collapse of the ERM. The values of the franc and the Danish krone then tumbled.[36]

These events led to the effective collapse of all hopes for implementing the timetable for monetary union as set out in the Maastricht Treaty. On 3 August John Major described the Maastricht timetable as 'totally unrealistic'. The crisis revealed the bitter divisions which exist about the future of Europe. Only two countries, Belgium and Ireland, are in favour of Stage Two of the Maastricht blueprint for a single currency going ahead as planned in January 1994.[37]

9.6 | **Conclusions: The future direction of the EU– Britain at the Heart of Europe?**

Now that the Maastricht Treaty has come into operation where does the EU go from here?

The Maastricht ratification process has been divisive not just in Britain but also on the Continent. The French narrowly endorsed the Treaty in a referendum, and debates in other countries have been equally acrimonious. This has disillusioned many of the new citizens of the EU. Moreover, with the collapse of the ERM in the summer of 1993 the EU has been forced to rethink the way forward to achieving an economic and monetary union. A few pointers for the future are worth noting as a conclusion.

Many Eastern European countries are desperate to enter the EU because of the economic advantages that they may gain. The EU is to expand, with the Scandinavian countries and Austria joining in 1995.38 This expansion will continue over the next two decades (see Figure 23), and it is possible that unenthusiastic members such as Britain may get left behind. The Maastricht Treaty specifies that 'any European state may apply to become a member of the Union'.

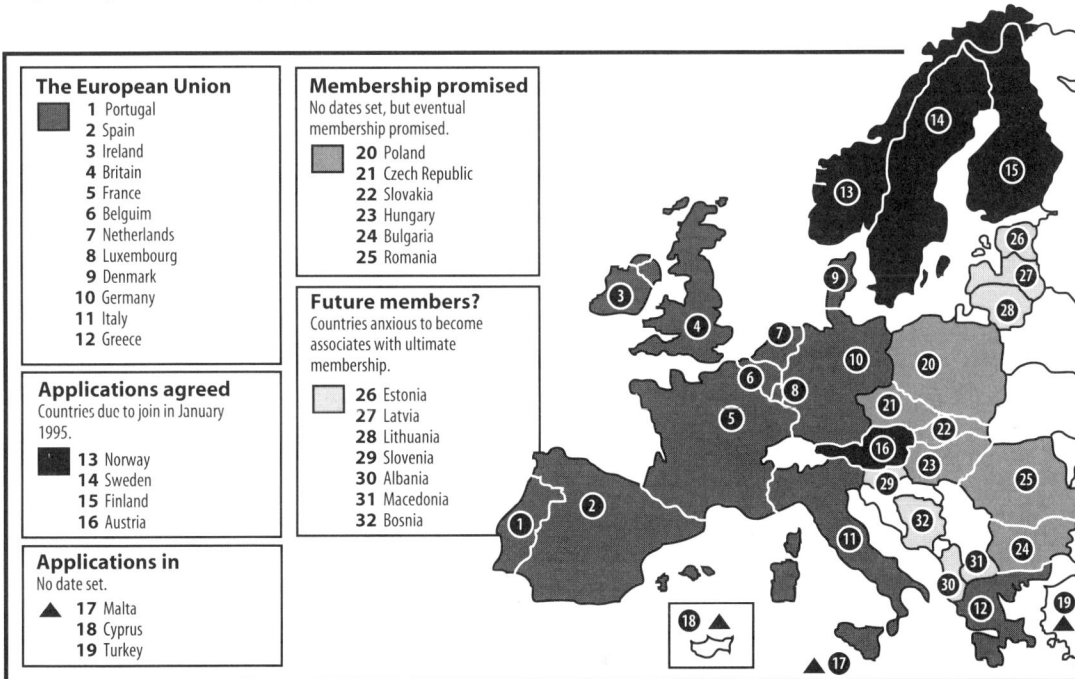

The European Union
1 Portugal
2 Spain
3 Ireland
4 Britain
5 France
6 Belgium
7 Netherlands
8 Luxembourg
9 Denmark
10 Germany
11 Italy
12 Greece

Applications agreed
Countries due to join in January 1995.
13 Norway
14 Sweden
15 Finland
16 Austria

Applications in
No date set.
▲ 17 Malta
18 Cyprus
19 Turkey

Membership promised
No dates set, but eventual membership promised.
20 Poland
21 Czech Republic
22 Slovakia
23 Hungary
24 Bulgaria
25 Romania

Future members?
Countries anxious to become associates with ultimate membership.
26 Estonia
27 Latvia
28 Lithuania
29 Slovenia
30 Albania
31 Macedonia
32 Bosnia

Figure 23 The expanding European Union.[38]

The EU has been associated with economic prosperity for much of the past twenty-five years and it is likely that as the countries of the EU come out of recession economic prosperity will return. In the longer term the UK must decide if it is to be at the heart of Europe and reap the benefits which, when it stood on the sidelines of the process before in the 1960s, it lost.

The collapse of the ERM was a disaster for those who hoped that Europe could now move quickly towards economic and monetary union. The Commission is in the process of drafting the EU's further development plans. However, the Union is paralysed by constant rows between it and Britain over enlargement and voting rights (in 1994[39] the implementation of the Social Chapter and plans for future economic intergration.[40] These rows have further damaged Britain's standing within the EU and the possibility has arisen that Europe may develop a two-tier currency system and a two-track speed approach to monetary union. There is a danger that the Germans may lead a small group of enthusiastic countries into an 'overnight monetary union'. This would be designed to achieve monetary union within a very short timescale thereby avoiding the risks of a longer-term approach to this goal. The risks of causing a permanent schism in the EU by pursuing such a scheme are very high. Such a move could split the Union into two groupings of nations, perhaps called the 'haves' and the 'have nots'. Such fears are fuelled by the British Prime Minister, John Major, talking of a multi-speed Europe, in which all member states would proceed at a speed of their own choosing.[41]

The timetable laid out in the Treaty does seem to be optimistic given the problems that have occurred with the ratification process and the collapse of the ERM. Everything is now pointing towards the intergovernmental conference on the next stage of European intergration scheduled for 1996. This will be a defining point for the EU and for Britain's position within it.

The Gulf War and the war in the Balkans have shown how difficult it can be to co-ordinate foreign and defence policies among the leading nations of the West, let alone Europe. The idealism of Maastricht has proved impractical in the context of the ERM crisis and the inability of the EU to decide a policy which would have prevented the system as it was known from collapsing. The idealism of Maastricht may prove impractical in the context of future international crises.

The EU will move towards greater unification because of Maastricht; whether Britain is a leading player in that movement remains to be seen. Britain appears willing to take the economic benefits on offer through membership of the Union but, via the concept of subsidiarity, is prepared to prevent any drive towards the creation of federal super state. All now rests on the intergovernmental conference of 1996 to decide the EU's future and Britain's position within it.

Questions

1. What is the Social Chapter?
2. (a) Describe the 'new pillars of the EU'.
   (b) Which do you consider the most important and why?
3. What reforms of existing EU institutions does the Maastricht Treaty propose?
4. What is the Committee of the Regions?
5. (a) Why did Britain leave the ERM?
   (b) Why did the ERM collapse?
6. Define the following terms: 'subsidiarity', 'opt-out', 'convergence', 'supranationalism'.

Essay questions

1. 'Maastricht has reduced the sovereign power of Parliaments across the EU community.' Discuss.
2. How has British sovereignty been diminished by membership of the EU?
3. Assess the evolution of the EU over the past twenty years.

Essay planning

This chapter has a very comprehensive essay plan. It is a research essay plan, and is a guide to the type structure, analysis and information that should produced in an in-depth essay on the European topic. In the examination this type of essay plan would produce an essay which could not be written in the time available. As an exercise using the plans of previous chapters as a guide, you should produce a condensed plan from the one given here.

2. How has British sovereignty been diminished by membership of the European Union?

First, you should define the term sovereignty:

'Sovereignty means that there is a final and absolute political authority in the political Union and no final or absolute authority exists elsewhere.'

British Sovereignty lies within in the supreme decision-making authority of Parliament. Until 1973 the British Parliament had the sole right to make laws and govern the country. Only this body could make laws which were applicable to whole of the UK and everyone who lived within it.

However, when the UK joined the EU, via the European Communities Act, 1972, the constitutional position and power of Parliament changed. Membership had profound constitutional, legal and political implications.

Britain now has to subscribe to a written constitution, the Treaty of Rome which resulted in three limits being placed on British sovereignty:

1. the direct applicability of EU legislation to the UK;
2. the institutional independence of the EU organs, the Commission, the Council of Ministers and the European Parliament;
3. the open-ended commitment to the ideas of the EU resulting in membership.

Direct applicability

Article 189 of the Treaty of Rome states that the EU institutions have the power to make laws which apply to every single member of the Union.

The 1964 *Costa vs NEL* case can be cited here as a further example of the direct applicability of EU legislation.

1. This means that the British Parliament is no longer the sole legislative force in the UK, because of membership of the EU. Its laws can now be overruled and updated by EU legislation. It is therefore subordinate to the European institutions.
2. The European Communities Act 1973 enables the institutions of the EU to make laws which are applicable to the UK without recourse to the British Parliament.
3. The European Court can make rulings which override those of our domestic courts. The House of Lords, formerly the highest court in the land, is thus subordinate to the European Court, with respect to interpreting European Law and its meaning in Britain.
4. In 1977 the European Court ruled that every national court must 'apply Union law in its entirety and protect the rights which this law confers on individuals'. Therefore any national law which conflicts with EU law must be set aside.

As the EU has developed, the 'open-ended commitments' to the ideas which lay behind the creation of the EU has meant a further erosion of British Sovereignty.

1. *The Single European Act, 1986* sought to create a single market in Europe by removing all national restrictions on the movement of goods and people.
    Example:
    This meant that Britain and the other member countries have been forced to remove their immigration controls for EU nationals, to allow 'the free movement of people' idea to be realised. This is an area of policy which would be a traditional primary concern for nation-states. Now it lies within the remit of this supranational organisation and is a good example of how far the Union has advanced since 1973.

2. Another example of an area of traditional national policy which has been changed via membership of the EU is passport and driving licence formats. There is now a European Union passport and driving licence for everyone living in the community. This means that the EU is now extending its influence into every angle of normal national life, and shows that the sovereign power of member nation-states to decide even relatively trivial matters, has been affected by membership.

3. At present, 50% of UK legislation originates from the EU. The Single European Act and the Maastricht Treaty are likely to increase this. Jacques Delors has predicted that by the beginning of the next century about 80% of the legislation enacted in the UK would have its origins in EU institutions.

The demise of British sovereignty through membership of the EU was predicted by some British politicians. Britain's continued membership of the EU means that British sovereignty will continue to decrease:

1. membership of the Exchange Rate Mechanism limited Britain's ability to construct its own economic policy. This amplified the effects of the economic recession;

2. the Maastricht Treaty aims to create an economic and monetary union which contains further commitments which will diminish Britain's freedom of action and independent decision-making power.

Conclusions

1. As time goes by Britain will become even more tied to Europe economically and politically.

2. British sovereignty has been curtailed by membership of the EU. The EU is 'the final and absolute authority' and therefore reduces the UK's sovereign rights as a nation state.

3. Britain cannot withdraw from the EU now because of its close trading links with the EU.

4. The referendum in 1975 was the last opportunity the UK had to withdraw.

5. Our future, many now believe, is unavoidably linked to that of Europe. The debate over Maastricht within the Conservative Government and its Party at large is perhaps the hard realisation of this fact. Britain can only apply the brakes to slow the process down, but not to stop the further loss of national sovereignty when a European Economic Union is created sometime in the future.

Notes and references

1. Morgan, K. O. *The People's Peace: British History 1945–1990* (Oxford, 1990) p. 89.

2. Smith, M. (ed.) *British Foreign Policy* (London, 1988), p. 16.

3. Whitehead, P. *The Writing on the Wall* (London, 1986), pp. 51–69.

4. *The Guardian*, 01.02.94.

5. *EEC Commission v. UK* (Case No. 124/81) 1983.

6. *The Times*, 14.05.93.

7. *The Guardian*, 23.05.94.

8. *The Guardian*, 2, 12.06.94.

9. Ibid.

10. Thatcher, M. *The Downing Street Years* (London, 1993), pp. 62–4, 83–6, 53–45.

11. Ibid., pp. 62–4, 83–6, 537–45 and Young H. *One of Us* (London, 1990) pp. 190–1, 551–2.

12. *The European: Maastricht Made Simple* (Milton Keynes, 1992), p. 6.

13. McKie, D. *The Election* (London 1992), pp. 194–7.

14. Ibid.

15. Ibid. p. 197 and *The Economist*, 14.12.91.

16. *The Economist*, 14.12.91.

17. Luff, P. *The Simple Guide to Maastricht* (London, 1992), pp. 8–13 and *The European: Maastricht Made Simple* (Milton Keynes, 1992), pp. 8–9.

18. Luff, P. *The European: Maastricht Made Simple* 1992, p. 12–15.

19. Luff. P. *The Simple Guide to Maastricht* (London, 1992), p. 22; *The European: Maastricht Made Simple* (Milton Keynes, 1992), p. 16.

20. *The Times*, 17 and 18.09.92.

21. *The European: Maastricht Made Simple* (Milton Keynes, 1992), p. 34.

22. *The Guardian*, 07.03.94.

23. *The Guardian*, 23.09.93.

24. *The Times*, 22.07.94.

25. *The Guardian* 23.05.94.

26. *The European: Maastricht Made Simple* (Milton Keynes, 1992) pp. 20–1.

27. Ibid.

28. Luff, P. *The Simple Guide to Maastricht* (London, 1992), p. 39.

29. *The Guardian*, 23.06.94. Students should be aware that the opt-out continues to be a point of friction between Britain and the other members.

30. *The Guardian*, 06.05.93, *The Times*, 24.07.93.

31. *The Times*, 24.07.93.

32. *The Daily Telegraph*, 14.07.93 and 15.07.93.

33. *The Times*, 20.07.93 and 03.08.93.

34. *The Times*, 13.10.93 and 02.11.93.

35. *The Times*, 17.09.92 and 18.09.92.

36. *The Guardian*, 30 and 31.07.93.

37. *The Guardian*, 03.08.93; *The Sunday Times*, 08.08.93 and Brummer, A. 'The Millstone that crushed ERM', in *The Guardian*, 03.08.93;

38. *The Guardian*, 11.06.94.

39. *The Guardian*, 02.03.94; 21.03.94; 30.03.94.

40. *The Guardian*, 01.06.94.

41. Ibid.

Further reading

Luff, P. *The Simple Guide to Maastricht* (London, 1992).

Nicoll, W. and Salmon, T. C. *Understanding the European Communities* (London, 1990).

Nugent, N. *The Government and Politics of the European Community* (London, 1989).

CHAPTER 10

The administration of justice

In every political system, law must be applied to the society, interpreted and enforced. Law must be applied evenly and equally to every citizen. In the Western world great value is placed on the construction, operation and interpretation of law. An attempt is made to balance the need for law with individual rights. The hallmark of most Western liberal democracies is the way in which these rights are guaranteed through the judicial system.

The judiciary are the third component of the trinity of the separation of powers: executive, legislature and judiciary. In different political systems, the characteristics and powers of the judiciary vary, but in its basic function the British judiciary is similar to that of the United States and France. The judiciary provides a system for enforcing the law fairly, an orderly method of dealing with infringements of the law and settling disputes between individuals and between citizens and government. It ensures that justice is done and that the Rule of Law is upheld. This chapter will examine the way that justice is administered in the UK and covers the following:

10.1   The Rule of Law.

10.2   The characteristics of the British judiciary.

10.3   The judiciary and court system in England and Wales.

10.4   The criticisms of the judiciary and the judicial system.

10.5   Administrative justice.

10.6   The courts and civil liberties.

Key concepts: law

This is a body of rules, whether formally enacted (passed by an assembly or executive) or customary, which a state or community recognises as binding on its members or subjects. In Britain this means those rules declared by Parliament, the courts and the EU as binding upon the population. Laws give us a framework for living in an orderly and peaceful society. They provide for the protection of individual rights and establish an acceptable system of behaviour for all members of a society.

Key concepts: justice

This means the exercise of fairness and impartiality in the creation and application of law. It means ensuring that laws are seen to be right and just and that they are applied with fairness, integrity and impartiality.

10.1 | The Rule of Law

The Rule of Law is a basic legal political ideology that is prevalent throughout Western liberal democracies. It means that every citizen should be equally bound by the law, regardless of their position in society, and that the law should be enforced impartially by an independent judiciary. The Rule of Law applies itself equally in every situation and controls relations between individuals, and between the government and the individual.

This means that:

1. no person is above the law and everyone should be presumed equal before the law;
2. no one should be punished except for a breach of the law;
3. fairness and consistent procedures should be applied to the solution of all legal cases;
4. the judiciary should apply the law independently of the other branches of Government.

In Britain, the Rule of Law has been exercised for many centuries. Many different citizens, from coal miners, Ministers of the Crown and members of the royal family, have been brought before the courts for breaches of the law.

Example:
In 1993 the High Court found the 1991 Home Secretary, Kenneth Baker guilty of contempt of court in a case involving the deportation of an alleged refugee. This case means that the courts in Britain may now stop a Minister taking an action, pending a court hearing on the legality of the proposed action.[1]

In Britain, however, there are a number of problems which hamper the operation of the Rule of Law:

1. The unwritten and conventional nature of the British Constitution means that the courts have little control over major aspects of our political system, e.g. what would the courts do if the leader of the governing party refused to resign as Prime Minister after losing his or her party's leadership election?
2. Ministers are given powers to make regulations which cannot be challenged in the courts, only their application may be reviewed by judges and deemed to be either *ultra vires* (*see Chapter 11*) or against the rules of **natural justice**.
3. The existence of the Rule of Law does not provide any guarantee of justice if the law itself is seen to be unfair. Parliament may sometimes change the law circumventing the judges or suspend certain laws.

Example:
The Criminal Justice and Public Order Act 1994 places limits upon a defendant's right to silence under police questioning.[3]

Key concepts: the independence of the judiciary

This means that judges should be free to apply the law in a fair and impartial way with no person being able to interfere or influence their deliberations. In Britain the independence of the judiciary has been guaranteed since the Act of Settlement in 1701, which stated that all senior judges hold office 'during good behaviour' and could only be removed by a motion to the monarch by both Houses of Parliament.

Key concepts: natural justice

This means that everyone is entitled to a fair hearing and that no person may be a judge in their own case, and that every case should be 'interpreted in accordance with common sense, common fairness and on the substantial merits of the case'. Any action which is unreasonable, or unfair, or shows an abuse of power can be deemed to be against natural justice.[2]

Questions

1. Define what is meant by the terms law, natural justice and justice.
2. (a) What is the Rule of Law?
   (b) What are the problems with the operation of the Rule of Law in the UK?
3. What is the difference between law and justice?

10.2 | The characteristics of the British judiciary

The judiciary in England and Wales are independent from political control and influence. This independence is considered important in ensuring the fairness of trials, the impartiality of judgements and the authority of the courts. The nineteenth-century constitutional expert A.V. Dicey described it as one of the two pillars of the British Constitution, the other being parliamentary sovereignty. This concept is now enshrined within the British political system and any attempt to tamper with it would face a severe political and public outcry.

The highest judges – the Law Lords – are appointed by the Queen on the advice of the Prime Minister, having consulted with the Lord Chancellor, who is the head of the judiciary. Lower court judges – high court and circuit judges – are appointed on the recommendation of the Lord Chancellor, from among experienced barristers and solicitors. In 1993, the Lord Chancellor Lord Mackay, outlined ideas to open up the judicial appointments system by advertising posts, filling some judicial positions by open competition and including lay people in the process of selecting judges.[4] By comparison, in Canada and Australia judges are appointed through a process involving a Commission of lawyers, politicians and lay people who select judges or advise on appointments.

1. Although judges are appointed on the advice of politicians, professional rather than political factors determine their appointment. This is unlike in the United States where the appointment of many judges lies firmly within the political arena, especially senior judges and justices of the Supreme Court.
2. Judges are immune from civil proceedings for anything said or done while acting in a judicial capacity.
3. Judges must conduct themselves properly. High Court judges, of the High Court or Court of Appeal, can only be removed from office by a motion of both Houses of Parliament, but lower court judges may be sacked for misbehaviour. This happened once, in 1983 after a circuit judge smuggled whiskey and cigarettes. Recently the Lord Chancellor issued a warning that judges convicted of drink-driving offences could face the sack.[5]
4. Judges must retire at 75.
5. Judges' salaries are paid for out of the Consolidated Fund which provides for their political impartiality from parliamentary debate.

6. Through the principle of parliamentary sovereignty members of the judiciary are subordinate to Parliament. The British Parliament is sovereign in all matters and Acts of Parliament take precedence over all other forms of law. This has been the theme of the British Constitution since the Revolution of 1688.[6] The British judiciary therefore has no option, unlike its United States counterpart, but to apply Acts of Parliament because Acts are part of the British Constitution (*see Chapter 2*):

●   It cannot strike legislation down because this is unconstitutional.

●   British courts have a new power under EU law to suspend the operation of Acts of Parliament that appear to breach EU law until a final determination is made (*see Section 10.5*).

●   British courts have the power to interpret the meaning of a statute once passed and the power to review the administrative actions of Ministers and others to determine whether they are *ultra vires*, i.e. beyond legal power. This power of statutory interpretation allows judges to declare the action of a public servant under an Act invalid, for exceeding the powers granted by the original act.

●   The interpretation of Acts of Parliament may be flexible or literal, meaning that judges either follow the letter of the law or the intention of the law. By interpreting the intention of the law judges attempt to interpret the intention of Parliament, by which they can become vulnerable to criticisms.

This interpretative power is known as **judicial review**. It allows the higher courts to review the decisions of all inferior tribunals, including lower courts, tribunals, special tribunals of professional bodies and the decisions of public authorities – central and local government. This allows the judiciary to shape the law and construct legal precedents. Since the 1960s the judiciary has been more willing to review administrative acts and executive actions, resulting in the quashing of a number of ministerial actions. This has meant that the courts are now playing a greater role than ever before in the determination of public policy, acting as a check upon executive power, in part because the number of applications for judicial review have risen significantly.

This has created the phrase 'judicial activism', which has been further increased by membership of the European Union (*see section 10.5*).

Example: Regina vs Secretary of State for Employment, *ex parte* Equal Opportunities Commission, 1994.
In this case the House of Lords held that UK legislation that gives part-time workers (most of whom are women) less protection than full-time

workers (most of whom are men) is incompatible with European Union law as to equality between employees. This meant that UK law was changed to come into line with EU law, because where domestic law comes into conflict with EU law, EU law takes precedent [7] (see Chapter 9).

By comparison, in the United States the written constitution establishes a much greater role for the judiciary in the political process, via the strict separation of powers and a system of checks and balances (*see Chapter 1*). The Supreme Court of the United States reviews the constitutionality of Congressional statutes and the actions of the executive branch. This means that it can declare an executive action or a Congressional Act unconstitutional and strike it down. Further judicial involvement in United States politics is provided through judicial interpretation of the first ten amendments to the United States Constitution, commonly known as the Bill of Rights. The Supreme Court is responsible for protecting the rights of individuals guaranteed under the Constitution. The exact meaning of these rights, e.g. freedom of speech, have changed over the past two centuries and the Supreme Court has revised its interpretations of them to reflect the changes in United States political and social attitudes.

In some states in the USA, state judges are elected or recommended to the governor or state legislature by a public commission. Senior judges, Supreme Court judges, are appointed by the President (executive) subject to approval by the Senate. This means that the judiciary in the United States has a much greater political colouring than in Britain. In the United States, the judiciary is more powerful than in Britain and judicial activism is a permanent feature of the constitutional arrangements. But students should remember that the US has a starkly different constitutional system to Britain.

Questions

1. What is meant by the term 'judicial review'?
2. What is the position of the British judiciary in relation to the concept of parliamentary sovereignty?
3. What are the main differences between the role of the judiciary in Britain and in the United States?
4. How is the independence of the judiciary achieved in Britain?

10.3 | The judiciary and the court system in England and Wales

The system of courts in England and Wales is divided between civil and criminal jurisdictions; however, there are a number of specialised administrative tribunals (*see section 10.5*). The system of courts is laid out in Figure 24.

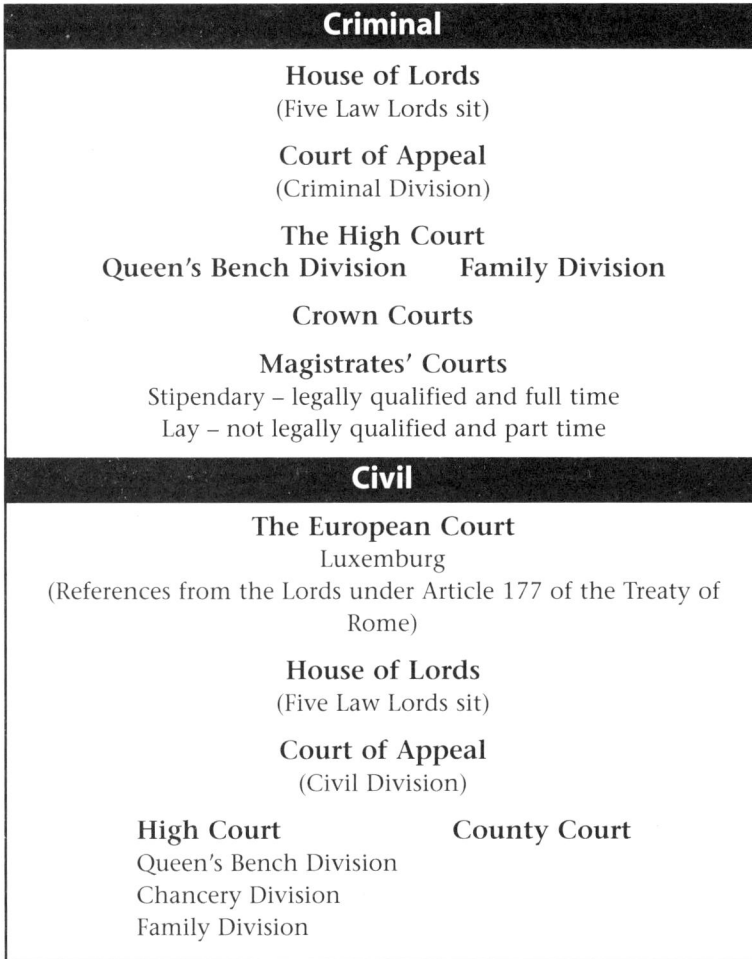

Figure 24 The system of the courts.

Criminal

House of Lords
(Five Law Lords sit)

Court of Appeal
(Criminal Division)

The High Court
Queen's Bench Division   Family Division

Crown Courts

Magistrates' Courts
Stipendary – legally qualified and full time
Lay – not legally qualified and part time

Civil

The European Court
Luxemburg
(References from the Lords under Article 177 of the Treaty of Rome)

House of Lords
(Five Law Lords sit)

Court of Appeal
(Civil Division)

High Court   **County Court**
Queen's Bench Division
Chancery Division
Family Division

All criminal cases begin in the Magistrates' Court. Nine out of ten cases are dealt with by this court, which has a variety of sentencing powers including fines, and a maximum sentence of sixth months in prison. More serious offences are referred by Magistrates' Courts to Crown Courts where a judge and jury are used to hear a case if the defendant pleads not guilty, or a judge alone for sentencing a defendant who pleads guilty. Serious cases in a Crown Court are presided over by a High Court Judge. Magistrates' Courts deal with some civil proceedings and some administrative functions.

Example: Licensing public houses.

Appeals from the Crown Court are usually taken to the Court of Appeal Criminal Division but they may be taken to the Queen's Bench Division of the High Court. Appeals are only possible on a point of law or a point of fact. Additionally, the Attorney-General has the power to refer to the High Court sentences which appear too lenient, allowing the High Court to increase the sentence imposed by the lower court.

Appeals may be made to the House of Lords if a point of law of general public importance is involved or that it is felt if the case should be considered by the highest court in the land.[8]

Civil courts

Civil cases involving small amounts of money are heard by County Courts while the remainder are heard in the High Court. The High Court is divided into three sections: the Queen's Bench, which deals with matters of common law, the Chancery which deals with equity cases and the Family Division which deals with domestic cases, the majority being divorces. It is the Queen's Bench Division which hears cases for *mandamus*, requiring a public body to fulfil a particular duty, and *ultra vires* cases.

Appeals from magistrates courts and county courts are heard by the Divisional Courts of the High Courts. Appeals from the High Courts are taken to the Court of Appeal Civil Division. Such appeals are usually heard by the Master of the Rolls sitting with two Lord Justices of Appeal. An appeal may be taken to the House of Lords with the permission of either the Court of Appeal or the Lords. Sometimes appeals on important points of law or precedent may go directly from the High Court to the House of Lords. With cases concerning European Union Law the House of Lords must refer the matter to the European Court rather than decide the case itself, but the lower courts, i.e. the Court of Appeal, may send a case to the European Court for an 'opinion', which gives the domestic court an indication of the thinking of the European Court on a particular matter which can be used to influence its judgement. This method saves both time and money. This has made the European Court the highest court of appeal in the UK civil court system; however, the Lords remains the highest 'domestic court' in the land.

Students should note that in all cases both the European Court and the Lords do not consider themselves bound by their previous decisions, i.e. precedent, changing the law 'when it appears right to do so'.[9]

Personnel

At the summit of the judiciary is the Lord Chancellor, the head of the judiciary (*see Chapter 1*). The Government has two other law officers, the Attorney-General and the Solicitor-General, both of whom are MPs and act as legal advisers to the Crown and the Government.

Beneath these political positions are the professional judges. The most senior are the Law Lords, the eleven Lords of Appeal Ordinary who are appointed by the Queen on the advice of the Prime Minister. Within their rank are:

1. *The Lord Chief Justice* who is the senior judge of the Queen's Bench Division of the High Court of Justice. He is head of the Criminal Division of the Court of Appeal, and is responsible for developing criminal law and sentencing policy.
2. *The Master of the Rolls* who is the most senior judge of the Court of Appeal (Civil Division) and as this Court hears a large number of appeals in civil law, is in a very influential position in the development of the civil law.

Beneath these judges are the Lords Justice of Appeal and the President of the Family Division, again appointed by the Crown on the advice of the Prime Minister. The Lords Justices are drawn from either High Court judges or from barristers of at least fifteen years' standing.

High Court judges, circuit judges and recorders are drawn from barristers of at least ten years' standing but solicitors of ten year's standing are eligible for consideration for appointment as a recorder.

Magistrates are appointed by the Lord Chancellor.[10]

Questions

1. Describe the structure of the civil courts in England and Wales.
2. Who are the Master of the Rolls and the Lord Chief Justice?

10.4 | The criticisms of the judiciary and the judicial system

Traditionally the British judiciary was seen to be independent, autonomous and divorced from the political process, existing to interpret and apply laws enacted by the legislature. In recent years it has become judicially active and this has meant that judges no longer operate in a political vacuum. They have begun to act as a check on the power of an all-powerful executive in reaction to what they see as Parliament's failings to act as a check on the power of the Government. Over the past ten years, politics and public opinion have begun to influence the judiciary to a much greater extent than before.

1. The judiciary is now more susceptible to public opinion.

   Example:
   Recent public concern about deaths caused by drink-drivers has influenced judges to pass more custodial sentences for such offences.

2. The judiciary has been criticised for its sentencing policies, which often do not strike the right balance and are too lenient.

Example:

A judge who imposed a fine of £500 on a 15 year-old boy found guilty of raping a similarly aged girl, saying that the money could be used to provide the victim with a holiday, was severely criticised by the press. The sentence was referred by the Attorney-General to the Court of Appeal because it was considered unduly lenient.

3.   The judiciary has been criticised for being ineffective guardians of the citizen's rights. Cases such as the Birmingham Six and the Guildford Four, which were referred back to the Court of Appeal by the Home Secretary, saw these convictions quashed. These cases revealed the inadequacies of the Criminal Justice system and drew into question the role and abilities of the judiciary. The overturning of the Birmingham Six and Guildford Four convictions led to the creation in 1991 of a Royal Commission on Criminal Justice (*see section 10.6*).

4.   In some cases the judiciary has been criticised for acting in the interests of the 'establishment'.

Example:

In the Ponting case in 1984 Mr Justice McCowan ruled that the nation, or state, and government of the day was one and the same thing. Therefore Ponting, who was accused of having breached the Official Secrets Act, could not claim in his defence that he had a duty to the nation and Parliament to reveal classified information about the Falklands War. This was a clear breach in the impartiality of the judiciary. Critics claim Mr Justice McCowan was attempting to ensure a guilty verdict on behalf of the establishment. However, the jury ignored his comments and found Ponting not guilty.

5.   Previously judges were not allowed by convention to comment on matters of public policy. However, in recent years this convention has been breached. In 1992, the new appointments of the Master of the Rolls, Lord Justice Bingham, and the Lord Chief Justice, Lord Justice Taylor, ushered in a new convention allowing senior judges to enter public policy debates, drawing the judiciary further into the political arena.

6.   Criticism has been levied at the judicial system saying that in the 1990s equality before the law is a myth. The cost of either a criminal and more especially a civil case can run into tens of thousands of pounds. Money can buy enormous advantage in litigation, increasing the chances of success for those with more money. The most wealthy can hire the best representatives, but the poor and even moderately well-off are often deterred from bringing claims which in legal terms may have good prospects of success.

Judges are seen to be unwilling to press for changes and critics claim that this unequal access to legal resources undermines the entire legal system. For this reason a nationally operated scheme was established in 1974 to help those of insufficient financial means to pay for any legal action that they wish to bring, or pay for their defence. The Legal Aid scheme covers both criminal and civil cases and is designed to ensure that those who cannot afford legal advice and representation are given an equal access to legal representation and advice.[11]

7. The judiciary has been criticised for being politically biased because of its social and educational background:

8. The overwhelming majority of judges come from a middle- to upper-class Oxford or Cambridge-educated background. With such a background, critics claim, most judges have conservative dispositions similar to the rest of their social class.

9. Moreover, because the judiciary is male dominated critics argue that it is insensitive in cases involving women, especially sexual offences cases.

10. Critics argue that the conservative background of the members of the judiciary leads them to unduly protect the status quo – possessing a built-in bias towards the government and the Conservative Party.[12]

In response to Griffith's criticism, Lord Devlin, a senior law lord writing in 1978, said that the politics of the judiciary 'are hardly more significant than those of the army, the navy and the air force; they are as predictable as those of any institution where maturity is in command'. Devlin argued that throughout the whole apparatus of the State, in every institution, civil service, judiciary or political party, the men at the top, especially senior judges, are seen by the young as showing too much concern with stability and too little with change. Devlin argued that the judiciary contained 'mature, safe and orthodox men' which was a good thing.[13]

Nevertheless, these concerns have provoked a debate about the judiciary and have led to the creation of pressure groups such as the all-party reform group, Justice, which campaigns for legal reform, e.g. a reform of the judicial appointments system.

Question

List and explain three criticisms of the judiciary in the UK.

10.5 | Administrative justice

With the increase in the size and complexity of the British State in the post-war period, Parliament sought to introduce cheaper and more effective ways of dealing with legal disputes arising out of the growth in the activity and responsibility of the State. This led to the creation of a system of administrative tribunals, which are concerned with the settling of disputes that are of more concern in an administrative context than a legal context. These bodies have judicial and administrative characteristics and determine disputes arising from the administration of statutes passed by the legislature. These disputes may be between citizen and state, arising directly from the administrative decision of a government department, or between citizens and other organisations.

There are now over 2,000 tribunals settling disputes concerning national insurance, pensions, housing, education, social security benefits, the National Health Service and immigration.

Disputes over injuries at work, industrial disputes or unfair dismissal are dealt with by industrial tribunals.

Unlike courts, tribunals do not use judges or lawyers so much as administrative experts. They are less formal and give more consideration to personal and local conditions than the courts. Disputes are settled in a cheaper, quicker and more common-sense manner, because unlike the courts they are not bound by a huge number of rules of evidence. It is possible to appeal against a decision, usually to a superior court or tribunal; however, in individual cases many tribunals give no right of appeal.

Example:
The National Health Service Tribunal, the Social Security Commissioners and the Immigration Appeals Tribunal.

Tribunals can be described as quasi-judicial, meaning that they hear appeals against decisions made by government agencies, or disputes between individuals and organisations. Tribunals are charged with the responsibility of establishing the facts of the case, and deciding what the statutory rights and entitlements of the aggrieved individual are. Most tribunals are composed of three members, though composition varies between tribunals. All have a chairman, often with legal qualifications, and two lay members, either part-time or full-time, representing the interests related to the concerns of the particular tribunal. Rights to legal representation are limited and usually claimants have to present their own case. Tribunals are generally held in public but they are not required, unless requested, to provide reasons for their decisions.

The mode of operation was established by the 1971 Tribunals and Enquiries Act. This established a Council on Tribunals which is responsible for the supervision of the administrative tribunal system and for reporting to Parliament and the Lord Chancellor on the functioning of the tribunals under its supervision.

Advantages of tribunals	Disadvantages of tribunals
• Cheap, quick and easy to use in general.	• Some are closed.
• Less formal than the courts.	• They do not have to give reasons for their decisions nor publicise their findings – justice is not seen to be done.
• Tend to be more local.	• Tribunal members are specially chosen, often from within the Department of State concerned, for a particular case. This affects their objectivity.
• Use specialists in particular field.	• Legal aid for preparation of a case is not available for a tribunal, except industrial tribunals.
• Not bound by rules of evidence.	• Some tribunals do not like legal representation, so aggrieved citizens have to represent themselves.

Over the past twenty-five years tribunals have become an integrated part of our justice system. They have, however, lost some of their flexibility by allowing a greater level of legal representation and by establishing principles of legal precedent, making them more like a court. They remain more efficient and cheaper to run than the courts system and they have helped to take some of the judicial load off the mainstream courts. Due to the growth of the administration and the welfare state these quasi-judicial courts have become an asset in the administration of justice.

Question

What is meant by the term 'administrative tribunal'?

10.6 | The courts and civil liberties

The judicial system in most countries has the task of protecting the citizen against abuses of power, administrative corruption, and ensuring that civil rights or liberties (*see Chapter 1*) are observed and maintained.

If civil rights are called into question it is the duty of the courts to resolve the disputes, often by reference to a constitution as in the United States or by precedent or common law, as in Britain. In Britain all civil liberties stem from the 'Golden Principle of the English Constitution', that people may do what they like so long as it is not prohibited by law. Furthermore, legal protection of our civil liberties is not enshrined in a Bill of Rights: rather such protection is afforded through common law, judicial precedent and a variety of statutes.

Examples:
1. *The right to vote is guaranteed by the Representation of the Peoples Acts, 1918, 1928, 1949, and 1969.*

2. *Freedom of speech includes the freedom of the press. This freedom is not written down in any law, but comes under the 'Golden Principle'. We have freedom of speech except in so far as law limits this, i.e. laws including treason, blasphemy, obscenity, libel, defamation, incitement to racial hatred and the Official Secrets Act.*

In Britain civil liberties are theoretically protected in the following ways:

1. The judiciary with its power of judicial review can act as scrutinisers and guardians of executive and police actions to ensure that civil liberties are not abused. Senior judges have always claimed that the judiciary exists to protect civil liberties but this is a controversial point because in recent times the attitude of the judiciary towards civil liberties has varied considerably.

    Example:
    In the mid-1980s the courts upheld the right of the state security services to tap phones. Nuclear disarmament campaigners lost their High Court battle against the Government over the monitoring of members' phones.[14]

Critics of the judiciary claim that too much power has become concentrated in the executive branch and that civil liberties are more vulnerable to abuse than ever before. They suggest that the courts are unable to deal with abuse of civil liberties because:

*   they are too weak;
*   the judiciary's background makes it unsuitable to deal with such cases and;
*   the unwritten nature of the British Constitution does not lend itself to the protection of civil liberties.

Critics argue that in the majority of civil liberty cases, the courts have identified the interests of the State with the interests of the Government of the day. They have accepted that government can avoid scrutiny of its conduct by calling to its aid the concept of 'national security', the definition of which judges are willing to leave to the executive. Critics argue that the judiciary's willingness to grant injunctions has meant that liberties have been extinguished without proper adjudication.

Example:
In the Spycatcher *and* Zircon Spy Satellite[15] *cases the judiciary appeared fully on the side of the Government. In the* Spycatcher *case (1986), the Court of Appeal agreed to the banning of the book,[16] on national security grounds, preventing British shops from stocking the book even though it was freely available across most of Western Europe and the United States. However, the House of the Lords ultimately ruled that the ban could not be upheld and* Spycatcher *became available in British bookshops.*

However, the other view of the role of the judiciary in protecting civil liberties is more complimentary. The judiciary in this view has proved itself to be effective protection, and through judicial activism it has sought to act as a check against executive power. The most recent example concerns the 'arms to Iraq' affair. During the trial of the Matrix Churchill directors who stood accused of illegally exporting arms to Iraq, the presiding judge ruled that government documents covered public immunity certificates and should be made public. As a result the trial collapsed and the directors were cleared. The subsequent judicial inquiry, the Scott inquiry, has shown the full extent to which senior government Ministers were aware of the export of arms to Iraq breaking their own guidelines.[17] Had the judge not acted, the accused may have been found guilty and an injustice would have occurred. This case restored some of the public's faith in the role of the judiciary as guardians of civil liberties.

2. Civil liberties are protected in that MPs can act as guardians of these liberties in both a legislative capacity, voting against Bills which remove liberties, and in a personal capacity, by taking up cases where persons have had their liberties compromised, although with the rise of party government this has been hampered.
3. The system of administrative justice protects civil liberties, in theory (*see Section 10.4*).
4. The power of the Ombudsman to investigate maladministration and provide remedies also protects these liberties (*see Chapter 3*).
5. Civil liberties are also protected through the European Convention on Human Rights to which Britain is a signatory country. Citizens may take a case to the European Court of Human Rights claiming a particular human right has been violated. (This is a separate and different institution to the European Court, which is part of the European Union, *see Chapter 9*.)

6. A variety of laws and practices relating to the criminal justice system, including the right to legal representation, the right to trial by jury, and the Bail Act 1976, protect civil liberties.

7. Civil liberty pressure groups are responsible for highlighting any reduction in the civil liberties of British citizens by new laws or executive action, often warning of the dangers to civil liberties which the most innocent of government initiatives may bring about.

    Example:
    When in August 1994 the Government announced proposals to introduce a new credit card-sized driving licence, which included a photograph of the licence holder, many civil liberties groups warned that this may lead to the introduction of a national identity card scheme via 'the backdoor'.[18]

8. Finally, the mass media have become influential in highlighting the need to protect civil liberties and investigating and reporting cases where civil liberties have been abused or an injustice has occurred.

    Example:
    The BBC programme Rough Justice *has investigated a number of criminal cases leading to the release from prison of a person wrongfully convicted.*

Civil liberties in Britain are protected in an uncoordinated and ambiguous manner. In many ways civil liberties in the past decade have been eroded via the inactivity of the judiciary, the unprecedented extension of police powers during the 1980s, the weaknesses of Parliament, and the massive centralisation of power. Some commentators argue that comparisons with other liberal democracies show that similar democracies have nothing like the same concentration of unqualified power at the centre of government as Britain.[19]

These factors have seen an increase in the ability of the judiciary to act as a check upon the powers of the executive and has led to calls for the introduction of a Bill of Rights which would enable the citizenry to know their rights precisely, provide a framework for rights to be protected in the face of an all-powerful executive, and afford the judiciary a clear opportunity – indeed the power – to protect civil liberties.[20] If a Bill of Rights is introduced it will, among other things, clarify Britain's civil liberties and enhance their protection (*see Chapter 2*).

Questions

1. What is a civil right?
2. In what ways are civil rights protected in Britain?
3. Name one civil right and describe how the courts have protected it.

Essay questions

1. How is justice administered in Britain?
2. Are the judiciary effective guardians of civil liberties?
3. Consider the view that the judiciary in Britain favours the establishment rather than the individual.
4. (a) What are the main issues regarding civil liberties today?
   (b) How adequately have the courts protected these liberties?

Essay planning

3. Consider the view that the judiciary in Britain favours the establishment rather than the individual.

This essay is asking you to discuss the claims that the judiciary are biased in favour of the establishment.

(a) Explain that in the post-war period the judiciary have been criticised on account of its background and that this has led to claims of pro-establishment bias on its behalf. Use the materials contained in *section 10.4*, especially the work of J.A.G. Griffith.
(b) Demonstrate using examples (from *section 10.7* and elsewhere), the alleged existence of a bias:
    (i) the experience of trade unions;
    (ii) civil liberties cases where the judiciary have ruled in favour of the establishment. (e.g. the Ponting case).
(c) These criticisms may be countered by using :
    (i) the Comments of Lord Devlin.
    (ii) counter civil liberties cases (e.g. Matrix Churchill).
(d) You may conclude by arguing that the traditional role of the judiciary (explain what this is) means that judges take the protection of the individual very seriously and through an increase recently in judicial activism, the judiciary has become a check upon the power of the executive.

This strongly counters any suggestions of bias – although the fact that members of the judiciary share a common background may give the impression of bias at times.

Notes and references

1. *The Guardian*, 28.07.94.
2. Walker, R.J. *The English Legal System* (London, 1985), pp. 42–3.
3. *The Daily Telegraph*, 26.04.94.
4. *The Daily Telegraph*, 09.07.93.
5. *The Times*, 21.07.94.
6. This estbalished the Supremacy of Parliament and of statute law. Prior to this event the British Courts were able to strike down statute laws.

7.   *The Times*, 07.03.94.

8.   Walker, R.J. *The English Legal System* (1985), pp. 179–228.

9.   Ibid. pp. 145–6.

10. Ibid. pp. 179–227 and Eddy, K. *The English Legal System* (London, 1988), pp. 12–23.

11. The Legal Aid Act 1974 consolidated all previous legislation relating to legal aid and advice.

12. See Griffith, J.A.G. *The Politics of the Judiciary*, 4th edn (London 1991).

13. Zander, M. *The Law Making Process* (1989), pp. 305 –11.

14. Drewry, G. *Judges and Politics in Britain* (1986), pp. 28–32.

15. For further details of both see Ewing, K.D. and Gearty, C.A. *Freedom Under Thatcher: Civil Liberties in Modern Britain* (Oxford, 1990), pp. 147–52 and Wright, P. *Spycatcher* (New York, 1987), pp. 152–69.

16. Wright, P. *Spycatcher* (1987).

17. See *The Sunday Times*, 06.03.94.

18   *The Times*, 10.8.94.

19. Ewing, K.D. and Gearty, C.A. *Freedom Under Thatcher: Civil Liberties in Modern Britain* (Oxford, 1990), p. 15.

20. See Zander, M. 'A Bill of Rights: The Debate Continues', *Social Studies Review*, Vol. 1, No. 3, 1986, pp. 32–6, and Drewry, G. *Judges and Politics in Britain*.

Further reading

Ewing, K.D. and Gearty, C.A. *Freedom Under Thatcher: Civil Liberties in Modern Britain* (Oxford, 1990).

Dowdle, J.L. 'The Factortame Case', *Talking Politics,* Vol. 6, No. 3, 1994.

Drewry, G. 'Judges and Politics in Britain', *Social Studies Review*, Vol. 2, No. 2, 1986.

Griffith, J.A.G. *The Politics of the Judiciary*, 4th edn (London, 1991).

Wade, E.C.S. and Bradley, A.W. *Constitutional and Administrative Law* (London, 1993).

Walker, R. J. *The English Legal System* (London, 1985).

Zander, M. 'A Bill of Rights the debate continues', *Social Studies Review,* Vol. 1, No. 3, 1986.

Zander, M. *The Law Making Process* (London, 1989).

CHAPTER 11

Local government in Britain

This chapter centres on a discussion of the need for local government and on the central–local government relationship in a unitary state. Local government may be defined as:

An institution incorporating local representation and administration established by central government with the aim of providing a range of services at a local level. Usually local government includes an elected group of representatives, called councillors, who are responsible for an administrative machine staffed by locally-employed people who are in effect a local civil service.

In this chapter we shall address the following topics :

11.1   The theories of local government.

11.2   Reform of local government in the 1960s and 1970s.

11.3   Local government finance in the 1980s and 1990s.

11.4   The central–local relationship.

11.5   Local government into the 1990s: the Heseltine Review.

11.6   Conclusions.

11.1 | The theories of local government

Since the 1960s local government in the UK has been the subject of a continuing debate over role and powers. In a unitary state some form of local government is a necessary to provide local services at an easily accountable level, but it creates a dilemma because it is a form of decentralisation. How much power should local government have and how much control should central government exert? These questions lie at the heart of the topic. The simple answer is that central government has over the past hundred years granted local authorities' powers and responsibilities that can be altered or removed at any time. In the UK, local government is a form of **decentralisation** and administrative devolution.

Key concept: decentralisation

Rather than organising all the functions of government and state at a national level, which could be inefficient and clumsy, governments have allocated a range of responsibilities to smaller administrative organs either on a regional or local level, e.g. the provision of social services. Decentralisation is more an administrative convenience than a democratic extension, and involves the allocation of administrative functions at a more efficient local level. In the UK powers have been given to local authorities to organise a range of services including the provision of refuse collection, education, and town and country planning responsibilities. Allied to the idea of decentralisation is the idea of devolution.

Key concept: devolution

This means the delegation of specific powers to a subordinate unit of government. In practice it means that central government establishes a system of regional or local executives and legislatures with specific roles and powers. This unit has a certain amount of freedom to use these powers within strict parameters to organise local services. This is a more limited and specific term than decentralisation, aimed at increasing both democratic representation and the provision of local services.

Key concept: centralism

This term means the concentration of executive and legislative power in a core of institutions of the State with very limited distribution of powers and authority to lesser administrative organs throughout the country. Central government tends to have responsibility for the control of urban planning and development and administers the provision of all the public services and amenities for the whole country from its central base.

Key concept: localism

This is the opposite of centralism and suggests an element of devolved power and responsibility to political and administrative institutions established in geographically definable areas, e.g. counties. These authorities provide a range of public services and tend to be given responsibility for the structural and social development of the local administration, e.g. urban planning.

In Britain neither decentralisation nor administrative devolution, are entrenched ideas. Local authorities in Britain have powers granted to them by Parliament, which at any time Parliament may remove or alter. Local government exists only at the pleasure of Parliament, or rather Whitehall.

By comparison in the United States where a federal system of government exists, the individual states have specific roles and responsibilities which are permanently granted to them by virtue of the written constitution. Over the past 200 years the range of the responsibilities of the individual state governments has been diminished by the increased responsibility and roles of the federal (central) government, but State governments are still powerful institutions in the United States today, and are certainly more powerful than local authorities in Britain.

Central to the debate over the nature of UK local government are the ideas of **centralism** versus **localism**.

If it is accepted that there is a need based upon administrative practicalities alone, even in a unitary state, for some form of localism or administrative devolution. Such ideas are furthered in liberal democracies by the principle that local people should not only elect a central government but that they should have some administrative and political control over their own community. Therefore local government should exist:

1. to enable local people to participate in making decisions for their own community;
2. to encourage pluralistic representation and accountability of local representatives for the decisions made;
3. to ensure an element of localism within a democracy providing for a form of local autonomy from central government;
4. to allow efficient and effective administrative devolution of central government services.

The need for local control

1. Local people should be able to decide what services their community should enjoy and how those services will be paid for.
2. Ideas of local democracy mean that a community should be able to elect representatives to a local assembly which is empowered to make policy for the local community.
3. Locally elected representatives with local knowledge are better equipped to decide in the interests of the community than a distant administrative central government department.
4. Financial control is central to the local versus central debate. Financial autonomy should allow local authorities to raise

their own independent revenue. It should be exercised by local councillors who are responsible to the local community for the level of local taxation they establish.

5. In principle 'localism' implies a high degree of administrative, financial and political control. Independent revenue gives a high degree of independence from central control.

6. Administrative devolution, in principle, allows local authorities the opportunity to apply central government policies to particular local circumstances.

The need for central control

1. In principle in a unitary state local autonomy must be balanced with the need for central control.

2. Administrative devolution requires an element of central control over the administrative actions of local government to ensure that adminstrative functions are performed effectively and efficiently. Close supervision and inspection of the services which local government is required to provide – police, education and social services – is performed by central government to ensure that uniformity in provision, quality and efficiency is achieved in relation to adapting each service to local needs.

3. In a unitary state, Parliament has higher democratic credentials than local government, possessing a duty of care for the whole nation and being responsible for monitoring local government. If the structures are found wanting it is the role of Parliament to exercise legal control over it, amending when necessary the structures and operations of local government.

4. Local government should be subject to control by the courts to ensure that their actions are both legal and just.

5. Financial control over local government has to be exercised by central government because:

- In the modern unitary state central government provides a substantial amount of funding for local government from the revenues of central taxation.

- The sheer scale of local government finances, now in the region of billions of pounds, means that it can, in certain cases, have damaging effects upon the economic policies of central government.

- Central government funding of poorer local authorities is vital to top up the revenues of poorer authorities which serviced poor areas of the country to ensure that services are provided and a degree of uniformity exists between authorities.

It is necessary to find a balance between these two positions to allow local autonomy and paternal control from the centre.

Questions

1. Distinguish between localism and centralism
2. What is decentralisation?
3. Outline a case (a) for local control and (b) for central control?

11.2 | Reform of local government in the 1960s and 1970s

By the 1950s the system of local government which had been established in the last century was proving to be inadequate and inefficient. Pressure to undertake a radical reform of the structure of local government resulted in the establishment of a number of Royal Commissions during the 1960s – a popular tool of government used to analyse a problem or issue in depth and suggest a range of measures. The reformers sought to reconcile the need for larger, financially viable authorities which would provide efficient provision of services and ensure localism. 'Modernisation' and 'efficiency' were the guiding concepts of the reforms.

The Herbert Commission Report on London, 1960

The Herbert Commission Report examined the provisions of local government in London and recommended the creation of a central authority whose responsibility would be to act as a strategic planning authority in London, responsible for the city's economic and social development. Herbert suggested that the number of small borough authorities should be reduced and that these units should be responsible for day-to-day services.[1]

The Herbert Commission's recommendations were implemented in 1965 with the creation of the Greater London Council (GLC) as the strategic planning authority for London, and thirty-three borough councils responsible for day-to-day services, e.g. refuse collection and public amenities.

The Redcliffe–Maud Commission, 1966–9

This Redcliffe–Maud Commission was established in 1966 to suggest possible reforms of local Government in England and Wales. Maud reported that:

1. the present system did not meet the needs of modern Britain and was not conducive to proper planning;
2. it was too fragmented with too many councils;
3. local government in Britain lacked a professional, highly trained staff;

4. local government in Britain should provide efficient services, attract and hold public interest, be able to deal with other parts of central government and most importantly, be adaptable.

The Redcliffe–Maud Commission was unable to agree about the means of reform. The Commission believed that local government had to meet demographic trends but it could not agree on its recommendations and wrote two reports, a majority report and an minority report.

The majority report recommended the creation of fifty-eight 'unitary' county authorities providing all functions, and three metropolitan authorities. The minority report recommended the creation of a two-tier structure based on city regions.

The majority Maud report was accepted by Harold Wilson's Labour Government but, after the 1970 General Election, reform of the system fell to the newly-elected Conservative Government of Sir Edward Heath. The Conservatives sought to create a two-tier system abolishing many smaller authorities in favour of creating larger metropolitan authorities. Many of the provisions of these reforms came under intense criticism for destroying small historical authorities in favour of urban giants which were distant from many of the localities which they served, and for confused allocations of functions.

The Local Government Reorganisation Act, 1972

1. The Local Government Reorganisation Act, 1972 established a two-tier structure of local government. On the first tier of local government in England the Act created the structure detailed in *Figure 25*.

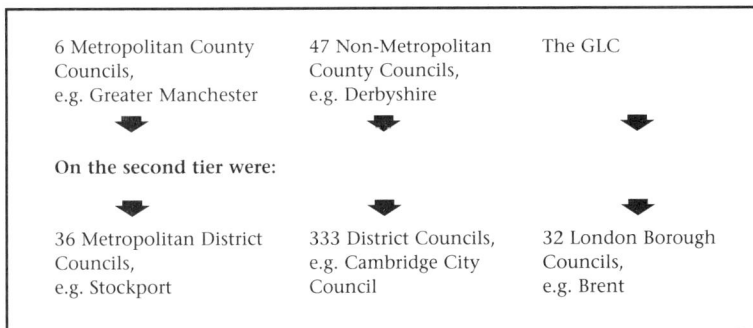

Figure 25 The first tier of local government.

Below this level many Parish Councils remained, but possessed few powers.

2. In Wales the Act created the two tiers shown in *Figure 26*.

Figure 26 The two tiers of local government in Wales.

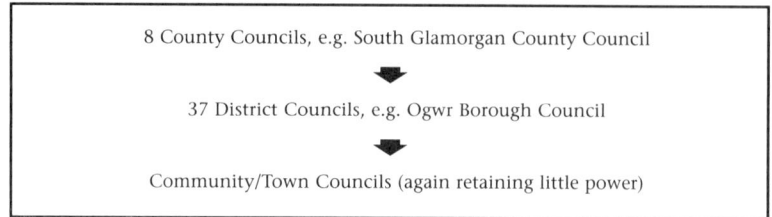

8 County Councils, e.g. South Glamorgan County Council

↓

37 District Councils, e.g. Ogwr Borough Council

↓

Community/Town Councils (again retaining little power)

The Act reflected the changing pattern of population distribution with the UK and sought to create authorities which were suited to the needs and distribution of the British population within newly defined geographic areas. The metropolitan counties were designed to serve populations of between 1.2 and 2.8 million people whereas the Metropolitan district councils were designed to serve populations of between 174,000 and 1.1 million. London was left undistributed until 1987.

The Act did:

1.   Redistribute authority and responsibility, giving the top tier responsibility for the more costly and politically significant services, e.g. strategic planning, transport, police, education, social services, while the lower tier undertook more local functions, e.g. housing, local planning, environmental health and leisure services.
2.   The special problems of the most heavily populated parts of the country were recognised with the creation of the six metropolitan counties – Manchester, Merseyside, West Yorkshire, South Yorkshire, West Midlands and Tyne and Wear – which were given major responsibilities, i.e. education, housing, police, transport.

The Act was an extremely unpopular piece of legislation and was heavily criticised on the following points:

1.   it destroyed a number of historic counties, e.g. the absorption of Rutland by Leicestershire;
2.   it was accused of creating an expensive, bureaucratic top tier in the form of the metropolitan county councils;
3.   it failed to address the issue of finance and as a result the new authorities immediately encountered financial difficulties.

Critics have since claimed that the aims of the Act, which were efficiency, intelligibility, and local autonomy, were never fully achieved. In the later half of the 1970s this new structure of local government was frequently lambasted in the press for overspending and waste. Subsequently, the topicality of local government and the nature of the central–local relationship became a constant topic on the modern political agenda. In 1979 the Conservatives came to power with a manifesto commitment to reform local government finance.[2] This commitment resulted in a huge series of reforms throughout the 1980s which altered the central–local government relationship radically.

Questions

1. (a) What were the main recommendations of the Redcliffe–
    Maud Report?
    (b) Were these recommendations implemented?
2. Outline the structure of local government in England and Wales after
    the 1972 Local Government Act.

11.3 | Local government finance in the 1980s and 1990s

The nature of reform during the 1980s was mainly focused on the financial aspects of local government. It is therefore necessary to discuss the basics of local government finance first.

Sources

Local government receives revenue from four principle sources: local taxation, central government, charges and borrowing and investments.

1. Local taxation has taken a variety of forms in the past twenty years. These taxes are raised and administered by the local authority and have been calculated according to income or size of property. In the 1970s local taxes were called 'the rates', a property tax which by the late 1970s had become heavily criticised. This gave rise to pressure for a reform of the local taxation system which the Conservative Party pledged to undertake in 1979.[3]
2. Since 1945, as the burdens upon local government have increased, it has become financially dependent upon central government funding, which took the form of a block grant known for some time as the Rate Support Grant. In the 1970s the block grant which each local authority received amounted to over 60% of its income. These grants were originally for specific purposes, but since 1958 they have been general grants, enabling local authorities to use the money how they wished. By the late 1970s this system of funding was being heavily criticised and during the 1980s it was reformed.
3. Local authorities gain revenue from charges for the services they provide, e.g. rents, commercial refuse collection, leisure centres.
4. A final source of local authority finance comes from borrowing money for long-term building projects from the institutions of the City of London, and their own investments. Local authorities borrow large amounts of money which they pay

back over many years. This is known as **capital borrowing** (*see Figure 27*).

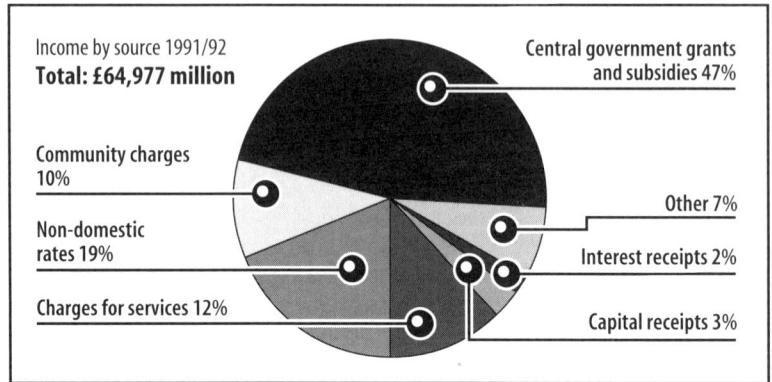

Income by source 1991/92
Total: £64,977 million

Central government grants and subsidies 47%

Community charges 10%

Other 7%

Non-domestic rates 19%

Interest receipts 2%

Charges for services 12%

Capital receipts 3%

Expenditure

Local authorities provide a range of services, education, transport, arts and libraries, etc. They spend a large amount of their annual budget on the daily provision of these services, the costs of local administration and capital investment projects. **Capital investment** means that large sums of money are allocated over a number of years to provide for large-scale spending projects, for example, new buildings like schools or leisure centres. The amount which the average authority spends on its different services is illustrated in *Figure 28*.

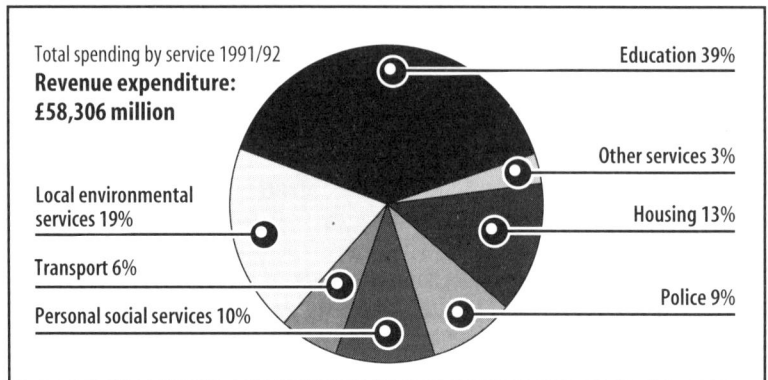

Total spending by service 1991/92
Revenue expenditure: £58,306 million

Education 39%

Other services 3%

Local environmental services 19%

Housing 13%

Transport 6%

Police 9%

Personal social services 10%

The annual spending on the provision of services is met by the levying of a local tax, central government financial support, revenue from charges and financial investments. Capital projects, which often cost millions of pounds, are paid for through local authorities borrowing capital. Such large-scale borrowing can affect the economic policies of central government. Throughout the 1970s central government became increasingly concerned over the level of local government capital expenditure and the effect which that had on macro-economic policy.

In the 1970s local authority expenditure and the problems surrounding its ability to raise revenue entered a crisis period and resulted in large-scale local rate increases. These increases caused alarm in Whitehall and led to the creation of the Layfield Committee of inquiry which was responsible for examining the whole matter of local government finance.

The Layfield Committee, 1976

The Layfield report was highly critical of the system of local authority finance, concluding that it was characterised by confusion and weak accountability. It recommended:

1. That either central or local government should assume greater responsibility for financial control.
2. Local authorities should be given greater responsibility for raising a larger share of their revenue through a local income tax and a reduction in the grant which local authorities received from central government.[6]

The Labour government failed to act on the central recommendation of the Layfield Committee, which was that the local taxation system should be reformed making local authorities more responsible for the revenue they raised. The Government indicated that a policy of greater control over local authority spending would begin.[7]

This policy was enthusiastically adopted by the Thatcher Government.

The 1981 Local Government Act

The 1981 Local Government Act reorganised the block grant system.

1. New controls were introduced to allow high-spending authorities to be identified, and powers were given to central government to penalise these high spenders.
2. The Rate Support Grant was replaced by a new block grant which was based on grant related expenditures; each local authority's projected expenditure was compared with what the Department of the Environment calculated that it should spend. This resulted in a reduction in the size of the grant if the calculation showed that the local authority was spending more than central government thought it should.

It was hoped that those authorities which overspent and had their grant reduced accordingly would reduce their expenditure or raise the level of local taxation which would make them unpopular. However, this did not work as effectively as the Government had hoped and it became necessary to take further action.

The 1985 'rate capping' Act

A 1985 Act introduced 'rate capping'. This Act enhanced the controls of central government over local authorities by giving the Secretary of State for the Environment the power to place a ceiling on the rate increases and spending budgets. This meant that a limit called the Standard Spending Assessment was set for each authority and the level of the rates had to be within this assessment. This allowed central government to place limits on the level of spending and rate increases. The new Act allowed the Department to designate local authorities whose spending was considered 'excessive', mainly, in its first years of operation, Labour councils.

If the local authority defied the rate-cap and refused to cut their expenditure to the standard spending assessment limit the Act allowed the government to impose a financial penalty upon the councillors themselves, called a surcharge. The Act also provided for the disqualification of councillors from office for five years.

The Audit Commission

The Audit Commission was established in 1982 to ensure that public money was used properly and that no illegalities occurred in finances of local government. The Audit Commission, which is appointed by central Government, is a regulatory body with powers to scrutinise local authority spending and conducts an annual audit of local authority accounts. The Commission is also responsible for ensuring the efficient use of public money by local authorities, and has produced a number of reports criticising the waste in local government and suggesting savings.

The abolition of the Greater London Council (GLC) and the Metropolitan County Councils

In 1986, fulfilling a 1983 election pledge, the Conservative Government abolished the GLC and the six metropolitan county councils. This removed a whole tier of government which the Conservatives believed was inefficient, expensive and extravagant. These councils – all Labour-controlled – were an element of opposition which the Government wished to see removed. Local government moral was further dented by the fact that many of its functions were not given to the new tier of authorities. Instead a whole range of quangos were established.

Example:
Transport, fire, police and waste disposal were given to a range of unelected bodies, such as the London Regional Transport Board.

The Community Charge

In its second term the Thatcher Government turned its attention to reform of the rate system, a pledge it had first made in 1979. A Green Paper, 'Paying for Local Government', was published in 1986.[8]

The paper recommended:

1. the abolition of the rates with a new form of local tax which every adult living in a local authority would pay regardless of income, the Community Charge (or Poll Tax, as it became known).
2. reform of the business rate. Local authorities would loose complete control over the business rate. This would now be set, collected and distributed by central government. The new rate was called the Uniform Business Rate.
3. reform of the grants system; part allocated according to need and part allocated on a per capita basis.

These recommendations were incorporated into the 1987 Conservative Manifesto and led to the subsequent Act which established the new tax.

The Community Charge was first introduced in Scotland in April 1989 and in England and Wales in April 1990. It was instantly unpopular in Scotland, and this feeling spread across the whole nation by the summer of 1990. The reasons for its unpopularity included the following:

1. The Government had publicly estimated that the average Community Charge bill would be £276. This was wildly inaccurate. Some bills were massively above this figure ranging between £300 and £600 per person.[9]
2. The tax hit the middle classes worst. The rates bill had been a single bill whereas the Community Charge was, for the average family, two bills – one for each partner. Many people suffered a huge increase in the amount of money they contributed to local government. In some areas the average family who had been paying a £500 rates bill were faced with a Community Charge bill of over £1,000.

However, there were exceptions to this and some authorities did issue bills which met the average or indeed fell short of it. In the London boroughs of Wandsworth and Westminster the Community Charge was very low, £148 and £188 respectively.

3. The new uniform business rate proved equally unpopular imposing similar tax increases on businesses.
4. The tax created a variety of public 'martyrs' who refused to pay, which fuelled non-payment campaigns. Some Labour MPs and councillors not only refused to pay but urged citizens not to do so. By the spring of 1991 over £1 billion of Community Charge bills remained unpaid.

Large-scale non-payment campaigns added to the already high costs of collection, and rather than making high-taxing local authorities unpopular, the Community Charge made the Conservative Government extremely unpopular. As public demonstrations and the levels of non-payment increased the Government sought to defuse the situation by promising greater central government financial support to mitigate the rate of the following year's Community Charge. However, local government elections that year were a disaster for the Government and it became clear that the Charge was becoming an unsolvable misery for the Conservative Party and its leader. It was a contributory factor in the events of November 1990.

The council tax

On taking office the Major Government pledged to replace the Community Charge. Michael Heseltine, then the new Secretary of State for the Environment, announced a wholesale review of every aspect of local government. In England a Local Government Commission was established to make proposals for a reorganisation, except in London and the metropolitan districts. Similar reviews were conducted by both the Welsh and Scottish Offices (*see section 11.5*). The Government offered to open membership of their review of local government finance to the opposition parties, but all refused to take part.[10]

Comment

The Government review examined a range of options, and in the April of 1991, after a number of delays, Michael Heseltine announced to the House of Commons that the Government would replace the Community Charge with the Council Tax. The Council Tax marked a return to a form of local taxation based on the value of property.

A Bill was introduced in November 1991 which was enacted in the Spring of 1992. The new tax would mean one bill per household and would be calculated using two elements, a property element based on the market value of the property, with a banding system dictating the tax payable, and a second element that assumed at least two adults per household. The scheme provided for a series of discounts (25% for single people and 100% for students).

The implementation of the council tax was completed relatively smoothly. All properties in local authority areas were registered and their market value assessed. Those with less expensive homes were to pay less than those with expensive homes. Each local authority set its charges across the band system, calculated on the basis of the total value of the properties in the area and its own expenditure requirement. In 1993 the average council tax for a band D property in London was £557.66. Outside London the average council tax for a band D house accordingly varies. In Cambridge the council tax in 1994 for a band D property was 551.86. The legislation provided an appeals procedure against a valuation of a property and by the end of 1993 one million appeals had been logged.[11]

The Council Tax seemed a fairer scheme of local taxation, taking some account of peoples' income according to where they live, and it has not caused the waves of public protest which arose over the Community Charge. The average household saved money with the introduction of this tax. Local authorities welcomed it because it was easier to implement and collect. With its implementation the Government ensured that during the new tax's phasing-in period no household would face too great an increase in its bill via the Council Tax Transitional Reduction Scheme. This scheme ensured that during the first few years of the new tax, the increase of some households bills would be limited. Rather than one large 'overnight' increase the scheme gave financial relief, allowing the increase to be staggered over a few years. This policy was designed to limit the degree of the financial pain which some households would feel in the first years of the Council Tax.[12]

Other aspects of local government finance remained untouched, i.e. the grants system, the centralised business rate, and capping – which now became Council Tax capping. These aspects of central government control over local government finance continue to cause resentment. The grants system continues to be a contentious issue. The standard spending assessments are misunderstood and often used by central government to cut local authority expenditure. Each year the Conservative Government publishes a list of authorities which are over-spenders and are to be capped. Over the past three years the list has become smaller and this event has become a moment of pure political theatre in the House of Commons. But this underscores a more serious point.

In summary:

1. Central government control over local government finance has increased dramatically in the past sixteen years.
2. Local taxation has undergone great turbulence in the past five years, but now a system is in place which should last for some time to come.
3. Central government has introduced a number of other reforms into local government practice which have changed many of its services and the way in which these services are delivered.

   Example: *Competitive tendering and market testing.*

Questions

1. What are the major sources of local authority finances?
2. What are (a) Council Tax capping, and (b) the standard spending assessment?
3. (a) What was the Community Charge, or Poll Tax?
   (b) Why was it replaced with the Council Tax?

11.4 | The central–local relationship

The central government–local government relationship is based on the fact that in a unitary state, central government can give and remove the powers and duties of local authorities. At the heart of this relationship is the question: what should the role of local government be in relation to central government?:

1. one view suggests that the relationship should be as *partners* to central government; co-operation, delegation and local responsibility being the key characteristics of this relationship.
2. another view sees local government in Britain acting as *agents* for central government, wherein local government is strictly controlled from the centre, implementing the policies and obligations placed upon it by central government. In this relationship the local authorities' freedom of action is limited.
3. a further view sees the need, even in a unitary state, for a degree of *delegation and local autonomy*. Local government is therefore another tier of democracy established by central government and should be equipped with the powers to raise its own revenue, elect its own representatives, be accountable to the community it serves and decide its own priorities, level of services and future development. In this perspective local government should be semi-autonomous.

The problem for 'Great Britain Limited' is finding a happy medium between these differing viewpoints. Inevitably in a unitary state local autonomy can never be fully realised. The needs and aims of central government take priority over those of local government and this can place the two on a collision course. In Britain, local government possesses some characteristics from all three of the above viewpoints. It does exert influence upon central government individually and collectively via local authority associations. In many respects it possesses a great deal of power on matters as varied as education and planning, but there is an endemic friction between the centre and periphery because the role of local government in the UK system has never been clearly defined.

A number of legal procedures can be used to control local authorities:

1. they may be sued for their actions or prevented from carrying out an act by an injunction;
2. their actions may be declared *ultra vires*. This means that an act or decision can be declared illegal and beyond the scope of the powers given to a local authority under an Act of Parliament. It means that a local authority cannot do anything which was not expressly allowed under the original Act of Parliament.

Example:
In Mixnam's Properties Ltd *vs* Chertsey Urban District Council, *the Courts held that local authorities were given wide powers to impose conditions as to the use of caravan sites, but that these did not extend to conditions relating to agreements for letting caravans to individual dwellers.*

3.   the courts could choose to use a rare set of powers called the prerogative orders to compel a duty to be performed or restrain the local authority from carrying out an action.

●   *an order of mandamus* requires the local authority to carry out a duty imposed on it by law;

●   *an order of prohibition* prevents a local authority from proceeding with an action where it appears to be exceeding its authority, failing to follow correct procedures or contravening the laws of natural justice.

These are a few of the legal remedies which can be used to control the actions of a local authority. The use of the courts to control the actions of local authorities is becoming rarer because of the costs involved, but perhaps the most frequently used are the doctrine of *ultra vires* and injunctions.

Administrative controls

The central administration in Whitehall has a variety of tools which it can use to control the actions of local authorities. Many of these controls stem from Acts of Parliament which place duties upon local authorities that are then, if necessary, monitored and overseen by Whitehall departments. Additionally, Ministers are given powers to control and scrutinise local authorities. These include regulations, power of approval, power of inspection, default powers, and persuasion and influence.

1.   *Regulations:* under some Acts of Parliament Ministers are given powers to make rules/regulations which affect the actions of local authorities. Furthermore some Acts give Ministers the power to authorise a decision of a local authority. These include compulsory purchase orders and clearance orders.

2.   *Approval:* often a local authority requires the approval of a Minister before they can go ahead with a plan or scheme.

Example:
Major redevelopment schemes require ministerial approval before they can begin.

3.   *Powers of inspection:* many of the services which local authorities provide are subject to government inspection. Local authority education services and social services are often inspected by Her Majesty's Inspectors to ensure standards are being met and attainment targets achieved.

4. *Default powers:* These are very important. If a local authority fails to carry out a duty which under an Act of Parliament it is obliged to perform, and if this failure continues a Minister may take over the function themselves by appointing an agent or commissioner to go to the local authority and ensure that the duty is performed.

   Example: The Clay Cross Council in 1972. Under the terms of the Housing Finance Act 1972 all local authorities were obliged to raise the level of rent for all its council housing. The Clay Cross Council refused to apply this rent rise and the Heath Government chose to appoint a Commissioner to take over powers from the Council because it had failed to comply with the Act of Parliament.[13]

5. *Persuasion and influence:* A Minister may use a variety of persuasive tools to encourage a local authority to follow government leads and adopt favoured schemes. Research reports, white papers and government circulars can be used to indicate central government thinking and influence the actions of local government. Furthermore, through ministerial meetings the leaders of councils can be influenced and persuaded to adopt or drop a course of action.

All of these methods may be used by Whitehall to control the actions and policies of local authorities, and moreover, they can compel local authorities to act. Most of these powers originate from the variety of Acts of Parliament which concern themselves with local government.

Legislative controls

The modern system of local government has been created by Acts of Parliament. These Acts create a variety of duties and obligations upon local authorities which can either compel local authorities to do things (mandatory powers), give them powers which they may chose to exercise if the need arises (permissive powers), or powers which can only be adopted via a certain procedure set down in an Act of Parliament (adoptive powers).

Parliament not only gives powers to local authorities, but it can also grant powers to them at their request via the Private Bill procedure. Private Bills may be laid before Parliament to give local authorities specific power to complete specific tasks. Private Bills are used to give local authorities permission to pass new by-laws, or begin major construction projects and redevelopments.

Conclusions

The nature of central–local relations suggests an unequal balance in favour of the institutions at the centre of the British state over the limited scheme of delegated power which can be described as local government. A whole range of controls exist which limit the freedom of action and decision-making capacity of every local authority in the country. These controls are exercised to varying degrees but the cumulative effect expresses the unitary nature of the British state. The most important are the collection of financial controls which have been amplified in the past sixteen years.

Local government in Britain today has very limited freedom of action through financial, administrative and legal restrictions. The Conservatives came to power with the aim of increasing central government control over local government. They have successfully achieved this aim, but interestingly, the main thrust of their reforms have been more in the field of financial controls than any other. Conservatives argue that while local councils have lost powers, these powers have not all passed to the centre. Rather some have been handed to the consumer of local services who now has the opportunity of exercising a greater say in the affairs of local authorities.

Example:
Parents and local community representatives on school governing bodies.

Alternatively, critics argue that these reforms have not only brought more central control but have changed local government's mode of operation through the introduction of policies like competitive tendering. They claim that the 1980s and early 1990s have been a period in the history of Britain in which there has been a large-scale redistribution of power back to the core. This is clearly reflected in the history of central local relations during the 1980s.

Questions

1. Name some of the ways in which central government affects the actions of local authorities.
2. What is the difference between the mandatory and permissive powers of local authorities?
3. How can the courts control the activities of local authorities?
4. Define the term *ultra vires*.
5. What was the importance of the Clay Cross case?

11.5 | Local government into the 1990s: the Heseltine Review

The Heseltine Review

In the past fifteen years the nature of the Government's reforms of local government have primarily concentrated on financial reforms and the imposition of greater central control upon local government finances. However, a number of other reforms have been introduced which have changed the nature of local government services.

Example: Competitive tendering
This policy compels local authorities to put a number of their services out to tender. This means that bids were invited from private firms to provide services previously performed by local authorities. Under the terms of the Local Government Planning and Land Act 1980 highway repair, building construction and maintenance work had to be put out to tender. This was known as **compulsory competitive tendering**. *Services like cleansing, catering and refuse collection were soon added to the list of services which had to be put out to tender.*

A range of other reforms have seen a reduction in the responsibility of local authorities as providers of services.

Example:
In the field of education, which has traditionally been a responsibility of local government, schools may now opt-out of local authority control. Other reforms have included the privatisation of local authority housing estates.

The Government now believes in the concept of **enabling authorities**, which would result in local authorities having a minimalist role acting as a regulator of services supplied through the private sector rather than a provider of public services.

This new view of local government in the UK has been accompanied by a complete review of the structure and role of local government in the UK designed to create enabling authorities.

A Local Government Commission, headed by Sir John Banham, was established to make recommendations for the reorganisation of local government in England.[14] The aim of this review was to replace the two-tier 1974 structure with a single tier of unitary authorities that combine the roles previously performed separately by district and county councils. A similar review was launched by the Scottish Office and the Welsh Office. The Government claimed that these new unitary authorities would promote local democracy,

Key concept: enabling local authorities

This is the idea that local authorities should provide opportunities for the community it serves to have a range of good services which are provided via tender schemes. The local authority should act as a regulator and monitor of a range of services, some supplied by outside contractors, ensuring the best possible cost, efficiency and quality. Such authorities follow a market driven ideology placing many of their services out to tender, ensuring good service at the cheapest cost to the council taxpayer. Furthermore, this policy should ensure the delivery of services closer to the customer.

reduce administrative costs and improve the delivery and quality of local services and from the Commission's terms of reference it was clear that Whitehall favoured the restructuring of local government into a single tier of unitary authorities.

Proposals for reform of the internal structures of local government were contained in a Department of the Environment (DoE) consultation paper in 1991 which discussed the possibilities of reforming the internal structures of local government. This suggested that internal structures should be adapted to promote more effective, rapid and business-like decision making, increase public interest and make better use of councillors' time.[15]

While at the DoE it became clear that Michael Heseltine himself favoured the introduction of directly elected heads of local councils; an individual popularly elected to head the local council, with his or her own manifesto which they would seek to implement. This system of popularly elected 'executive' heads of local authorities is found in the United States and some parts of Europe. In this system the people directly elect a mayor who has a range of executive powers to organise and administer the local community. Such mayors can become quite powerful national politicians, especially if they are the leaders of a big city like Paris or New York. This idea was unacceptable to many in the Major Cabinet because they feared that it would create a new and effective echelon of opposition with many of Britain's urban centres controlled by Labour Party mayors. A DoE working party was established in 1991 to consider reform of the council committee structure, the appointment of council managers and directly elected mayors.[16]

The Welsh and Scottish reviews were completed in 1993. The Welsh review recommended the establishment of twenty-two[17] new unitary authorities providing all the local government services in their areas. The old system of eight county councils and thirty-seven district councils would be swept away and replaced with new authorities possessing the old names of Wales.

Example:
The old county names of Monmouthshire, Cardiganshire, Flintshire and Denbighshire would return.[18]

The new emphasis on unitary authorities was further demonstrated by the publication of the Scottish Office review in July 1993, which proposed a similar scheme for Scotland. The review recommended the creation of a single tier of local government in Scotland through a restructuring which would produce twenty-eight local authorities, including four unitary councils for Glasgow, Edinburgh, Dundee and Aberdeen, replacing the existing nine regional and fifty-three district councils and making a saving of over £65 million a year.[19]

Key concepts: unitary authorities

This refers to the idea that instead of having two local authorities with divided responsibilities for a local community there should be one local authority which performs all the functions and services of local government for an area. The review which the Major Government launched favoured the restructuring of local government in Britain to create these all-embracing single local authorities.

In England the Banham Commission has been slow in reporting its recommendations,[20] but these have included recommendations to create unitary authorities and two-tier authorities.

Example:
In the summer of 1993 it proposed the abolition, as expected, of Avon and Cleveland in favour of a single tier of local authorities in each area.[21] In November 1993 it recommended the retention of a two-tier structure with some adjustments in Durham, and in Derbyshire the Commission proposed a restructuring which would retain a two-tier structure.[22]

The Commission has encountered serious criticism. Proposals for two-tier authorities have not been well received by the Government, which had expressed a preference for unitary authorities wherever possible, and some of its ideas have upset the local government lobby.[23] It has been accused of failing to ask what functions local government is intended to serve and has been criticised for its methodology and costings.

Questions

1. What is the aim of the Local Government Commission?
2. What is meant by the terms (a) unitary authorities, and (b) enabling authorities?

11.6 | Conclusions

The importance and significance of local government within the British state has grown in recent years. Local government is now a highly charged political issue across the ranges of its functions and roles, including finance, structure, and central–local relations. Twenty years ago local government existed on the periphery of party politics: now it orbits the centre.

1. The major political parties regard local elections with increased importance, pouring money and personalities into local election campaigns.
2. The numbers of authorities that each party controls is important for the prestige and moral of the party, and indicative of possible parliamentary seats.
3. The control of local government by central government has increased dramatically in the past sixteen years, most notably in finance. It is reasonable to suggest that local government will never again pose the worries for Her Majesty's Treasury that it did during the 1970s.
4. The Conservative Government will restructure local government in England. If this has not happened before the

next general election the next election manifesto will probably contain commitments to a restructuring.

5. In the past sixteen years the roles and powers of local government have been diluted. The Government's aim is to create councils which no longer directly provide but instead enable the delivery of services in partnership with the private sector. These new authorities will take British local government into the new millennium.

6. The development of local government in Britain during the 1980s ended until recently the *regionalism* debate. During the 1970s there was a debate about the structure of local government and centralisation in the UK. Proponents of a decentralised system of government in the UK advocated a regional structure of local government. This scheme would be based on the larger counties possessing cultural identities including Cornwall and Yorkshire, and less culturally distinctive regional concepts such as the North East of England and East Anglia. The regional government debate was very much linked to the devolution debate and both seem to have faded in the post-1979 period. However, during the 1992 General Election campaign the topic surfaced briefly. Both the Liberal Democrats and Labour are committed to moves in this direction.[24]

7. The changes that have taken place have resulted in centre–local conflict. This was inevitable given the nature of the changes and the inherent conflict within a unitary state between the desire for local autonomy and the need for central control. The poor state of centre–local relations after many years of new legislation and changes was acknowledged by John Major in February 1993 when he told a conference of Conservative councillors that it was time the skirmishing between central and local government came to an end, saying, 'Let us stop battering one another around the head and get on with good government.'[25] For the foreseeable future, under the shadow of the Local Government Commission and tight central control of local authorities' revenues and expenditures, local government will continue to undergo reform until the purest form of enabling authorities has been created, and these factors will mean that centre–local relations remain poor.

Essay questions

1. Is the relationship between central government and local government an equal or an unequal partnership?
2. What is the nature of central–local relations in the UK?
3. Are local councils anything more than the agents of central government?
4. Discuss the changing nature of the relationship between central and local government.

Essay planning

4.   Discuss the changing nature of the relationship between central and local government.

This essay requires you to analyse how central–local relations have changed in recent years. An answer to this question must encompass the following points:

(a)   A description of the traditional role of local government in a unitary state: local democracy, provider of local services, administrative devolution, and financial responsibility.

(b)   Explain that in the 1960s the size of local authority budgets began to cause central government concerns which led in the late 1970s to moves to control local government finances.

(c)   Explain how local government finances were brought under stricter control in the 1980s. Use material from sections 11.2, 11.3 and 11.4. Include a brief discussion of:
(i)   rate (council tax) capping
(ii)   reduction of central government grants
(iii)   reform of the local tax system, to make local government more accountable for its spending.

(d)   Explain that in tandem with financial changes the Conservative Government sought to introduce, in line with its general philosophy, private market forces into local government to make it more efficient, i.e. competitive tendering and to reduce the roles of local government. It also sought to change the very characteristic of local government, from a provider of public services to a regulator of privately supplied services.

(e)   You have to emphasise throughout the essay that the changing relationship has seen an increase in central control over local government finance and a centrally inspired re-organisation of the services that local government supplies and now a structural re-organisation to make it more efficient.

You may conclude with an analysis that thirty years ago a purer form of localism existed, and that this has been replaced by a higher degree of centralism.

Notes and references

1.   See *The Herbert Commission Report on London*, Cmnd 1164 (London, 1960).

2.   Travers, T. 'Community Charge and other Financial Changes', in Stewart, J. and Stoker, G. *The Future of Local Government* (London, 1989), p. 10.

3.   Willetts, D. *Modern Conservatism* (London, 1992), p. 58.

4.   *The Guardian*, 2, 03.05.94.

5. Ibid.

6. See The Layfield Committee Report, Cmnd 6453 (London, 1977).

7. Travers, T. 'Community Charge' (1989), p. 10.

8. See 'Paying for Local Government', Cmnd 9714 (London, 1986).

9. Travers, T. 'Community Charge' (1989), p. 19.

10. *The Guardian*, 2, 30.04.93, pp. 10–11.

11. Ibid.

12. 'The Council Tax: The Transitional Reduction Scheme.' The Department of Environment, 14014 (London, 1993).

13. Harvey, J. and Bather, L. *British Constitution and Politics* (London, 1982), p. 390.

14. *The Guardian*, 04.03.93.

15. 'The Internal Management of Local Authorities in England: A Consultation paper.' Department of the Environment, 1991.

16. This reported in July 1993 and its recommendations are contained in 'Community Leadership and Representation: Unlocking the Potential.' Report of Working Party on Internal Management of Local Authorities (London, 1993).

17. *The Guardian*, 02.02.94.

18. *The Guardian*, 04.03.93 and 'Local Government in Wales: A Charter for the Future', Cm, 2155.

19. *The Guardian*, 09.07.93 and 'The Structure of Local Government: Shaping the Future – The New Councils', Cm, 2267 (London, 1993).

20. McKie, D. *The Guardian Political Almanac, 1993/4* (1993), p. 187.

21. See Robbins, L. *Politics Pal 1994* (Leicester, 1994), p. 42.

22. *The Guardian*, 09.11.93.

23. *The Guardian*, 05.7.94, 15,06.94 and *The Times*, 16.06.94, 12.07,94, 14.07.94 and 16.07.94.

24. *The Times*, 24.06.94.

25. McKie, D. *The Guardian Political Almanac,* (1993) p. 183.

Further reading

Alexander, A. 'The Decline of Local Government – Does Local Government still matter?', *Contemporary Review*, Summer 1989.

Bryne, T. *Local Government in Britain* (London, 1992).

Butcher, H. Law, I. and Mullard, M. *Local Government and Thatcherism* (London, 1990).

Greenwood, J. 'Local Government Reform', *Talking Politics*, Vol. 4. No. 2, 1991/2.

Hollis, G., Ham G. and Ambler M. *The Future Role and Structure of Local Government* (London, 1992).

Kingdom, J. *Local Government and Politics in Britain* (London, 1991).

Stewart, J. (ed.) *The Future of Local Government* (London, 1989).

Travers, T. *The Politics of Local Government Finance* (London, 1986).

Wilson, D. 'Central-Local Government Relations', *Talking Politics*, Vol. 5, No. 3. 1993.

CHAPTER 12

Elections

Most countries which are classified as representative democracies hold elections through which their citizens are able to choose their representatives and leaders. In elections people are able to choose their local representatives, their national representatives and the political complexion of the government. Sometimes, as in the USA, people are able to elect directly their head of state, e.g. President Clinton was elected in a nationwide election in 1992.

This chapter will examine the following :

12.1 Elections: terms and concepts.

12.2 The present UK voting system.

12.3 Arguments used for retaining, and replacing the present first-past-the-post system.

12.4 Alternative voting systems

12.5 The proportional representation debate.

12.6 The role of referendums and by-elections

12.7 The 1992 General Election result.

12.1 | **Elections: terms and concepts**

In Britain, every adult over the age of 18 is entitled to vote (there are a few restrictions upon this rule) in local government elections, general elections and European parliamentary elections.

An **election** is a mechanism which allows people to chose representatives to hold office and perform particular functions. It allows people to chose who governs them and permits them to hold those in office accountable for their actions. However, elections are not the only way in which those who exercise power in society are chosen, e.g. civil servants are appointed. Elections are normally governed by electoral laws, which lay down the procedure and the rules of the election. Elections may be direct,

Key term: elections

In a representative democracy, there must be some means to allow people to choose who should govern. This is achieved through popular elections where individuals are selected by the people to fill certain offices of state in Parliament or government. In France the President is elected by popular vote for seven-year terms and in Britain MPs are elected by popular vote for five-year terms.

Key concepts: the franchise and universal suffrage

This is the right to vote in elections. When every adult in the country is entitled to vote regardless of income, race or sex, and barring certain restrictions such as convicted felons of the mentally impaired, a country is said to possess universal suffrage. In Britain there has been universal suffrage since the 1920s, but in South Africa all the people have only enjoyed the franchise since April 1994.

Key term: a constituency

This is a term used to describe a territorially defined representative district in which the residents are able to vote and elect a representative to a local or national assembly.

Key term: electoral system

This is the term used to describe the method by which votes in an election are translated into seats in a legislature or other elected institution. In Britain we use the *majoritarian* model whereby candidates are elected by counting all the votes in a constituency and the seat is given to the candidate with a simple majority of votes.

Key concept: the mandate

This term refers to the idea that when a government is elected it can claim that its leaders and policies have been endorsed by the electorate and that it therefore has the right to implement its manifesto. In addition to an instruction from the people to implement their party's programme, governments claim to have a 'doctor's mandate', which is a mandate to do anything that is necessary when economic, social or defence problems arise, i.e. to act to deal with an 'illness'.

when the votes of the electorate are given for candidates for the office concerned, or indirect when the electorate first chooses representatives or delegates, who then chose from the candidates for office. Elections may also be single or multiple, depending upon whether the election is to fill a single office, such as a member of the House of Commons or to elect several candidates at once, such as the elections held annually for the National Executive Committee of the Labour Party.

In Britain there has been universal suffrage only since the 1920s. Representatives are elected to the House of Commons, the European Parliament, and local government. In the United States similar elections take place involving more than 490,000 positions.

The right to vote is known as the **franchise** and most people vote in **constituencies**. The country is divided into representative districts which vary in size geographically but are designed to contain a uniform size of population. In Britain in a general election there are 650 constituencies, each electing one Member of Parliament (MP). General elections can take place once every five years but there is no system of fixed-term elections for the House of Commons. This means that within five years of the last general election the Prime Minister may exercise the prerogative power and ask the monarch for a dissolution of Parliament ahead of when the general election was actually due.

Example:
In May 1979, the Conservative Party won the election under the leadership of Margaret Thatcher. The next general election was not due until May 1984, but in June 1983 Margaret Thatcher asked the Queen to dissolve Parliament and call a general election. Similarly, in 1987 a general election was requested one year ahead of when it legally would have to be.

By comparison, both our European parliamentary and local government elections are fixed-term elections, held every five years and every four years respectively. This system of fixed-term elections is popular in other countries; in France the President is elected for a fixed term of seven years, in the United States the President is elected for four years and the US Congress is also subjected to fixed-term elections.

Questions

1. What is meant by the term 'mandate'?
2. What is an election?

12.2 | **The present UK voting system**

The UK has an election system which uses a pluralist majoritarian model whereby candidates are elected by counting all the votes in a constituency and giving the seat to the candidate with a simple majority of votes. This system is described as being a plurality system because it elects candidates who secure less than 50% of the total votes cast, but more votes than the number of votes obtained by the nearest rival. This system is known as the **first-past-the-post system**. Under this system all the ballot papers in a constituency are counted and the candidate with a clear majority is declared the winner (*see Figure 29*).

Name	Party	Votes
Ian McDonald	Conservative	23,540
Joan Beckett	Labour	20,120
Chris Maun	Liberal-Democrats	10,920
Nick Gould	Save the NHS	29

Figure 29 A sample election result using the first-past-the-post system.[1]

In this case the Conservative candidate, who has more votes than his nearest rival is declared the winner.

In terms of the election of a government, under this system the party that gains a majority of seats in the House of Commons becomes the governing party and its leader becomes the Prime Minister. This means that once the party has gained over 326 seats in the Commons they are said to have won by passing the winning post of 326 seats (*see Figure 30*).

General Election Result 1992 for Great Britain				
	Total Votes	Share of Vote (%)	No. of MPs	Share of MPs (%)
Conservative	14,049,508	42.8	336	53
Labour	11,557,134	35.2	271	42.8
Liberal-Democrats	5,998,446	18.3	20	3.2
Nationalists	786,348	2.4	7	1.1
Others	433,870	1.3	0	0
(Excludes Northern Ireland's General Election Results)				

Figure. 30 General election result for 1992 for Great Britain.[2]

The winning figure of 326 is half the number of seats in the House of Commons plus one.

Key term: an election campaign

This is a period prior to polling day when the political parties name their candidates, publish their manifestos and organise events in each constituency and nationally to encourage voters to vote in a general election. British election campaigns normally last for three weeks and the political

The British **electoral system** has been the subject of much debate regarding whether it is fair. If one considers the 1992 result one can clearly see that minor parties do not receive a fair proportion of seats in the House of Commons compared to the number of votes

parties employ marketing consultants to advise them how to get their message across. In the 1980s and 1990s the media became increasingly important in 'getting the message across'. There is no legal limit on the amount that each national party can spend. In 1992 the Conservatives estimated that they spent £10 million on the national campaign. By comparison Labour spent £7 million and the Liberal Democrats £2 million.[3] However, there is a legal limit to how much each candidate can spend and in 1992 this was between £6,000 and £7,000. By comparison in other countries election campaigns can be even more sophisticated, costly and media orientated; in America the Presidential campaign lasts for over two months and candidates spend over $20 million.

Key term: manifesto

This is a policy document published by a political party at the time of an election which sets out what that party would do if it were to gain power. Manifestos provide the electorate with information about the principles and policies that a party stands for. If a party wins office they set about implementing their manifesto. In 1979, the Conservative Manifesto contained a commitment to introduce legislation to allow council tenants to buy their council houses. This commitment was enacted through the 1980 Housing Act.

which they collected. Under the present system, critics argue, third parties are discriminated against. They suggest that the first-past-the-post system should be replaced with a fairer system known as **proportional representation** (PR) which would ensure that third and fourth parties received a better allocation of seats in the Commons, but within this suggestion is an argument about which system of PR should be adopted in Britain.

Question

Explain the first-past-the-post system

12.3 | Arguments for retaining and replacing the first-past-the-post system

The debate over the present system is a popular question with examiners and it is a debate of recurring topicality, and interestingly, entered the mainstream of British politics during the 1992 General Election campaign. The arguments in favour of retaining the present first-past-the-post system rest upon two points:

1. stability and effective government
2. the MP–constituency relationship.

Stability and effective government

Supporters of the present system argue that it provides a mechanism for the stable transfer of power from one government to the next and effective government with a mandate from the people to implement its manifesto and a working majority of seats in the House of Commons.

The present system also has provided the country with strong governments with working majorities able to pursue their policies in the national interest even if some are initially unpopular (*see Figure 31*). This means that the successful party is able to form a government and implement its **manifesto** through its Commons majority. Voters are able to vote for parties which have a defined programme, contained in a manifesto. Supporters argue that since 1945, the first-past-the-post system has provided Britain with strong majority governments, unlike many of its partners in Europe which have suffered from weak and ineffective governments. Since the end of the Second World War Britain has had ten governments with large enough majorities to enable them to implement their manifesto pledges.

Example:

Italy has had forty-eight different governments from 1945 to 1992.

Proponents of the British system point out that Italy's political instability is the result of its having proportional representation, resulting in often weak coalition governments. In 1993 the Italian people voted by a large majority in favour of adopting a first-past-the-post electoral system with the hope of gaining strong, stable and effective governments (*see Figure 31*).[4]

Government majorities since 1945		
Year		Overall majority
1945	Labour	147
1950	Labour	6
1951	Conservative	16
1955	Conservative	59
1959	Conservative	99
1964	Labour	5
1966	Labour	97
1970	Conservative	31
1974 (Feb.)	None	
1974 (Oct.)	Labour	4
1979	Conservative	44
1983	Conservative	144
1987	Conservative	102
1992	Conservative	21

Figure 31 Government majorities since 1945.

MP–constituency relationship

Supporters of the present system argue that the concept of the MP–constituency relationship is a strength of the present system. An MP represents all the citizens who live in the constituency whether they voted for him or her or not, and during **surgery** times deals with the problems of any constituent. An MP does not ask whether the person voted for him or her or not. The introduction of a system of PR would weaken this traditional link and change the nature of MP–constituency relationships.

The alternative argument that the present system should be replaced rests upon the following points:

1.   The stability which the present system affords is not concrete

Critics argue that the proponents of restructuring the British system overstate the case that the present system provides stability and strong government. They suggest that this first-past-the-post system can produce instability as easily as it produces stability. It is, they argue, a double-edged sword. In 1950, 1964 and 1974 the party majorities were either very small or non-existent, which created weak and unstable governments. Within a short time on these three occasions, general elections had to be held to try to establish a better majority and therefore a modicum of stability.

Key term: surgeries

This term refers to MPs' practice of making themselves available to their constituents at regular intervals so that people may meet with them and bring matters to their attention. MPs normally hold these meetings in the party offices in the constituency or in a public building, e.g. a church hall. These times allow MPs to have contact with the voters in the constituency and an opportunity to fulfil their traditional role as redressers of grievances.

With equal force they suggest that strong government with large majorities is not necessarily good for democracy. The Thatcher Governments of 1983 to 1990 enjoyed majorities in the House of Commons of over 100 seats, but it can be argued that this did not lead to better government. Critics argue that mistakes were still made and policies were forced through the legislative process by strict whipping of Conservative MPs in the face of legitimate criticisms and widespread public opposition. Critics argue further that the majoritarian system produces large-majority governments on the basis of less than 50% of the popular vote.

Example:
Examples of large seat majority governments with less than 50% of the vote

Year	*Party*	*No. of Seats*	*Majority*	*Share of vote (%)*
1966	*Labour*	*363*	*97*	*47.9*
1983	*Conservative*	*397*	*144*	*42.4*
1987	*Conservative*	*375*	*102*	*42.3*

2.   The unfairness of the present system

Critics argue that the present system is completely unfair to smaller parties. The mechanism of the first-past-the-post system means that the dominance of two parties is encouraged and the electoral success of the smaller parties are squeezed and reduced between the two giants. In 1983 the Liberal–SDP Alliance (the forerunners of the Liberal Democrats) received 25.4% of the popular vote compared to Labour's 27.6 %. Labour won 209 seats whereas the Alliance only won 23 seats. Under the present system, Peter Kellner and others suggest that minor parties have to struggle to get over 33% of the popular vote before they can begin to pick up large numbers of seats across Britain.[5] Critics add that a system of proportional representation would better translate the level of national support which the smaller parties receive in the country into a higher proportion of seats in the House of Commons.

3.   The perpetration of the two-party system

The present system encourages the phenomenon of safe seats. 70% of all the seats in the House of Commons are safe, i.e. have a large unshakeable majority. These are predominantly Conservative or Labour seats. The smaller parties have very few safe seats. Of the remaining seats, 25% are marginals, in which the real contests of a general election are fought.

In a general election a simple swing in support from the Conservatives to Labour can result in the seat changing hands. This is calculated in percentages and is known as the *electoral swing*.

Example:

In 1992, 2% of the voting population changed from voting Conservative to Labour.[6]

During each election both parties draw up lists of target seats which they wish to win, with the intention of increasing or gaining a majority in the House of Commons. It is a two-party race and shows how the two parties dominate the present electoral system.

Critics argue that the first-past-the-post system encourages this two-party contest and the adversarial nature of British Politics.

Questions

1. What is 'adversarial politics'?
2. Outline three arguments in favour of retaining the present electoral system.
3. What is meant by the term 'majoritarian model'?
4. Describe one major advantage and one major disadvantage of the British electoral system.

12.4 | Alternative voting systems

There are a number of different systems of proportional representation. The range and differences of these systems reveals the problems associated with any reform in Britain and raises questions concerning the system which Britain should adopt, including whether we should adopt multi-member constituencies? The Labour Party's Plant Report made a number of recommendations which are discussed later, and represents the most recent example of mainstream political thinking on the matter.

The most common systems are outlined in *Figure 32*.

ATV – Alternative transferable vote system. This is used in Australia. Each citizen lists the candidates in order of preference, 1, 2, 3, etc., and the votes of those who have the least number of votes are transferred, according to the other preferences until a candidate has half the vote. This is used in single member consitituencies.

AMS – Additional member system. A proportion of MPs are elected in single member constituencies on a plurality basis, i.e. more votes than their nearest rival but less than 50% of the total votes cast, and others are elected by a second vote from party lists which are produced regionally. This allocation ensures a proportionality between the votes and overall totals of MPs. This system was used in the previous West Germany.

Continued...

Key term: adversarial politics

This term refers to a characteristic of British politics where ideologically different political parties oppose each other in the search for power. Parties construct a series of policies based around their ideology and present these to the electorate. This is accompanied by opposition towards and criticism of policies of other parties. Such politics are marked by confrontational attitudes in the House of Commons with parties furiously opposing each other and committing themselves to amending the other's policies. The central thesis is that British party politics has developed an adversarial nature because of the simple majority electoral system, and that the style of adversarial politics has resulted in inconsistent and damaging policies produced by single-party governments. Nationalisation and privatisation are two very good examples of this trend.

Figure 32 Alternative voting systems.

STV – **Single transferable vote.** This system is used in legislative election in the Republic of Ireland and Malta, and in European parliamentary and local elections in the Province of Northern Ireland. It utilises preferential voting in multi-member constituencies. Each elector lists the candidates in order of preference rather than selecting one candidate. In the Republic of Ireland there are three-, four- and five-member constituencies. In this system a quota is calculated from the minimum number of votes required to win. Surplus votes after a candidate has achieved a quota are transferred to other candidates according to the voters second and third preferences if insufficient candidates are elected after the first calculation. This redistribution process is repeated until all the seats are filled.

The list system. Each party presents a list of candidates. The voter then casts a vote for one of those lists, and the candidates are declared elected normally according to their ordering on the list. In some systems voters can amend the content or the ordering of the lists. Various calculation methods are used to produce a result in terms of numbers of seats per list. This system is used in Belgium, Finland and Israel.

The proportional representation debate burst onto the mainstream political agenda during the 1992 General Election campaign. Towards the end of the 1992 campaign the issue arose of a political deal between the Labour Party and the Liberal Democrats if there were a hung Parliament. Central to this debate was whether Labour, being the larger partner in such a coalition, would agree to a Bill which introduced a system of proportional representation into election practice.

This was the first time that proportional representation entered the core agenda of British politics and some say influenced the result of that election.[7] In the 1970s the issue of proportional representation had entered the political scene but remained on the periphery. In 1976 the Hansard Society published a report emphasising the merits of an AMS system and suggesting how it could be grafted onto the British system. However, nothing came of it despite widespread academic support.

Since 1987 there has been a developing public awareness over the issue of electoral reform through the activities of such pressure groups as Charter 88, advocating wholesale constitutional reform. This increased awareness led in 1990 to Neil Kinnock agreeing that the Labour Party should examine the problem of electoral reform within the context of a reformed second chamber and regional assemblies in the UK. The Plant Commission was established and in a preliminary report in 1992, Plant recommended a system of proportional representation for the European parliamentary elections and for the proposed Scottish Parliament. A final report was published in April 1993.

1.   Plant recommended the replacement of the first-past-the-post system in elections for the House of Commons, but did not

propose the adoption of a strict proportional representation system. Rather, Plant proposed the supplementary vote electoral system which was based on the principles of the system used in France, and the alternative vote system.

2.   The supplemental vote system would give voters two choices and they would be able to express a first and second preference if they wanted to. Any candidate who wins more than 50% of first preference votes is elected automatically on the first count. But if none of the candidates reach 50%, then second preferences are added to the votes of the top two candidates (other candidates having been eliminated). Whichever candidate gains the biggest total wins the seat.[8]

Plant's recommendations were rejected by the former Labour leader, John Smith. However, the new leader Tony Blair is in favour of a referendum on electoral reform for the Commons although he is 'personally unpersuaded for the need for reform'.[9] Electoral reform has the potential to split the Labour Party; however, some in the Party fear that Labour will fail to gain a large enough electoral swing in the next election to give it a majority government, and will therefore have to form a pact with the Liberal Democrats to allow it to take office. The Liberal Democrats, they fear, will demand the introduction of a Bill to reform the electoral system as the price of their support.

Questions

1.   What was the Plant Commission?
2.   Explain two methods of proportional representation.

12.5 | **The proportional representation debate**

Arguments for proportional representation

The arguments used to support the introduction of proportional representation (PR) are as follow:

1.   Increased fairness

Proponents of (PR) argue that smaller parties would benefit through the introduction of a PR system. They would gain seats truly reflecting their electoral strength in the country. Proponents of PR argue that it would more truly reflect the electoral representation and strength of the parties, producing a fairer result. Parties would win seats in proportion to the amount of votes which they gained.

14

Key term: consensus politics

This term is sometimes used to indicate a basis for political debate and decision where outcomes are to be produced by agreement, as far as possible. Coalition government produced by PR would have to work to final agreement on the decisions and policies to be adopted.

The term is also used to describe the basis of political agreement between the political parties, established within a country, about the nature and operation of the political system. This can extend itself into the area of policy. In Britain between 1945 and 1979 a consensus existed between the major parties meaning that there existed a set of common assumptions, and continuity, between the policies pursued by both the major parties when they were in power. This was known as the *post-war consensus*. There were differences in some of the policy areas but on a broad range of common topics, e.g. economic policy, welfare policy, defence and foreign affairs their policies were very close. This consensus broke down in 1979 when both major parties moved in opposite directions.[11]

Example:

If the 1992 General Election had used one of the following systems of proportional representation the results would have been as follows:[10]

Party	Votes Won %	STV Seats	%	AMS Seats	%
Conservative	42.0	275	42.2	346	45.9
Labour	35.4	237	36.4	283	37.7
Liberals	18.0	102	15.7	89	11.9
SNP	2.1	17	2.6	10	1.3
Plaid Cymru	0.4	3	0.5	4	0.5

Accordingly both systems would see the level of representation of smaller parties which presently in the House of Commons increase. Under the single transferable vote system the Liberal Democrats would gain eighty-two more seats than they did in 1992 under the first-past-the-post system.

2.   Create a better MP–constituency relationship

Critics of the present relationship claim that one MP is unable to effectively deal with the numbers of constituency problems which are brought to their attention. It is also claims that many staunch supporters of a party which has lost the seat do not seek the help of their MP because he or she is not of their political persuasion.

Example:

Critics of the present system ask if it is possible that a staunch and ardent Conservative voter would be unable to ask a left-wing Labour MP, like Tony Benn, to deal with their problems.

They argue that the different interests of the constituency and the workload would be better served by multi-member constituencies where burdens and interests are shared between MPs. Through the adoption of one system of proportional representation this could be achieved.

3.   Advantages of coalition government

Supporters of proportional representation argue that coalition governments are not weak entities racked by indecision. They suggest that coalition government is not the inevitable result of PR. In Spain PR has produced majority single-party governments, and in Australia and Germany PR has produced stable coalition multi-party governments which have ruled each country successfully for many years. Coalition government could bring to an end the adversarial nature of our political system and create a new form of consensus politics in the UK.

The present government with a majority of twenty-one, which has fallen to sixteen is not a good example of strong decisive government.

4.   European dimension

Finally supporters of PR argue that Britain should follow the example of its European partners where the system of PR is widely used. Britain is the only country which uses the plurality system for elections to the European Parliament, as in 1994.

Arguments against proportional representation

Arguments used against the introduction of proportional representation are as follows:

1.   Representation

Critics of PR as a system to be adopted in Britain argue that the present first-past-the-post (FPTP) system does produce Parliaments which reflect the plurality of society. They suggest that although PR may produce a mathematically fairer result, it is questionable whether it necessary for a Parliament to be an arithmetically perfect reflection of society.

2.   Coalitions

This is the most popular criticism of PR. This electoral system, in its endeavours to produce mathematically fair results, often does not produce enough seats in an assembly for one party to form a majority government; rather coalitions are often produced instead. Through coalitions, policies are often fudged and compromises made to seek accommodation with the other party which becomes the partner in government. Coalitions are often weak and fragile arrangements which may break down. New agreements have to be reached in order to form a new government.

Critics of PR cite the Italian post-war experience where coalition governments have abounded composed of sometimes three parties working together. These have consisted of centrist and centre-right coalitions composed generally of one major party and up to three minor parties. Since 1948 Italy has had forty-eight different governments, many of these lasting between six to eighteen months.[12]

Example:
Between June 1972 and November 1974 a total of five different governments held office.[13]

This has created serious problems for the long-term development of the country and suggests why the Italian electorate in 1993 voted to replace PR with a FPTP system.[14]

Critics argue that this instability could result from the introduction of PR in Britain. Compromises would be reached and policies watered down in the hope of reaching agreement with the prospective coalition partner. This would mean, they argue, that election manifesto commitments would be dropped without the electorate being able to influence the process. This process, known as 'horse trading', would take place behind closed doors with major policies being dropped at the behest of a small group of individuals who hold sway over important decisions. Critics conclude that it is not fair that such smaller parties should, within coalitions, wield power totally out of keeping with their actual electoral strength.

3.   Extremism

Critics of PR argue that it can provide small, extremist political parties with representation in a legislature on the basis of a small proportion of votes, unlike the FPTP system. They suggest that the British National Party could gain a Parliamentary seat under PR, and question the likely results of this for British society.

4.   MP–constituency relationship

Finally, critics of PR argue that the British concept of MP–constituency relations is a worthy and strong dimension of British political life which has worked well and should not be altered. The introduction of multi-member constituencies would break the readily identifiable link between people and Parliament that presently exists. Furthermore, it would spread confusion and separatism within the community of the constituency. Different party MPs would give different interpretations to policies affecting the constituency and people would have to express a party preference in order to see an MP. This would be harmful.

Conclusions

1.   In the past sixteen years there has been a growing public awareness of the issues of electoral reform but widespread popular support for it has yet to materialise. In 1992 the topic entered the election campaign agenda briefly, which was significant because it spread awareness among the electorate that perhaps all was not right with our electoral system and that it could be reformed.

2.   The major political parties stand at opposite ends on the issue. The Conservatives are against any electoral reform at all. The Labour Party after Plant seems no nearer to resolving its position on the issue. Tony Blair has revealed his thoughts on the matter but until the result of the next election is known, it is likely that Labour will not tackle the issue until all prospect of their winning another general election through the FPTP system has evaporated. The Liberal Democrats, who have a radical constitutional reform agenda, are in favour of electoral

reform and wish to introduce a system of single transferable vote (STV). If Labour are forced to enter a coalition with the Liberals after 1996 or 1997 the price will be PR.

3. If any form of regional assembly is established in Scotland or Wales and a form of PR is used to elect those assemblies, as was the suggestion of the Plant Commission, the case for the introduction of PR for elections to Westminster will be even stronger.

Questions

1. What, in your opinion, are the two most convincing reasons for the introduction of PR into Britain? Explain your reasons.
2. Give the main arguments against the introduction of PR into Britain.
3. What is consensus politics?

12.6 | The role of referendums and by-elections

Referendums

A referendum is vote by an electorate of a state or other political unit on a specific policy proposal, or on the ratification or amendment of a constitution. Such votes may be considered binding or advisory upon a legislature. In a referendum the electorate is asked to express its opinion on a policy issue and is usually asked a question to which the answer is yes or no. Voters go to polling booths and express a preference either yes or no, or A or B. In the UK the referendum system has been used only three times. The two best examples are:

1. In 1975 the electorate was asked whether it wished Britain to remain a member of the European Union. This was an example of a binding referendum. A campaign was held in which arguments for and against continued membership were presented and this gave the electorate the chance to be involved in the European decision. This first ever referendum was judged a success because 63% of the electorate voted. Of this 67% favoured continued membership.[15]

2. In 1978 a referendum was held in Scotland and Wales over the issue of devolution. This referendum was to decide whether the electorate in Wales and Scotland wished to have a system of self-government with national assemblies established in Cardiff and Edinburgh. In this case, however, a simple majority was not acceptable and this referendum required a

qualified majority of the electorate to be in favour of the idea. In Scotland only 33% of the population voted in favour, when 40% was required by the Act establishing the referendum and in Wales only 12%. This referendum ended hopes for a system of devolved power to Wales and Scotland. In Scotland the issue has never quite been laid to rest and continues to inhabit the political scene.[16]

Since 1978, referendums have not been used in Britain to decide national issues. However in other parts of Europe they are frequently used, and in the United States referendums are used by many states to decide issues such as local tax rates.

Example:
In Holland in 1992/3 there were two referendums over the Maastricht Treaty and in France in 1993 a similar referendum was held to gain the electorate's approval of this important Pan-European agreement.[17]

France has a long history of using national referendums to decide a whole variety of issues. Since the founding of the Fifth Republic in 1958 there have been seven referendums.[18]

Example:
In October 1962, on the method of electing the President and in April 1972, on approving Britain's entry into the European Union.[19]

Within the context of European politics referendums have become topical in the past few years in Britain. The prime reason for this has been the Maastricht Treaty. Many of those who opposed the Treaty because they believed that it would create a European federal super state argued that the British people should be given the right to decide whether they wished to be part of the new European Union, as envisaged within the Treaty. This included Margaret Thatcher and other Euro-sceptics.

The issue of a British referendum on Europe will figure prominently in the controversy over the future of the EU in the run up to the European intergovernmental conference in 1996, which will review the implementation of the Maastricht Treaty and decide the next stage in the development of the EU. In the summer of 1994, the British Government seemed to be at sixes and sevens over the issue of a referendum after the intergovernmental conference in 1996, neither endorsing the idea nor completely ruling it out. Such a referendum would possibly decide Britain's attitude towards greater integration, federalism and a single currency. In this context, therefore, it is worth considering the arguments for and against the use of this electoral device to gauge the electorate's opinions.[20]

Arguments against the use of referendums in Britain

1.   Undermining parliamentary sovereignty

Britain is a representative democracy where power is invested in the hands of Parliament through elections. This implies that at a general election the people elect their representatives (MPs) into Parliament, giving them a mandate to implement their ideas and govern in their best interest. Referendums are thus believed to undermine Parliament and the role of an MP as an accountable legislator. In the wake of the first Danish referendum in June 1992 John Major told MPs,

'I am not in favour of a referendum in a parliamentary democracy and I do not propose to put one before the British people …I do not believe it would be generally acceptable to the House of Commons or in the interests of good government in this country.'[21]

2.   Referendums are the devices of 'demagogues and dictators'[22]

Referendums are tarnished with the reputation of having been used by extremist political regimes. Hitler used a referendum to approve Germany's withdrawal from the League of Nations.

3.   The phrasing of the question and the number of issues

Referendums generally ask a question and critics argue that the way in which this question is phrased can influence the result. This was the case in the 1970s.

Opponents of referendums argue that there are so many issues which could be put to a referendum that governments could indulge in frequent referendums which could limit their freedom of action and the implementation of innovative policies.

Arguments for the use of referendums in Britain

1.   Popular sovereignty

In the modern British Parliament, sovereignty is exercised by the party with the largest majority. This has created an 'elected dictatorship'[23] which is often elected on a minority of the popular vote. Parliament is ruled by the party and this has stifled British democracy. If we were to adopt the use of referendums as a useful tool to allow the electorate to express its wishes, the sovereignty of the people would be restored and we would create a participant democracy.

2.   *Carte blanche* mandates

In the present electoral system political parties who win general elections with a majority of seats in the House of Commons, claim to have a mandate from the people to implement their entire manifesto. Elections are not often fought on single issues and mandates are often so general that once in office governments can pursue policies which many of the electorate did not endorse. Sometimes constitutional issues arise which had never been aired during an election campaign and for which a government cannot claim to have a mandate. The introduction of referendums in between general elections would allow the electorate to have greater say over major policy decisions and prevent governments from becoming too powerful and out of touch. There use would enhance democracy and ensure that major constitutional issues are addressed to the people.

3.   The nature of the question

Referendums can pose precise questions and give governments precise answers.

4.   Other countries

Referendums are used in many other democracies across the world and it is unfair to label them the tool of 'dictators and demagogues'. Equally there is little evidence that they weaken the Parliamentary system.

In Europe they are used to resolve major issues, as in the Netherlands and France over the Maastricht Treaty, which the party system cannot always easily resolve. This was the reason why in 1975, Harold Wilson, the Labour Prime Minister, used the device of a referendum to avoid a damaging party split over membership of the EU. A binding referendum was seen as a way of resolving an issue which the party system could not easily tackle.

5.   British tradition

Supporters of this idea argue that it is wrong for those who are opposed the use of referendums in Britain to suggest that they are an anathema to the British way of life. Referendums have been used at a local level to test public opinion on a variety of issues. They have worked successfully and without confusion.

Example:
In West Wales a regular ten-year referendum was held to decide whether public houses should open on a Sunday. In the 1990 referendum the electorate of that region voted narrowly in favour of Sunday opening.

By-elections

These are elections for a parliamentary or local government seat when it becomes vacant prematurely, i.e. before the next election. Sometimes the elected representative resigns but more often it is because the person who is the MP or local councillor has died.

The most prominent by-elections are Parliamentary and in 1993 there were three by-elections for seats in which the sitting MP had died[24] and again in 1994 there was a whole spate of by-elections caused through deaths of MPs.

By-elections are seen as important when they occur in seats held by the party in office. A number of those in 1994 were in Labour seats which did not attract much media attention. However, over the past sixteen years all by-elections in Conservative seats have attracted great media attention and have been viewed as an accurate indication of the electorate's thinking towards the Government, its popularity and the popularity of the opposition parties.

Between 1988 and 1992 there were twenty-four by-elections. Ten of these were in Conservative seats and seven were won by either Labour or the Liberal Democrats.[25] Since the 1960s, the Liberal Democrats have always done well in by-elections, although in subsequent general elections they tend to loose many of the seats which they had gained through this form of election. In 1992 they lost all three seats including Eastbourne where they had gained a 20% electoral swing in 1990 providing them with a majority of over 4,000 votes.[26]

Questions

1. (a) Define the term 'referendum'
   (b) When and why have they been used in Britain?
2. Outline (a) a case for and (b) a case against the use of referendums
3. What importance may be attached to by-elections and their results?

12.7 | The 1992 General Election result

The 1992 General Election was the most open election for years, with no clear indication of whether the Conservatives would hold onto office or Labour would take office for the first time in thirteen years. In the two previous elections, 1983 and 1987, the Conservatives entered the campaign ahead of Labour and the only aspect of the result in question was how big the Conservative majority in the House of Commons would be. When the election was called at the end of March 1992 Britain was experiencing the worst economic depression since the 1930s and few commentators expected the Conservatives to be returned with a majority. Opinion was divided between an outright Labour victory or a hung Parliament, where no party had a working majority. Most people's money was on the latter horse.

The election campaign which takes place in the three weeks between the dissolution of Parliament and Election Day is important. Each party presents its policies and ideas to the

Figure 33 John Major, with his wife Norma, celebrates victory in the 1992 General Election.

electorate via a number of techniques: senior politicians touring the country meeting with voters and canvassing, door-to-door leafleting, the publication of a manifesto and party political broadcasts. During a campaign the issues are debated and each party attempts to take hold of the election agenda giving it an advantage over its rivals. In 1992 the campaign was of greater significance because fewer voters had made up their minds before the election began than had been the case in 1987 or 1983. These people are known as 'floating voters' and are the target of most campaigns. In 1992, 73% of the electorate had made up their minds before the election, leaving the remainder to swing the balance either way. According to a Harris exit poll in that year, 21% of voters made up their minds during the campaign, so the campaign was to prove vital and decisive. After the election an internal Labour inquiry concluded that Labour had made mistakes during the campaign which contributed to its defeat.

The result, a Conservative fourth victory, shocked many of the opinion pollsters who predicted a Labour lead or level pegging. The Conservatives actually gained 8%. Arguments have raged to find a reason why the polls got it so wrong.[27] The reasons put forward are that

1. the polls sampled the wrong people or insufficient numbers from each social strata based on inaccurate census or statistical data;
2. a late unseen swing which the polls failed to see. This could have been the result of media influence. MORI have produced some evidence to suggest that the Tory tabloids may have caused a 2% swing, enough to take twenty marginal seats. Or it could have been the fact that about 10% of the electorate claim to have made up their minds in the final twenty-four hours of the campaign.
3. hostility towards pollsters which led many people to lie when answering questions.

Whatever the reason it was the worst result for the opinion polls since they were invented.[28]

The worst shock of course was for the Labour Party. It was its fourth consecutive defeat – a crushing blow for Neil Kinnock whose modernisation of the Labour Party failed to oust the Conservatives despite the recession and the aftermath of the Poll Tax débâcle. Labour did enjoy a 2% swing, which cut the Tory majority from 101 to 21 but why, when it seemed that Kinnock was on his way to Number 10, did they loose?

Some have suggested the answers to this are as follows:

1. The campaign

Within the campaign one may identify certain aspects that went wrong for Labour and right for the Conservatives.

a. *The Economic policy*   The Conservatives correctly assessed that Labour's weak point would be economic policy. The shadow budget that John Smith produced, designed to lay Labour's economic policies before the electorate, gave the Conservatives and the pro-Tory tabloids a target to aim at. Despite John Smith's assertions that eight out of ten taxpayers would be better off under Labour, the Conservative 'Double Whammy' that under Labour taxes and prices would go up, hit home to the voters who mattered most, the new post-1979 middle classes. Moreover, the Conservatives promoted successfully the idea that if people voted Tory, the recovery would begin the day after the election. Labour was unable to persuade the electorate of its view that the Conservatives were responsible for the recession nor could it persuade them to vote to support its economic policies. The electorate continued to fear and distrust Labour on the economy. In the BBC/NOP exit poll the Conservatives led Labour by 53% to 35% as the party most likely 'to take the right decisions on the economy'.[29]

b. *The NHS*   If there was one single issue over which the majority of the electorate cared and on which Labour should have triumphed it was the NHS. Unfortunately, its attack upon the Tories was blunted by the row over a party political broadcast. The broadcast explaining the story of a little girl waiting for an ear operation was seized upon by the pro-Conservative press and turned on its head. Instead of being a debate about the state of our hospitals it became a debate about the morality of the use of such scare stories. This harmed Labour's image, although on the dominant issues of the campaign, education, unemployment and health, its policies were clearly preferred to those of the Conservatives. However the voters did not vote on these issues. If they had, Labour would have won. Rather they voted on issues where the Conservatives had the preferred policies – the economy and taxation.

c. *The image of John Major*   During the campaign the Conservatives promoted the image of John Major as an ordinary man with working-class roots. His face was on the front cover of the manifesto and he toured the country getting close to the people. This was compared to the team approach which Labour adopted and which avoided any great promotion of Neil Kinnock on his own. Labour felt that Kinnock was vulnerable to Conservative and media attack and chose to promote instead the 'team' which would give them a better chance of winning. The Conservative approach worked: throughout the campaign Major led Kinnock as the person likely to make the better Prime Minister.

d. *The Sheffield Rally*   In the second week of the Campaign on 1 April in Sheffield, Labour staged the largest political rally ever seen in Britain. A rally that was to be a defining moment in the campaign was attended by 10,000 people. The day before, three polls had put Labour well ahead of the Tories, set to take power with a majority of 20 seats. This alarmed many in the Party who sensed that the campaign would now, given that a Labour victory was a foregone conclusion, concentrate on whether Labour could be trusted with power. At Sheffield the process began which undermined Labour's lead and indicated to many voters that they could not be trusted with power.

The rally was too triumphalist: Labour had another ten days to go. They forgot the words of one of their own former leaders, Harold Wilson, who said 'a week is a long time in politics'. The image of Neil Kinnock on a stage, acting as if it were a rock and roll event appalled his own supporters, prospective voters and, in retrospect, himself. He has said since, 'I completely let my defences drop' in response to the atmosphere which greeted him on stage. The press seized upon his actions on stage questioning whether the public wanted this man as Prime Minister. This rally severely damaged the Labour campaign and the respectful and safe image which Neil Kinnock himself had spent eight years building. On the Sunday after the election, *The Observer's* inquest into the defeat summed up what Sheffield had done with a headline, 'How the glitz turned to ashes'.[30]

e. *The PR debate*   In the days after Sheffield, Labour added to its woes by suggesting that it was willing to work with other parties over constitutional issues such as PR, by offering the Liberal Democrats a place on the Plant Commission. Given that both the Liberal Democrats and Labour manifestos contained commitments to constitutional reforms Neil Kinnock sought to reassure the electorate that Labour would be willing to work with others on this area of policy. Unfortunately, rather than being portrayed as a strength the talk of co-operation or consensus building with other parties was portrayed in the press as a sign that Labour was opening negotiations with the Liberals in preparation for a hung Parliament. This was seen as a weakness and was compounded by the media suggesting that Neil Kinnock would do anything for power. Talk of electoral pacts dominated the remaining campaign agenda. By 5 April it was clear that Labour had lost control. The Conservatives cited the Opposition PR debate as evidence that if disaffected Tory voters voted for the Liberal Democrats they would be allowing a Labour Government in through the back door. This message encouraged many disaffected Conservatives to renew their loyalty to the Party in the polling booths on 9 April.[31]

In the final days of the campaign the Conservatives renewed their attack on Neil Kinnock as a leader rather than on the Labour Party's policies. The Opposition from 1 April onwards had pressed, and continued to press, the self-destruct button. The Conservatives were able to avoid all talk of the economy, health, and education and in the closing stages of the campaign sat back and watched the votes drift back.

2.   In addition to the actual campaign there are a number of other reasons why Labour lost the election. These include the following:

a. Labour was unable to persuade voters to trust it. The distrust and fear of a Labour Government based on the experiences of the 1970s remains, it seems, an unexorcisable factor. A large proportion of the voting public remember the International Monetary Fund (IMF) crisis and the 'Winter of Discontent', and those that do not are easily persuaded to stick with what they know, that is a Conservative Government, when images of the period are shown in party political broadcasts. Labour's strategists in 1992 knew that they had to build an image of trust. They failed to do this.

b. A majority of the media were openly hostile to Labour in 1992. In his speech on the morning of 10 April, accepting defeat, Neil Kinnock laid heavy emphasis on the role of the press in the defeat of Labour. The hostility which newspapers such as *The Sun* generated is hard to convert into electoral support but according to a Mori poll based on a large sample of 22,700 voters, there was a 4% swing to the Tories among *Sun* readers in the last week, and a 9% swing among *Daily Express* readers.[32] *The Sun's* final headline of the election on 9 April ('If Kinnock wins today will the last person to leave Britain please turn out the lights') shows how hostile they were to Neil Kinnock personally and how influential they must have been.

c. The inaccuracy of the opinion polls predicting a lead for Labour probably did more to capture reluctant Conservative voters than to keep complacent Labour voters at home. The electoral turnout was high and the Conservatives received 14 million votes in 1992, the highest ever received by one party.[33]

d. A last minute swing to the Conservatives occurred in the final days of the campaign. This may have happened for a variety of reasons, but whatever the combination, in the last few days the electorate thought again about the prospect of Neil Kinnock in Number 10 and switched their vote. The BBC's *On the Record* programme had a panel of floating voters whose voting intentions were surveyed throughout the campaign. After the election they reported that 11% of those who said the week before they would vote Liberal Democrat switched to the Conservatives in the final days of the campaign.[34]

e. Labour failed to achieve a uniform swing of support across the country. The average swing across Britain from Conservatives to Labour was only 2%. This was simply not enough for Labour to reduce the Conservative majority to zero and increase its own numbers to over 326 allowing it to form its own majority government. In some regions of the country Labour achieved very good swings, in London between 5–6%, and in certain parts of the

Midlands between a 5–7% swing. Yet in the South East and South West the Labour swing was between 3.3% and 4% overall, providing Labour with only five extra seats, and it was in these regions that the Party had to achieve a higher swing if it was to stand a chance of forming the next government.

Conclusions

Labour simply failed to get its message across. It was unable to persuade the electorate that it was ready for office and could be trusted. In 1992, even though the Conservatives were responsible for the deepest recession for 60 years, the electorate trusted John Major's ability more than Neil Kinnock's to correct the problems and rebuild the British economy.

Neil Kinnock himself became a factor and was a vote loser. John Prescott has said that twelve months before the election the polls were indicating this fact but that little could be done.[35] The Conservatives and the press centred on him in the campaign, and to some extent belittled his Welshness and his background. This was the first election in which the personality of the Opposition leader had been so criticised and abused. It was an ugly aspect of the campaign and undoubtedly did much damage to Labour's prospects. In the final analysis a large number of factors contributed to Labour's defeat, perhaps principally it failed to get its message across to the new home owners that they would not suffer under a Labour Government. The debate over 1992 will continue, but one thing is certain: …history already records the question not as 'How did the Conservatives win?', but 'How did Labour lose?'

Questions

1. Explain why the opinion polls failed in 1992
2. What, in your view, were the three most important reasons why the Labour Party lost the 1992 General Election? Explain your choice.

Essay questions

1. What are the arguments over Britain adopting of some form of proportional representation to replace the first-past-the-post (FPTP) electoral system?
2. 'Referendums are useful ways for politicians to gauge public opinion, but that is all.' Discuss this statement in reference to the arguments for and against the use of referendums in Britain.
3. 'Proportional representation would weaken the British Government.' Discuss.
4. Discuss the case for and against electoral reform in Britain.

Essay planning

3. 'Proportional representation would weaken the British
    Government.' Discuss.

In this case you must use the material in the section on the
arguments for and against PR to assess the effects of PR upon the
British system of Government. You need to argue:

(a) that PR would weaken the present system using material in
     sections 12.3 and 12.5 explaining the strengths of the present
     system over the possible weaknesses of PR.
(b) that this may not necessarily be the case. Use the materials to
     suggest that PR may produce:
     (i)   fairer government;
     (ii) more representative government;
(c) in your conclusion you may wish to argue that PR would
     remove the adversarial characteristics of British politics,
     producing a more co-operative political alignment between the
     political parties which would produce better government. You
     may also briefly explain where the major parties stand on this
     issue.

Notes and references

1. Completely fictitious example.

2. *The Daily Telegraph*, 11.04.92.

3. *The Guardian*, 08.09.93 and 26.0.94.

4. *The Guardian*, 22.03.94.

5. BBC European Election Special, 12.06.94.

6. *The Daily Telegraph*, 11.04.92.

7. See *The Economist*, 11.04.94. Also this factor has been cited on
    the ITV biographical documentary on Neil Kinnock.

8. *The Times*, 02.04.93.

9. *The Guardian*, 24.06.94.

10. Robbins, L. 'The PR Debate', in *Political Update, 1992–93*
    (Leicester, 1993).

11. Heywood, A. 'A New Political Consensus', *Talking Politics,*
    Vol. 4, No.2, 1991/92, pp.

12. Hancock, D. et al. *Politics in Western Europe* (London, 1993),
    pp. 540–1.

13. Ibid.

14. *The Guardian*, 22.03.94.

15. Whitehead, P. *The Writing on the Wall* (London, 1986), pp. 134–40.

16. Ibid., pp. 294–302.

17. *The Guardian*, 05.03.93.

18. Hancock, D. et al *Politics in Western Europe* (1993), p. 110.

19. Ibid.

20. *The Guardian*, 10.05.94.

21. Ibid.

22. Ibid. Clement Atlee, Prime Minister 1945–51.

23. Lord Hailsham, The Richard Dimbleby Lecture, 21.10.76.

24. McKie, D. *The Guardian Political Almanac, 1993/4* (London, 1993), p. 332.

25. McKie, D. *The Election: A Voter's Guide* (London, 1992), pp. 278–87.

26. Ibid. p. 282.

27. Denver, D. 'The 1992 General Election,' *Talking Politics*, Vol. 5, No. 1, 1992, and Crewe, I. 'Voting and the Electorate', in Dunleavy, P. *Developments in British Politics*, Vol. 4, (London, 1993), pp. 92–122, and Eatwell, R. 'Opinion Polls in 1992,' *Talking Politics*, Vol. 5, No. 2, 1993, pp. . and *The Economist*, 11.04.92.

28. Eatwell, R. 'Opinion Polls in 1992' (1993), pp. 70–1.

29. Crewe, I. 'Voting and the Electorate' (1993), p. 114.

30. ITV biographical documentary on Neil Kinnock, No. 4.

31. *Sunday Times* and *Sunday Telegraph*, 12.04.92.

32. Marsh, D. 'The Media and Politics', in Dunleavy, P. *Developments in British Politics*, Vol. 4, (London, 1993), p. 342.

33. *The Daily Telegraph*, 11.04.92.

34. BBC television, *On the Record*, 12.04.92.

35. ITV biographical documentary on Neil Kinnock, No.4.

Further reading

Bogdanor, V. *What is Proportional Representation* (London, 1984).

Crewe, I. 'Why did Labour Lose?', *Politics Review*, September, 1992.

Denver, D. *Elections and Voting Behaviour in Britain*, 2nd edn (London, 1994).

Denver, D. and Hands, G. (eds) *Issues and Controversies in British Electoral Behaviour* (London, 1992).

Denver, D. 'The 1992 General Election: In Defence of Psephology', *Talking Politics,* Vol. 5, No. 1, 1992.

King, A. *Britain at the Polls, 1992* (London, 1992).

McKie, D. *The Guardian Political Almanac, 1993/4* (London, 1993).

McKie, D. *The Election: A Voter's Guide* (London, 1992).

Rose, R. *What are the Economic Consequences of PR.* The Electoral Reform Society (London, 1992).

CHAPTER 13

Voting behaviour

During general elections, European parliamentary elections and local government elections political parties present ideas and policies to the electorate in the form of manifestos. This process presents the electorate with a vast array of choices, including which policies are the best for them or their community, which party they feel most affinity with and which leader they have the most confidence in. Given that voters have this choice, how do they decide how to vote? The analysis of this decision is a complete science within political science.

This chapter contains the following:

13.1   What is voting behaviour?

13.2   Post-war voting behaviour, 1945–75.

13.3   The way people voted in the 1980s.

13.4   Voting behaviour in the 1992 General Election.

13.1 | What is voting behaviour?

Political scientists examine the way people vote according to a number of basic factors. These are class, age and sex, party identification, regional voting and issue voting. However, the nature of some of these factors have changed over the past twenty years and are discussed later in the Chapter (*see section 13.3*).

1.   Social class

Society is composed of various classes of people, which in Britain are characterised as working class, middle class and upper class. Various definitions of these classes are used by those who study voting behaviour but for our purposes we shall classify the classes according to the British Market Research Society's scheme (see below). Students should note that there are a number of other schemes which may be employed to divide the population into classes[1] and these will be addressed later (*see section 13.3*).

A	Professional	upper middle class
B	Managerial	middle class
C1	Clerical	lower middle class
C2	Skilled manual	working class
D	Semi-skilled Manual	working class
E	Un-skilled/non-workers	working class

This scheme divides the population according to occupation, income and lifestyle to produce a 40/60 split between the middle and working classes. An analysis of voting behaviour using this simple classification produced, until the late 1970s, a pattern of voting behaviour based upon class lines, known as a **class-based** alignment. This meant that within the working classes there was majority support for the Labour Party, and majority support from the middle classes for the Conservative Party. However since the 1979 General Election this phenomenon has weakened, leading to a class de-alignment, meaning that there is now a greater amount of cross-class voting, i.e. more voters from the working classes vote Conservative while more voters from the middle classes vote Labour or Liberal. (This is discussed in *section 13.3*.)

2.   Age and sex

Within the classes people vote differently according to their age and sex. Older people tend to be less radical in their outlook on life that younger people and psephologists (people who study voting behaviour) have found that between various ages people vote differently, mainly because their interests and concerns change. Similarly there are differences in voting behaviour between the sexes.

3.   Party identification

Many people identify with a political party for a considerable part of their lives. During the period 1945–70, 80% of voters identified with one of the two main parties. They are described as 'partisans'. Butler and Stokes claimed that most voters had a strong partisan self-image, regarding themselves as Labour or Conservative.[2]

4.   Issue voting

Since the late 1970s voters have become more concerned with the issues debated during an election. Electors are more discerning and consider the problems which the country faces and the ideas that each party presents to solve those problems.

5.   Regions

Since the later 1970s psephologists have studied the voting patterns by region. In this way, psephologists can discover regional trends and suggest which political party will perform best in which part of the country.

These are the basic factors which are used to analyse the way Britain votes. The most important of these is 'class' and class-based voting has undergone a massive change since 1979 (*see section 13.3*).

Questions

1. What is meant by the term 'voting behaviour'?
2. Give three explanations of how voting behaviour is classified.

13.2 | Post-war voting behaviour, 1945–75

Until the mid–1970s voting behaviour followed a predictable pattern. David Butler and Donald Stokes were perhaps the most influential psephologists during this period and they argued that the two main features of the British political system at this time – a class-based partisan alignment, and the predominance of a two-party system – allowed psephologists to explain voting behaviour easily.

1. Class was the most important influence upon how people voted.
2. The majority of the electorate had a strong partisan self-image which meant that they thought of themselves as either Conservative or Labour, leading to each casting their vote in support of their party. Using Butler's and Stokes' determinations of class (similar to the British Market Research Society scheme), Ivor Crewe found that in the 1964 General Election, 62% of non-manual workers voted Conservative and 64% of manual workers voted Labour, confirming the Butler and Stokes thesis. However students should note that between a quarter and a third of the working class did, at times, vote Conservative which accounted for a considerable proportion of the electoral swing between elections and changes of the party in power.
3. The second feature of the post-war period 1945–75 was the predominance of the two-party system. In this period the Conservative and Labour Parties dominated the political scene. Between 1945 and 1966 their combined vote averaged 87.5%.[3]

These factors were linked. Quite simply if there were two classes, there would be two parties to represent those classes. There was little room for a third party, although the Liberals survived on very small percentages of the vote.

As has been mentioned earlier, within the system there was a proportion of the electorate that did not follow this pattern. These have been described as **deviant voters** and were defined as manual workers who did not vote Labour and non-manual workers who did not vote Conservative. The number of deviant voters fluctuated between elections but their existence was central to determining the results of the election. Explanations of this phenomena included:

1. Embourgeoisement theory

This suggested that as members of the working classes became more affluent they would adopt middle-class attitudes and values which would lead them to vote Conservative.

2. Middle-class radicalism

This theory, promoted by Frank Parkin, argued that members of the middle classes whose occupations emphasised either a notion of service to the community or human betterment or welfare, i.e. social work and teaching, were outside the mainstream of capitalism and would vote Labour as a means of furthering the ideas which led them to select such social occupations.[4]

Therefore between 1945 and 1970, the two major parties could rely on a predictable level of support and fought campaigns to persuade the 20% of the electorate which would change their vote in elections to vote for their party, its leader and policies.

By the late 1970s this system began to break down and the predictable two-party, two-class model collapsed because of the following factors:

- The relationship between class and voting began to weaken because of the diminishing size of the old manufacturing-employed traditional working class.

- A class de-alignment began to occur with the rise of the new working class who switched their electoral support to the Conservatives. In 1979 the Conservatives gained a 9% electoral swing of support from C2 voters.[5]

- Both major parties' share of the vote declined from a 90% average to a 75% average in elections during the 1980s and in 1992. The electoral stability which the former status quo provided has been replaced by electoral fluidity, or volatility, making election campaigns more important. Issue voting has since increased in importance.

Key concepts: the new working class.

These are members of the C2 class, skilled manual and supervisory workers who are the largest socio-economic class group. They are employed in the new technology industries and the service sector, and many have benefited from the Conservative policies pursued since 1979 increasing as a class their proportion of home ownership and personal disposable income.

Questions

1. What were the major features of voting behaviour in the 1945–79 period?
2. Why did some working-class voters vote Conservative while some middle-class voters vote Labour?
3. What is the new working class?

13.3 | **The way people voted in the 1980s**

The 1979 General Election was a watershed in British political history. It saw an end to class-based voting that had existed since 1945 and before, and ushered in a period of class de-alignment voting and voter volatility. The Conservatives won the 1979 General Election for a whole host of reasons, but their victory heralded a breakdown of class-based politics which has supported their unbroken possession of power for over sixteen years.

Gender and age

In the 1960s more women voted Conservative than did men but by 1987 this gender gap had disappeared. In 1987 an equal 44% of men and women voted Conservative, and 33% of men and 31% women voted Labour. Prior to the 1980s men and women voted differently along age lines. The reasons for this varied; women were perceived as more Conservative than men because more women stayed at home, fewer women worked, and the majority of those were employed in jobs that would not bring them into industrial conflict. This meant that they were less supportive of trade unionism and ultimately of the Labour Party. In the 1980s, with an increase in the number of working women, the rise of the career woman and the socio-economic changes of the period the voting behaviour of women came to match that of men.

In relation to age it was noted during the 1980s that young males voted Conservative because they were attracted to Margaret Thatcher's strong image and with the growth in the number of so-called 'yuppies' (young urban professional people) in the mid-1980s the Conservatives' command over the younger voter increased.

Example:
In 1983 the majority of full-time students voted Conservative.[6]

Class

This period saw a reduction in the size of the working classes and an increase in the size of the middle classes. Between 1979 and 1992 the working class, defined as manual workers excluding the self-employed, supervisors and technicians, declined from 41% to 34% of all voters while the managerial class grew by 3% from 26% to 29%.[7]

1. Social changes created a new working class which strongly identified its position and economic prosperity with the Conservative Party. This new class of non-union worker, living in the South of England, owning their own homes and

employed in the private sector had prospered during the 1980s, and had turned away from the Labour Party. In 1987, 42% of the C2 class voted Conservative, 35% voted Labour and 21% voted for the Alliance. During the 1980s these skilled workers turned away from Labour, helping to provide the Conservatives with their electoral success.

2. Voters who had benefited from the Conservative policies of the 1980s tended to attach more importance to their own prosperity than to the problems of society. Thus Ivor Crewe suggested in analysing the 1987 General Election that voters thought first of the prosperity of their family, rather than the greater good of society, when entering the polling booth. Crewe found that in 1987, 55% of those responding to a Gallup survey, commissioned by the BBC, believed that the Conservatives were more likely to produce prosperity and a rise in living standards than the other parties.[8]

3. The level of class de-alignment which occurred during the 1980s has attracted some debate. Ivor Crewe has argued that there has been much de-alignment between class and party, whereas Anthony Heath et al.[9] have argued that less de-alignment has occurred than Crewe suggests. The results of the 1987 General Election suggest that the Conservative share of the A+B vote has declined and, by comparison, the level of support of the Labour Party among C2 voters has been reduced to the benefit of the Conservatives.

The 1987 General Election results and social groups were as follows. The figures are percentages of the overall vote[10].

SOCIAL GROUPS	CON.	LAB.	ALL.
AB professional	57	14	26
C1 white collar	51	21	26
C2 skilled	40	36	20
DE	30	48	20

These figures are indicative of the loss of support which Labour suffered during the 1980s. Some of this support moved to the centre parties. These figures show the superior level of support which the Conservatives enjoyed during the 1980s in both the C1 and C2 (skilled) classes. Crewe argues that both the non-manual classes and the manual classes have changed their voting preferences from their own class party since 1979.[11] He suggests that the changing social composition of the classes is the main explanation. 'The growth of the public service professions has eroded middle class solidarity with the Conservatives . . . and the expansion of non-union private sector employment has undermined working-class loyalty to the Labour Party.'[12]

4. The party membership decreased and partisanship weakened with an increase in the numbers of floating voters.

Regional voting

This showed that Labour were strongest in Scotland, Wales and the North of England, while the Conservatives remained strongest in the South East and South West. The Midlands became a Conservative stronghold during the 1980s and if Labour are ever to win a general election they have to regain seats in the Midlands.

Third parties

In the mid-1970s there was a growth in the electoral support of third parties at the expense of both major parties. In 1979 the electoral support for third parties fell. This recovered during the Liberal-SDP Alliance of the mid-1980s. In 1983 and 1987 the Alliance gained 25.4% and 22.6% of the popular vote respectively, although this did not translate into more than twenty-or-so seats in the Commons because of the nature of the first-past-the-post electoral system (*see Chapter 12*). Nevertheless, this degree of electoral support left the Alliance well placed to take 44 Conservative seats in the next general election.

Issues

The Conservatives timed their general elections to occur while they carried majority support on the political issues of the day. This was especially true in 1987, when conditions of low inflation, falling unemployment and an increase in the standard of living made them certain winners. This was paralleled by an increase in the importance and influence of issues upon the way people voted during elections. The electorate became more discerning about the ideas which political parties presented on the issues of the day. These included defence and low inflation in 1983, low taxation and economic growth in 1987 and unemployment, health and education in 1992. However, the importance of issues in an election is debated by writers. Some issues are more important and influential than others. Crewe argues that although one party may have a lead in the opinion polls on a particular issue or number of issues, it does not necessarily lead to electoral success. In 1992 Labour led the Conservatives on health, education and unemployment but lost the election because on economic issues they failed to persuade the electorate that their policies would be better than those of the Conservatives.

Questions

1. Give three voting behaviour factors which account for the electoral success of the Conservatives in the 1980s.
2. Analyse the relationship between class and voting behaviour in the 1980s.

13.4 | **Voting behaviour in the 1992 General Election**

The election result of 1992 surprised many commentators and politicians. Analysis of this election revealed a reversal of a number of the voting behaviour trends of the 1980s, but these changes were small and it will take at least one more general election to confirm these new patterns of voting behaviour. The 1992 General Election showed a small increase in popular support for both major parties, rising to 78% of the total vote. Although the Liberal Democrats only gained 18% of the vote, their support in the South placed many of their candidates in good second places in many Conservative seats and left 44 Conservative seats vulnerable to them in the next election.[13]

Class

The Conservative vote in classes A+B and C1 remained steady but in 1992 the majority of C2s voted Labour as opposed to Conservative. This undermined the theories of the 1980s that the C2s were the all important factor for parties to win general elections, because despite this success the Conservatives still won the election as shown below:[14]

SOCIAL GROUPS	CON.	LAB.	LIB-DEM.
AB professional	57	17	20
C1 white collar	49	28	19
C2 skilled	35	40	17
DE	29	48	14

The year 1992 saw an increase in the level of support among the new working classes for Labour. In the South, Labour gained 36% of the new-working-class vote compared to the Conservatives 38%, and Labour won a majority of the new-working-class owner-occupiers over the Conservatives, 39% compared to the Conservatives 38%. Furthermore, Labour took a majority of the non-union vote, 43% compared to 34% for the Conservatives. These figures suggest a reversal in the class de-alignment of the 1980s, possibly because during the economic recession of 1989–94 the new working class's southern owner-occupier suffered most .[15] Many had voted Tory but blamed the Conservatives for the recession, which had hit them so hard that a sizeable proportion switched to Labour. The Liberal Democrat vote in classes A+B, C1, C2 and DE fell. These votes were primarily redistributed to Labour.

Regional voting

Labour remained strongest in the North, Scotland and Wales while the Conservatives remained strongest in the South and Midlands. Labour failed to make the breakthrough in the Midlands that was required, although patches of red returned to the political map south of The Wash. Figure 34 shows how Britain voted, region by region, and reveals a continuing north–south divide in political geography. Labour's vote in the South East rose by 4% and in the South West by 3.3% but the Liberal Democrat vote in these regions placed them second to the Conservatives with 23.4% and 31.4% of the vote respectively. This showed that Labour failed to gain the trust of the majority of those people in the South who were disaffected with the Conservatives. Many believe that while this 'Opposition vote' remains spilt the Conservatives will remain in office.

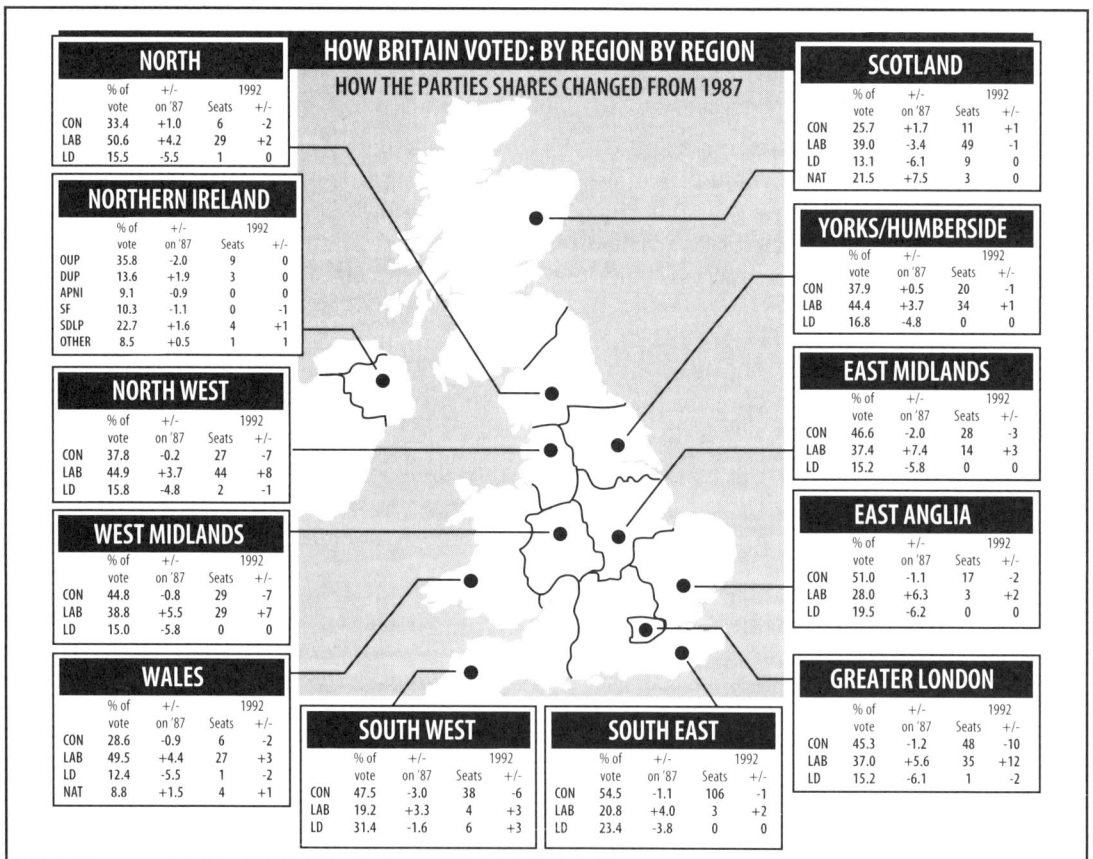

HOW BRITAIN VOTED: BY REGION BY REGION
HOW THE PARTIES SHARES CHANGED FROM 1987

NORTH

	% of vote	+/- on '87	1992 Seats	+/-
CON	33.4	+1.0	6	-2
LAB	50.6	+4.2	29	+2
LD	15.5	-5.5	1	0

NORTHERN IRELAND

	% of vote	+/- on '87	1992 Seats	+/-
OUP	35.8	-2.0	9	0
DUP	13.6	+1.9	3	0
APNI	9.1	-0.9	0	0
SF	10.3	-1.1	0	-1
SDLP	22.7	+1.6	4	+1
OTHER	8.5	+0.5	1	1

NORTH WEST

	% of vote	+/- on '87	1992 Seats	+/-
CON	37.8	-0.2	27	-7
LAB	44.9	+3.7	44	+8
LD	15.8	-4.8	2	-1

WEST MIDLANDS

	% of vote	+/- on '87	1992 Seats	+/-
CON	44.8	-0.8	29	-7
LAB	38.8	+5.5	29	+7
LD	15.0	-5.8	0	0

WALES

	% of vote	+/- on '87	1992 Seats	+/-
CON	28.6	-0.9	6	-2
LAB	49.5	+4.4	27	+3
LD	12.4	-5.5	1	-2
NAT	8.8	+1.5	4	+1

SOUTH WEST

	% of vote	+/- on '87	1992 Seats	+/-
CON	47.5	-3.0	38	-6
LAB	19.2	+3.3	4	+3
LD	31.4	-1.6	6	+3

SOUTH EAST

	% of vote	+/- on '87	1992 Seats	+/-
CON	54.5	-1.1	106	-1
LAB	20.8	+4.0	3	+2
LD	23.4	-3.8	0	0

SCOTLAND

	% of vote	+/- on '87	1992 Seats	+/-
CON	25.7	+1.7	11	+1
LAB	39.0	-3.4	49	-1
LD	13.1	-6.1	9	0
NAT	21.5	+7.5	3	0

YORKS/HUMBERSIDE

	% of vote	+/- on '87	1992 Seats	+/-
CON	37.9	+0.5	20	-1
LAB	44.4	+3.7	34	+1
LD	16.8	-4.8	0	0

EAST MIDLANDS

	% of vote	+/- on '87	1992 Seats	+/-
CON	46.6	-2.0	28	-3
LAB	37.4	+7.4	14	+3
LD	15.2	-5.8	0	0

EAST ANGLIA

	% of vote	+/- on '87	1992 Seats	+/-
CON	51.0	-1.1	17	-2
LAB	28.0	+6.3	3	+2
LD	19.5	-6.2	0	0

GREATER LONDON

	% of vote	+/- on '87	1992 Seats	+/-
CON	45.3	-1.2	48	-10
LAB	37.0	+5.6	35	+12
LD	15.2	-6.1	1	-2

Figure 34 Regional voting in the UK in 1992.[16]

Gender and age

In 1992 the gender gap returned. More women voted Conservative, 44%, whereas only 38% of men voted Conservative. The effects of the economic recession may account for this change as more men became unemployed and the number of women in part-time employment increased.

If one analyses the gender gap in terms of age, more younger women than men voted Labour. However as the age groups are divided, one finds that the Conservatives had clear leads among the older age groups and very young (18–24) but Labour had a narrow lead among the 25–34 age group and the two parties were equal in the 35–44 bracket. One explanation for the Conservative lead in the 18–24 age group is that because these people have formed their political opinions during the 'Thatcher Decade' they are inclined to vote Conservative because they have grown up during a period where privatisation and the free market have been the dominant ideas. Moreover, having never experienced a Labour Government they are more inclined to believe in what they know, rather than trust an unknown quantity. Furthermore, none of the political folklore of the last Labour Government is positive. By comparison it is worth noting that in 1966, 51.2% of the 18–24 generation voted Labour.

Issues

In 1992 the dominant issues of the Campaign were the economy, low taxation, the NHS, pensions and education. Labour were already strongly placed on the social issues before the election, but they failed to convince the electorate that on tax and the economy they could be trusted. The Conservatives successfully and confidently led on these issues towards the end of the campaign. The electorate were persuaded that the Conservatives could bring the economy around. During the campaign most polls gave the Conservatives a lead over Labour on the economy. An NOP poll on 2 April gave the Conservatives an 8% lead over Labour on the issue of taxation, and a Harris exit poll found that 49% of voters cited taxation as the most important issue effecting their vote.[17] Ivor Crewe argues that if everybody had voted on the two issues which they cared most about Labour would have won in 1992. In 1992 the Conservatives won because the economic considerations overrode emotions, and people voted Conservative because they believed the Conservatives could bring economic prosperity. They voted with their pockets to send the Conservatives back into office.[18]

The 1992 General Election revealed a number of subtle changes in the way people vote but the patterns of the 1980s have been recorded over three elections and after only one election in the 1990s it is too early to say what new forms of voting behaviour will be recorded as the British people move into the next century. 1992 showed that the Thatcher legacy remains, but that the changes which were recorded and influenced by her in the 1980s were not as permanent as some had supposed, leaving instead a volatile electorate. This leaves the question, 'Can Labour win?' – which needs to be addressed elsewhere.[19]

Questions

1. What were the characteristics of class based voting in the 1992 General Election?
2. Explain three factors of voting behaviour in reference to the 1992 General Election.

Notes and references

1. See Heath, A. et al. *How Britain Votes* (London, 1985), see also O'Donnell, M. *A New Introduction to Sociology* (London, 1987), pp. 526–35.

2. See Butler, D. and Stokes, D. *Political Change in Britain* (London, 1974).

3. Crewe, I. 'Voting and the Electorate', in Dunleavy, P. et al. *Developments in British Politics*, Vol. 4 pp. 94–101.

4. See Parkin, F. *Middle Class Radicalism* (MUP, 1968).

5. Crewe, I. 'Voting and the Electorate,' in Dunleavy, P. et al. *Developments in British Politics*, Vol. 4, pp. 98–107.

6. Conservative Central Office Poster, 1984.

7. Crewe, I. 'Voting and the Electorate,' in Dunleavy, P. et al. *Developments in British Politics*, Vol. 4, p. 101.

8. *The Guardian*, 15.06.87.

9. Crewe, I. 'Voting and the Electorate,' in Dunleavy, P. et al. *Developments in British Politics*, Vol. 4, p. 98. See also Heath, A. et al. *How Britain Votes* (1985).

10. *The Sunday Times*, 12.04.92.

11. Crewe, I. 'Voting and the Electorate', in Dunleavy, P. et al. *Development in British Politics*, Vol. 4, p. 100.

12. Ibid. p. 100.

13. McKie, D. *The Guardian Political Almanac, 1993/4* (London, 1993) pp. 327–8.

14. *The Daily Telegraph*, 14.04.92.

15. Ibid.

16. *The Sunday Times*, 12.04.92.

17. Robbins, L. *Politics Pal, 1993* (Leicester, 1993), p. 10.

18. Crewe, I. 'Voting and the Electorate', in Dunleavy, P. et al. *Developments in British Politics,* Vol. 4, p. 114.

19. See Crewe, I. 'Why did Labour lose (yet again)?', *Politics Review*, September 1992.

Further reading

Butler, D. and Stokes, D. *Political Change in Britain* (London, 1974).

Crewe, I. 'Voting and the Electorate', in Dunleavy, P. et al. *Developments in British Politics*, Vol. 4.

Crewe, I. 'Why did Labour lose (yet again)?', *Politics Review*, September 1992.

Denver, D. 'The 1992 General Election: in Defence of Psephology', *Talking Politics*, Vol. 5, No. 1, 1992.

Heath, A. et al. *How Britain Votes* (London, 1985).

McKie, D. *The Guardian Political Almanac, 1993/4* (London, 1993).

O'Donnell, M. *A New Introduction to Sociology* (London, 1987).

Robbins, L. *Politics Pal, 1993* (Leicester, 1993).

Robbins, L. *Politics Pal, 1988* (Leicester, 1988).

CHAPTER 14

Exam technique

This chapter discusses some techniques which students may employ to convert their knowledge of politics into competent and high-scoring examination answers. Most exams seek to test a candidate's knowledge and understanding of basic political concepts, ideas, structures and processes. Students are expected to interpret and analyse information presented in a variety of forms and to evaluate arguments. Examinations now contain a variety of styles of questions which are designed to fulfil these criteria. Within exam technique there is a huge range of different ideas and methods that can be taught. This chapter will provide a mainstream approach dealing with the following:

14.1   Short answer techniques.

14.2   Data/stimulus response questions.

14.3   Self-test data response questions.

14.4   Essay techniques.

14.1 | Short answer techniques

The short answer questions are primarily intended to test students' factual knowledge across the **whole syllabus** and their ability to analyse and distinguish between different concepts and ideas. These questions require short and succinct answers, not mini-essays and not lists of notes. Time does not allow for long and complex answers. Throughout this book, every chapter contains one or two sample short answer questions. They are accompanied throughout with 'Key concepts' and 'Key terms', both of which are indicative of the types of answers which students should produce.

At the beginning of the exam students should read the whole paper through and mark off those questions that they feel confident to answer. They should then plan their answers for each section. It is good to quickly write a rough list of points for a short answer question. These questions come in two forms, single and double. Usually the double questions are spilt in such a way that the (b) question is designed to test knowledge and analytical abilities more than the (a) question.

Example:

1. (a) *Define the convention of collective responsibility.*

    (b) *How does this work in practice?*

There are two ways that students can prepare for this section of the exam:

(a) By doing plenty of model answers to these questions from the sample questions in the book, which are designed to be self-tests.

(b) Memorising the main concepts explained in Chapter 1 and under the headings of 'Key concepts' and 'Key terms'.

Sample answers

1. What are administrative tribunals?

Administrative tribunals are bodies with both judicial and administrative characteristics, created by governments to determine disputes arising from the administration of statutes passed by the legislature. These disputes may be between citizen and state arising directly from the administrative decision of a government department, or between citizens and other organisations. Tribunals are staffed by professionals and lay persons and are designed to provide a speedier, cheaper and less formal method for the settlement of disputes than could be provided by the courts. Examples include tribunals concerned with disputes over taxation assessments, welfare payments and discrimination in employment.

2. Define corporatism

This refers to the tendency for a state or international organisation to work closely with a variety of groups in the making of public policy. Corporatism has increased as the state has become more involved in the social and economic organisation of the country involving more and more relevant groups in the policy making process. Essentially this concept envisages a social partnership between the institutions of the state and interested groups. The European Union possesses a corporatist attitude which encourages the participation of groups from across the countries of the Union in the policy-making partnership.

14.2 | Data/stimulus response questions

These questions are increasingly popular with examiners. They are usually compulsory and are designed to test understanding and interpretation of data by the student. They are invariably restricted to the central institutions of the syllabuses: Parliament, the Prime Minister and the Cabinet, the role of the civil service, civil liberties and the administration of justice, the party system and the electoral system.

They present the student with a piece of information, either a piece of prose or some statistics, on one of the above and ask a series of questions related to the information in front of the student and on the topic in general. They are designed to provide material to assist and 'stimulate' the student's responses to the questions in front of them. Usually there are three types of questions:

1. Those where the answer is contained within the material. (It is staring you in the face.)
2. Those which require an answer partly constructed from the material on the paper and from your own understanding and learnt knowledge.
3. Those which test your deeper knowledge and understanding.

Example: The 1992 General Election result for Great Britain[1]

	TOTAL VOTES	SHARE OF VOTE %	NO. OF MPS	SHARE OF MPS %
Conservative	14,049,508	42.8	336	53
Labour	11,557,134	35.2	271	42.8
Lib-Dems	5,998,446	18.3	20	3.2
Nationalists	786,348	2.4	7	1.1
Others	433,870	1.3	0	0

(Excludes Northern Ireland's general election results)

1. *How does the above data illustrate the character of the British party system?*
2. *How might this data be used to support the case for electoral reform?*

In this case, question 1 asks you to examine the data and use it to explain the nature of the British party system, and question 2 asks you to use some of the data and your own knowledge to present a case for electoral reform.

This is a rather simplistic example but it serves to illustrate the nature of the questions. Remember that the main aim of these questions is to examine your ability to use and evaluate the material given. You should read and study the material presented very carefully before reading the questions. Once you have read the questions, find and highlight the answers in the material. Those questions which test your deeper knowledge will require you to plan an answer, because a short essay is the best way to answer. In the case of question 2 above, you would have to use some of the data in the case that you present for electoral reform.

Example:
The unfairness of the present electoral system.

The Liberal Democrat performance could be used to illustrate this point: 5,998,446 votes gave them only twenty seats and 18.3% of the popular vote translated into only 3.2% of seats.

Data response questions are not simple but they are straightforward and students who have revised thoroughly should be able to score highly on them. However, there are some common mistakes which apply to the whole exam but have particular relevance here:

- Students do not read the materials fully or with enough care.

- They do not think about their answers to these questions.

- They get their timing wrong. The simpler questions can be dealt with quickly leaving time to concentrate on the longer mini-essay style questions.

- They panic when they see a table of numbers. Look at the table carefully and take your time. In many ways statistics are easier to study than a piece of prose.

- Prose-based questions sometimes require the student to find a quote within the passage and explain it (*see question 1, section 14.3*). Students make silly mistakes by misreading the question or the prose.

Finally, the best way to tackle such questions is through practice. Use some of the examples in this book and practice answering questions from past papers. You should familiarise yourself with these types of question so that they hold no fears and allow you to answer them confidently.

14.3 | **Self-test data response questions**

1.   Study the following extract and then answer questions (a) to (c)

'A week before the war began a Cabinet Minister said John Major was lacking in one small but important attribute. It was the reverse of the Thatcher problem. There was insufficient distance between Mr Major and his colleagues. They appreciated his courteous attention to their feelings, but a Prime Minister had to be slightly apart.

If war comes, the Minister suggested, it would take care of the problem. It has. The gravity was there from day one of hostilities when the 'War Cabinet' swung into action and Mr Major addressed Parliament and people with sureness, calmness and dignity.

In a few weeks between arriving at No. 10 and turning himself into a war premier, John Major signalled to his colleagues that collective Cabinet Government really was back – restored in full. How did he do it? One colleague said: "The Prime Minister sums up, but he doesn't prejudge the question, so that changes the discussion. It has a rather odd effect on Ministers." He went on to say, "In the old days", using a phrase that shows just how quickly Mrs Thatcher has been consigned to political history, "a Secretary of State would discuss a proposal with the Prime Minister. If after one meeting or, perhaps, two he persuaded her it was right she would say: "We'd better put it to cabinet." Then he wouldn't have to worry about it because he'd gone through the difficult part. Now he has to persuade the Prime Minister and he has to persuade a lot of other people in the Cabinet as well. It's all to the good, but it's going to produce a lot more effort." '

(Source: Adapted from P. Hennessy, in *The Independent*, 21.01.91.)

(a) Explain how John Major 'signalled to his colleagues that collective Cabinet Government really was back'.
(b) (i)   How did war effect the authority of the new Prime Minister?
      (ii) What other factors affect the authority of the Prime Minister?
(c) Compare and contrast the relationship between the Prime Minister and the Cabinet under Margaret Thatcher with that under John Major?

(London Board, Paper 1, January 1993)

2.   Study the following extract and then answer questions (a) to (c)
'The evidence for arguing that by the mid-twentieth century Parliament had become little more than a rubber stamp for which ever of the two major parties was in power is compelling ... In some respects this paints too stark a picture ... Nevertheless, back-bencher MPs were not particularly well equipped to keep a check on the government.

There can be no doubt that significant changes have taken place in the role of the House of Commons. That role has changed dramatically – the British parliamentary system remains executive-dominated, but it has changed nonetheless. Parliament in general and the Commons in particular is more assertive, more critical, more demanding and significantly less subservient.'

(Source: M. Rush, 'Recent Parliamentary Developments', in *Developments in Politics*, Vol. 2, 1991.)

(a) What is the case for and the case against the view that 'by the mid-twentieth century Parliament had become little more than a rubber stamp'?
(b) According to the author, how has the role of Parliament changed?
(c) To what extent are MPs now 'well equipped to keep a check on the government' ?

(London Board, Paper 1, January 1994)

3.   Study the data below and then answer questions (a) to (c)

CANDIDATE	% OF VOTES PER SECTION			
	MPS	MEMBERS	TRADE UNIONS	TOTAL %
Blair	60.5	58.2	52.3	57.0
Prescott	19.6	24.4	28.4	24.1
Beckett	19.9	17.4	19.3	18.9

(Source: *The Guardian*, 22.07.94.)

(a)   What is one member one vote?
(b)   Using the figures above explain how the Labour Party elects its
      leader.
(c)   Explain the method for electing the Conservative Leader?

4.   Study the data below and then answer questions (a) to (c)

% OF VOTES					NUMBER OF SEATS			
GENERAL ELECTION	CON.	LAB.	LIB.	OTHERS	CON.	LAB.	LIB.	OTHERS
1970	46.4	43.0	7.5	3.1	330	287	6	7
Feb. 74	37.8	37.1	19.3	5.8	297	301	14	23
Oct. 74	35.8	39.2	18.3	6.7	277	319	13	26
1979	43.9	36.9	13.8	5.4	339	269	11	16
1983	42.4	27.6	25.4	4.6	397	209	23	21
1987	42.3	30.8	22.6	4.3	376	229	22	23
1992	41.9	34.4	18.0	3.7	336	271	20	23

(Source: McKie, D. *The Guardian Political Almanac, 1993/4* (London,
1993) and *The Election: A Voter's Guide* (London, 1992).)

(a)   How does the above data illustrate the existence of a two-party
      system?
(b)   How does the table support the case for electoral reform?
(c)   In what period and how does the above data suggest that the
      party system may have been changing?

5.   Study the following extract and then answer questions (a) to (c)

'British Members of Parliament are not delegates mandated by their
constituents to follow a particular line. Rather, they are
representatives elected to serve all their constituents from
whichever party they come and the nation as a whole. In practice
this idealistic description is qualified by MPs overriding allegiance
to party. MPs are in the main middle class, middle aged and male.'

(Source: Politics Briefing, No. 3. Parliament and Reform.)

(a)   What is meant by the term 'representative'?
(b)   Why is the House of Commons accused of not being truly representative?
(c)   What are the four major roles of a backbencher?

14.4 | **Essay techniques**

The essay questions are either single questions or subdivided questions. They are designed to:

1.   Test your knowledge of a topic and your ability to use this knowledge.
2.   Test your ability to analyse, evaluate and criticise.
3.   Test your skill in presenting a case using only the relevant material with clarity and coherence.

Essays require a good knowledge of the main topics of the course. They do not ask you to write everything you know about the topic in question, for example, the Cabinet or pressure groups. Rather they ask a specific question on one particular aspect, requiring the student to *think* about what they are going to say in reply to the question. It is useful to underline the key words of a question in order to clarify what the question is asking.

Example:
Would a Bill of Rights provide greater protection of civil liberties in Britain?

In this example the key words are *Bill of Rights, greater protection of civil liberties*. This question asks you not to write everything you know about civil liberties or all the arguments for and against the introduction of a Bill of Rights in Britain. It asks you to assess:

(a)   How are civil liberties (a term which needs explanation) protected in Britain now?
(b)   Give a critique of this protection.
(c)   Explain what a Bill of Rights is, and how it is theoretically meant to afford greater protection.
(d)   Assess whether it would provide greater protection than presently exists and if you believe that it would explain your reasoning.

This question requires you to produce an answer which incorporates a **only a few** of the arguments for and against the introduction of a Bill of Rights. This question and others like it link topics together. In this answer you would have to combine material from Chapter 10 (The administration of justice) and materials from Chapter 2 (on the Constitution).

These questions ask for key lines of analysis and not over-long definitions, background information or lengthy explanations of the whole topic. In all your essays your analysis should include plenty of examples to illustrate the points that you are making. Although the essay plans in this book give the key lines of analysis they do not direct the student to every example that may be used. Some have references to key writers, but in general it is up to the student to select and include the necessary material in their answers.

Some essays are more straightforward than others because they ask for an (a) versus (b) explanation. They simply require the student to produce a range of arguments for and against a particular idea, but they do require a demonstration of more than simple learning. Students should attempt to show their analytical skills in these essays by writing conclusions which draw all the strands of the argument together. Furthermore, if time allows, contemporary reference to the topic is always a point scorer.

Example:
'State (a) the case for and (b) the case against electoral reform.'

In the conclusion of an answer to this question students could explain the contemporary position of the major political parties on this issue.

There is a massive amount of different advice about how to write a good essay. I have attempted to address the main points. All answers should be thought about first and should be planned. In the exam room students should write out a sketch answer to the question. The essay plans contained in this book should give an indication of what should be written. These are 'ideals' and are here to provide the student with something to learn. Students will not necessarily be able to reproduce such plans in the exam. Generally, a plan should focus on the question and list the main points and the examples that the student wishes to make in answer to the question. The plan should not take more than a few minutes to write. It is advisable to write as many practice essays and prepare as many plans as possible.

This chapter has sought to give general advice on preparation for the exam, but it should be stressed that there is a vast science on exam techniques. In reality only hard work throughout a course, and self-disciplined and comprehensive revision will produce results. Good Luck !

Note

1. *The Daily Telegraph*, 11.04.92.

INDEX

E

Q

T

U